A Home for Nickel

A Home for Nickel

◆

A Sea Turtle's Story

Jim Gamlin

iUniverse, Inc.
New York Lincoln Shanghai

A Home for Nickel
A Sea Turtle's Story

Copyright © 2007 by Jim Gamlin

All rights reserved. No part of this book may be used or reproduced by any means, graphic, electronic, or mechanical, including photocopying, recording, taping or by any information storage retrieval system without the written permission of the publisher except in the case of brief quotations embodied in critical articles and reviews.

iUniverse books may be ordered through booksellers or by contacting:

iUniverse
2021 Pine Lake Road, Suite 100
Lincoln, NE 68512
www.iuniverse.com
1-800-Authors (1-800-288-4677)

Because of the dynamic nature of the Internet, any Web addresses or links contained in this book may have changed since publication and may no longer be valid.

The views expressed in this work are solely those of the author and do not necessarily reflect the views of the publisher, and the publisher hereby disclaims any responsibility for them.

ISBN: 978-0-595-44650-6 (pbk)
ISBN: 978-0-595-70024-0 (cloth)
ISBN: 978-0-595-88974-7 (ebk)

Printed in the United States of America

To Mike Bier
Without whose involuntary phone call and constant support, neither I nor one very special turtle would be where they are today.

Contents

ACKNOWLEDGEMENTS..................................... ix
CHAPTER 1   SPRING 1998 IN THE BEGINNING 1
CHAPTER 2   GENESIS 5
CHAPTER 3   IN THIS WORLD YOU WILL HAVE
             TROUBLE 9
CHAPTER 4   THINGS TO WONDERFUL FOR ME TO
             KNOW 13
CHAPTER 5   EXODUS 17
CHAPTER 6   JOURNEY 23
CHAPTER 7   ARRIVAL 27
CHAPTER 8   RESURRECTION 31
CHAPTER 9   YOU ARE MY FRIENDS 37
CHAPTER 10   ROTUNDA 40
CHAPTER 11   MESSENGER 44
CHAPTER 12   ISLANDS 48
CHAPTER 13   I JUST HAD TO GO BACK TO THE
             ISLAND 54
CHAPTER 14   CHAINLINK 60
CHAPTER 15   CAROLINE STREET 73
CHAPTER 16   TINA AND THE TARPON 82

CHAPTER 17	SAVE-A-TURTLE	89
CHAPTER 18	FISH STORY	116
CHAPTER 19	CHANGE OF PLANS	125
CHAPTER 20	ENCOUNTERS	134
CHAPTER 21	ENDS AND BEGINNINGS	137
CHAPTER 22	FOLLOWING MALACHI	144
CHAPTER 23	A STRANGER INVITED IN	148
CHAPTER 24	JANUARY 2002	152
CHAPTER 25	JULY 2002	156
CHAPTER 26	YOU DIDN'T CHOOSE ME, BUT I CHOSE YOU	162
CHAPTER 27	INTERLOPER	166
CHAPTER 28	END RUN	168
CHAPTER 29	IMPASSE	172
CHAPTER 30	UPS AND DOWNS	175
CHAPTER 31	TO GOOD TO BE TRUE	180
CHAPTER 32	BARRY	183
CHAPTER 33	WORTH THE WAIT!	186
CHAPTER 34	REVELATION	193
CHAPTER 35	HOME	196
EPILOGUE		201

ACKNOWLEDGEMENTS

Thanks to all the people who helped with this project, among them, Save A Turtle's Mike Bier, Jeanette Hobbs, Pat Wells, Herb and Yea Bernett, Don and Margie Jensen, Jeri Sears, Patty Anthony, Tropical Mike Hall, Elaine Mason, and Edna Bier
Megan Conti from Florida Fish and Wildlife Conservation Commission.
Matt Finn, Maura Krause from the Goodland, Florida area, Glenn Harman and Tammy Langer from the Clearwater Marine Aquarium. Tina Brown from the Turtle Kraals Museum in Key West. My photographers Ann Lyssenko, and Carol Flisak. The Turtle Hospital's Ritchie Moretti, Sue Schaf, and Corinne Rose. The Karen Beasley Sea Turtle Hospital's Jean Beasley. And of course the Shedd Aquarium's Bryan Bortman, George Parsons, Michelle Sattler, and Bill Gwozdz..

1

SPRING 1998
IN THE BEGINNING ...

The sun rose early this time of year, having nearly reached the summer solstice, its rays warming the South Florida waters and slowly bringing life to the myriad of creatures inhabiting that area of the mangroves. Hermit crabs of various description scuttled along the bottom in search of a prize looking like little pirates wearing three cornered hats in their borrowed shell homes. Flocks of birds perched in the trees and floated in the air, Egrets, Roseate Spoonbills, and Brown Pelicans, were included in the avian mix. Underneath the water, juvenile Mangrove snapper, and an assortment of angelfish and jacks surveyed the submerged tangled root forest of the mangrove trees that was their aquatic home, having survived another night. If one listened closely you could hear the staccato popping of pistol shrimp using the oversized claw they possessed to fire off a warning shot defense of their burrows or to stun an early morning breakfast. The sun's rays also gave life to a creature that dated back millions of years, who was also awakening from his nap in the sea grass bed in which he had made his home for the night.

Pete, a Green sea turtle poked his head through the air water interface that was the ocean's surface. He surveyed the thin longitudinal blue line of the horizon that was this ancient mariner's perspective on the world and took a few breaths of the warm humid air, his throat expanding and contracting like a small balloon, the brown mosaic of the scales on his head glistening in the sun as the sea water dripped off droplet by droplet.

Pete was a member of the group of reptiles known as sea turtles, among that tribe would be included, the Loggerhead, Leatherback, Hawksbill, Ridley, and the Green sea turtle, Chelonia mydas, the genus and species of which Pete was a member. He would begin the day as previous generations of his clan had, first warming himself in the life giving rays of the sun that were not only important for animation, but also for absorption of essential nutrients his body and shell needed to insure survival. As his flippers and appetite came to life, Pete began his feeding routine. Slowly surveying the bottom as turtles do, he started to make mechanical snaps at the surrounding sea grass pasture, sometimes grabbing a mouthful of the greenery, and sometimes missing altogether. When successful, he pulled up stems and roots, or broke leaves off at their terminus. This resulted in little fragments of the plants floating to the surface in the wake of Pete's feeding activity that left a telltale trail of aquatic flotsam on the ocean. Many years ago when the hunting of sea turtles was legal, turtle fisherman would look for the presence of these trails of plant debris to indicate the location of the animal. The unsuspecting turtle would in this way lead the hunters to the spot where they could harpoon the quarry. Pete no longer had to worry about this particular threat, he was now a protected animal as were all other sea turtles. There were still plenty of other dangers to his survival that he had to overcome. As Pete worked along the ocean floor his snapping flushed out a variety of creatures. Crabs, shrimp, and small fish darted out of the emerald forest. Seahorses, clinging to their now severed green plant hitching posts, sculled as rapidly as was possible in their slow motion world in search of a new holdfast for their prehensile tails, coiled like tiny rams horns. Some of these unfortunate animals were inadvertently included in Pete's meal as welcome but unsought after additions.

In this same submerged garden he took little notice of the long straight tracks of bare sand that seemed to cut their way through the sea grass like so many lines scratched by some giant hand onto a green slate. These tracks were outboard motor scars cut by the propellers of boats traveling at sometimes very high speeds through the grass beds. By feeding in that area of the bay, Pete had unknowingly placed himself in danger. The long days of summer would increase the boat traffic, which included fisherman and sightseers. This day would not be any different.

Pete had already experienced a previous close call with a boat. He had been feeding just as he was today, when a high pitched buzzing and splashing sound caught his attention. He popped his head up to the surface, and then he felt the impact. The force sent him spinning Frisbee-like through the water, tumbling wildly until he came to rest on the bottom. He remained there for several minutes, reconnoitering, a green shower of minced grass floating like confetti around him. He could feel a sharp pain in his shell which would go on to bother him for several weeks. That time he had been fortunate, only having suffered a glancing blow from the passing boat.

But on this spring day of 1998, with the Florida sun beaming down, Pete was encouraged by its warming radiance to commence with his feeding activities.

While he was immersed in this endeavor, all at once at the underwater limits of his vision, he began to perceive a shadowy shape off in the murk. Pete silently floated to the surface and inhaled a quick breath of air, then resubmerged once again and scanned the surrounding water for the telltale elongated, sinuous profile of an advancing shark. While he hovered there he could make out now a shorter distance away what appeared to be a large head in a brown bathing cap poke through the surface and then disappear making a kind of "ploop" sound as it submerged.

Pete remained motionless, but at the same time he slowly sank, as his brain processed the information which would decide if a dash for life was necessary, or if it were just another false alarm in a world of life or death decisions that are made by all forms of wildlife in their daily fight for survival.

Then Pete saw it! Like a large dirigible materializing out of the mist, the head and shell of a Loggerhead sea turtle entered into his vision field. This turtle was much larger and older than Pete. It's broader brown head and weathered form showed that this was indeed a veteran ocean traveler. The shell it possessed was home to barnacle hitchhikers, a crop of algae, and even a small remora fish that had attached itself to the underside and waited opportunistically for the turtle to crush up a meal. This would result in a snowstorm of crumbs that the fish could dart out and eat safely in the shadow and protection of the big vehicle to which it was attached.

The Loggerhead may have been attracted by the crabs and lobsters that were being flushed out of the sea grass by Pete's feeding activities. The larger turtle was a much less discriminating feeder than Pete. When it comes to Loggerhead feeding cuisine, their motto can be described in these words—eat first and ask questions later. While crabs and lobsters are a favored fair, these turtles diet also can include but are not limited to, plastic bags, which may or may not be mistaken for jellyfish, hooks and fishing line, and other assorted objects or garbage. When these are eaten they can at best result in indigestion, or at worse, the demise of the turtle.

The Loggerhead quickly located a slipper lobster in Pete's trail. The odd looking creature that resembled an animated door stop attempted to kick and scuttle itself out of harms way, but it was too late. One crushing bite from the turtle and it was all over. Clouds of debris and shell filled the water where seconds before there had been a living animal. The remora came to life next, darting out to swallow the suspensed morsals, as did other opportunistic fish, most of them juvenile wrasse who being in the immediate area joined in the feast.

Pete watched as the Loggerhead swam away. The massive animal of nearly three hundred pounds was impressive to behold and commanded respect because of its size alone, not to mention the aura of ancient survival that it carried. Then it faded into the murk, gone from his view and memory. After it left, things settled down and returned to normal as they always had, but by the end of this day, Pete the Green sea turtle's life would change forever.

2

GENESIS

By any standard of measure, Pete was already lucky to be alive. As with any sea turtle, the deck is stacked overwhelmingly against one individual surviving to adulthood, even less is the chance of ever successfully reproducing. Pete had already beaten the odds to this point at least.

His struggle for survival had begun many years earlier, when one night a weathered old female Green sea turtle emerged from a dark but glistening ocean, and made her unannounced beach landing among the gently breaking waves that looked like so many white pompadours, disappearing as they reached the shore. When the female came to shallow water, she could feel the ocean's surge pushing her forward as if to accent the urgency she felt in returning to a destination instinct told her was the nesting beach. As her lower shell started to scrape the sand, she ceased her swimming motion. Coming to a stop at the waters edge, she cautiously surveyed the surroundings. The turtle took in the silence, breathing in the cooler night air, looked up at the pinpoints of light that were the stars, and felt the still warm sand that had not radiated all of its heat back to the atmosphere. It was a good feeling. The beach was a familiar place, she having been here many times before. The darkness of the night was a comfort to her, camouflaging her intention from the eyes of the unknown predator that she knew surely must be out there. Blinking her own eyes, she at once began the laborious task of dragging her no longer buoyant body off the water's perimeter and advanced inland. The flippers that just a few minutes before had with one thrust caused her to effortlessly fly through the water, now seemed poorly suited for the ordeal of sliding her almost three hundred pound body over land.

The flippers would move forward, stretching out as if still swimming, but now grabbing sand instead of water, found a purchase and she pulled herself along, the rear flippers also thrusting one by one lending aid. Once, twice, three times, countless times, this example of reptilian calisthenics was repeated until the horizontal chin-ups she was doing were complete and the nesting sight had been gained.

Resting momentarily, the female then began the purpose for which she had come. Kicking and flapping with her flippers, she sent dry loose sand flying in every direction into the surrounding darkness until she had removed as much of it as she could by that method and having reached moist sand stopped. The female then looked about, as if to survey in some way or marvel at what she had just accomplished. She was satisfied. The turtle now laying in a crater of sand, next cupped her rear flippers as if you would cup one of your own hands, and commenced with the next task, digging the nest. Throwing flippers full of sand one after another, the excavation continued until the project was after some time, finally completed. What appeared to be tears were flowing from the turtle's eyes, trapping some of the sandy grit that had inadvertently been thrown into them during the dig.

After a period of time the female began the ultimate purpose of her landward trek, the actual laying of the eggs. Shortly she started to deposit them two or three at a time, all the while remaining in a hypnotic like trance, oblivious to her surroundings and all the while vulnerable to whatever predator, man or beast that came upon her. As it had been in the past and again so this time her luck held out, and once more she remained undiscovered until the nest was complete. It consisted of nearly one hundred eggs containing the essence of new life, already beginning the wonder of transformation into tiny embryos.

She next set to the task of covering the nest, her flippers again working in the substrate to replace the displaced beach into the hole on top of the eggs. That done to her satisfaction, she threw the sand in a scattering pattern to hopefully obliterate any sign that she had been there, then began her march back to the ocean. Summoning the strength to repeat the effort that had brought her inland, she dragged and pushed herself, eventually arriving at the goal of the sea's welcome edge.

With the first taste and feel of its salty brine, she was rejuvenated, and her body once again in the element for which it was designed became buoyant. With a few powerful kicks of her flippers she flew through the water, no longer a trudging beast but an elegant aquatic aviator, soaring ever farther and farther out into her ocean home, possibly never to return as the years were advancing on her. The only evidence that she had been there was the tank tread track her body and flippers had left in the sand as she had exited the beach. As the Green sea turtle faded off into the sea, the tiny germ of one little creature remained behind, already beginning to knit itself together into its final form.

The days went by, one at a time, as they always have. The sun rising and setting, the rain and clouds coming and going, the mangrove pods plopping into the nearby sea, until slightly less than two months later, Pete, now a tiny replica of his mother and father, began to stir in his eggshell cradle. A big event was scheduled to occur on this date. For he and his siblings it was their last day in the sandy nest that had been home since their mother created it. It had been decided that this very night they would emerge from the sand and enter the world!

Pete and his mates had to this point been fortunate. The nest had not been discovered by a foraging animal such as a raccoon looking for a scrambled egg dinner. Nor had it been inadvertently dug up by another nesting turtle. None of these calamities or any other had come their way. And now filled with excitement that could not be contained, the little turtles with the use of a tiny egg tooth, started to tear through their shells and then dig and push upward through the sand. Already the unforgiving struggle for life began at this early stage as the first casualties started to appear and take their toll on the troop. Some of the hatchlings had been born too weak to break out of their egg shell prison and get to the surface. The light of day and the warmth of the sun would be an experience they would never realize. Pete however, was among the chosen. He and most of the other turtles in the nest one by one erupted from the sand like lava from tiny volcanoes and commenced with an amphibious assault in reverse, heading for the invisible but instinctive call of their objective ... the ocean!

The tiny soldiers moved surprisingly fast compared to their ponderous mother as they gallantly flip-flopped and hopped along. Forging ahead, they took little notice that some of their number had become disoriented by artificial lighting coming from the behind the beach. Instead of heading to the ocean, they reversed their course and proceeded inland toward the siren call of the beckoning lights. They quickly were entangled hopelessly in thick vegetation that held them like barbed wire where they awaited death that was certain to come later that day from the sun's heat or the jaws of a passing animal. But Pete continued on, his tiny heart beating within his shell, perhaps more determined than the others to reach his goal.

A troop of raccoons making nightly patrols had to their delight come upon the hatchlings running to the ocean. These masked bandits began to greedily pick them off one by one, crunching them into oblivion. All the while, Pete was traveling over the sand, making progress, inch by inch, foot by foot, not to be defeated.

Still another obstacle presented itself as ghost crabs started to appear from their burrows. They rattled sideways across the beach, interrupting the broken field run of the turtles and grabbing several in their claws, mechanically waving them in the air like some trophy, only to later dismember and devour the victim below the sand. A few of the hatchlings through violent wiggling and flapping were able to break loose from the crab's clutches, usually losing a flipper in the process. Then they would limp with three legs to the safety of the ocean, where they would be forced to deal with its dangers, being already at a disadvantage. Pete, with death exploding all around him passed by unnoticed. On and on he went, his eyes always focused ahead to what he instinctively knew was over his small horizon.

Luckily, there were no birds that night. In daylight, their strafing flights would have descended on the tiny brigade with an aerial assault, relentless in their attack. On the ground, still more turtles became entangled in washed up sea grass and other debris, only feet from their final goal, destined to drown in what for them would be the ironic arrival of the now unwelcome tide.

Despite all of these countless obstacles, miraculously, Pete had come this far unscathed, his determination far outweighing his diminutive size. He could not pause or rest, and then, just at the right time, there it was … the initial touch of water on his tiny frame. With its first feel he frantically began to kick his flippers but was met with an incoming wave that tumbled him backwards. He righted himself and then buoyantly flapped through the water, swimming for the first time in his life. Out and out he went, swimming, breathing, flapping, and then breathing again. Striking farther and farther seaward, on his way to a home of unknown location where he would spend the early part of his life, never looking back or thinking about the carnage of the beach forgotten behind him. Pete and a small flotilla of his fellow survivors were on their way.

3

IN THIS WORLD YOU WILL HAVE TROUBLE ...

Having now survived for nearly nine years and reached almost two feet since his escape from the nesting beach, Pete continued his day of leisurely feeding and cruising in the sea grass flats. In what would soon be a decade of life, he had glided through a crystalline blue world. Pete had sailed through schools of Sergeant Major fish at times so dense that the fish were forced to part only inches from his head, only to re form their school an equal distance from his tail. He had traveled down the corridors of both dense spur and groove coral fortresses and to distant patch reefs that seldom if ever had seen human presence. Pete had foraged for food only feet from piles of egg shaped ballast rock that secretly marked graves of Spanish galleons, silent for centuries, that had met a violent demise by slamming aground on the reefs themselves. Or caught in some form of tropical storm, hurricane or gale, were driven onto shallow sand, crushing their teredo worm riddled hulls, never to return to Spain. The rotting hulks of these ungainly ships remaining entombed for countless years as monuments to man's futile efforts against the power of nature. One minute the ocean is a thing of beauty and peace, the next a source of sickening fear that brings dryness to the mouth and nauseates the stomach.

In Pete's world this day was a particularly spectacular one. The sun's rays had heated the water to a tepid bath, and he soaked up its warmth. The surface of the ocean consisted of a light chop, so Pete didn't have to battle against any currents when he came up to breathe. His visibility was not impaired by high waves or rollers that would have elevated him one second and lowered him the next. The warm water and air, full belly and overwhelming tranquility of the day started to make Pete groggy as he floated on the surface. The eyelids grew heavier and heavier, then slowly closed a little, and then a little more, until he slipped into a dream world of blue horizons, white sand beaches, mangrove forests, and sea grass beds. He fell into a sweet trance, deeply involved in his dream, rocking comfortably in his ocean hammock.

In the next instance, Pete's restful sleep was abruptly altered by an unknown force as he felt crushing pain and the feeling of air being inadvertently expelled from his lungs. He waited for the dream to be over and the relief that would come with it, but this was not a dream. At the same time, he was driven rapidly across the surface of the ocean, and in the next instance he was submerged and spinning corkscrew fashion downward in the dissipating wake field. As the inertia of the boat's collision with Pete weakened, he found himself underwater, in need of air, confused and throbbing with pain. Then instinct took over and he looked upward to the surface and the essential air just beyond the blue boundary. The breath which he sought there seemed so close. Pete began to frantically kick, but now instead of the effortless glide he expected, his action resulted in sharp jolts of numbing pain and he gained the sea's surface with a great effort and without the use of his rear flippers whose movement caused him much discomfort. He greedily sucked in the air. The first breath thirstily filled his lungs and as they did he could feel a pain that grew more intense as they expanded. Once they filled to capacity he paused, then made his first exhalation letting out the air with a gasping sound. Filled with excruciating pain, confusion and disorientation he tried to grasp what fate had befallen him, he however did not live in our world but was from one beyond the shore and would never be able to understand what had taken place, only wonder why.

The strike of the boat had damaged his spinal cord. The rear flippers that had helped propel and steer him through so many miles of ocean were for all intents and purposes silenced, and had only limited movement. The beauty and tranquility of the morning earlier that day was now only a longed for memory.

Pete lay there on the ocean's surface, now just an immobile green speck on a flat blue background, no longer the free ocean traveler, but a piece of aquatic flotsam at the mercy of the wind and current. The only thing in his favor at this point was his full stomach that he had worked so diligently to fill for most of the morning and afternoon. He just floated on the waves that earlier in the day had rocked him peacefully, but now only brought pulses of pain, finally dozing off into a fitful stupor, only to reawaken and then slip off again. As he fell into this sleep pattern of the feverous, sick, or dying, his fate was more and more totally in the hands of a higher force.

Time passed. The hours turned into days and the days into weeks. Pete began to get weaker and weaker, all the while losing weight. Only having the use of his front flippers, he was unable to forage effectively for food. And if this was not already a big enough handicap in a now hostile sea, he was also unable to submerge fully. Due to some aspect of his trauma, he was like a semi buoyant cork, repeatedly floating back to the surface when not swimming. He adapted to his handicap after awhile and became adept at diving with the use of his front flippers alone, the rear ones trailing along like some kind of odd hitchhikers, but as soon as he stopped kicking he would slowly float back to the surface once again. This made it nearly impossible to feed on the sea grass that at times was just within the reach of his jaws, unfortunately, just as he snapped at it, he would float frustratingly upward and out of its range. Sometimes with a great effort he would be able to get a taste of a few blades but by the time it was swallowed the water had often deepened and there would be no second chance.

The days past by and Pete's weight loss became more severe. He grew weaker and weaker. Like a shipwrecked sailor floating in a raft he was a prisoner on the surface, where the hot sun, once his friend began to dry out his shell and raise his body temperature to critical levels. He would hope for the occasional lapping wave or maybe a tropical shower to cool him down, and that relief would always come. At times it would seem as though it was meant for him to survive, and at other times not.

It had been over a month now and Pete was rapidly deteriorating and starting to die. Helplessly floating on the ocean, he had heard the now all too familiar sound of other boats passing by that had mercifully not struck him again and ended his life, although that might have been a blessing. Several times sharks had passed within inches. Checking him out and sizing him up as a possible target. He had seen the double dorsaled brown shapes approaching with their sinuous, slow, lazy, confident swimming action, then pass by with cold fixed eyes searching him for signs of life or the scent of death. They were most likely docile nurse sharks, not the more aggressive lemon sharks that would have been less cautious and more prone to attack. From that end, Pete was spared.

Off and on during the endless days and nights, he would slip into a deep sleep where he once again glided through a blue world and dove painlessly down into the sea grass, effortlessly flying with each thrust of his restored flippers, dancing with schools of spectacularly colored fish, joy filling his heart. Sometimes bright clear skies were overhead, and sometimes wonderful starlit nights. In Pete's dream the ocean was always peaceful and warm, his stomach always full, and his safety was certain. Then he would awaken to only things remembered and wished for.

Pete had only a few days left now, perhaps hours. He had grown weak and emaciated, was unable to use his rear flippers or dive, and could not feed or escape danger. All he could due was float and trust to the currents and wind to carry him were they may.

    The water grew shallower and warmer under him now, and if you cared there was the smell of land in the air, but Pete did not care and he paid little notice. While the waves pushed him closer and closer to his final resting place, he continued to dream of the world left behind, far out past the breaking waves, out on the open sea. And then there he was, washed up under the cathedral of mangrove roots along with other bits of ocean debris. He lay there in the shade for several hours, or was it days, and then felt what surely must be the warm comforting hands of death start to take hold of him and lift Pete up into the sky.

4

THINGS TO WONDERFUL FOR ME TO KNOW...

In the scheme of nature, seemingly small insignificant occurrences often have unforeseeable consequences. When a snail dies, its shell may provide a home for a hermit crab. The crab having no shell of its own to protect it, must forever throughout life forage about the shoreline and ocean floor looking for an abandoned one of just the proper size and weight. When it finds a prospective new piece of shell real estate, the crab must decide if the move will benefit it, a move up in the world if you would, to a better neighborhood. Just as a prospective buyer checks out a potential new property, so the hermit crab will also check out the new shell offering. The crustacean moves closer to the potential home, it's antennae with their chemo receptors quiver with excitement as it samples the air or water currents for the smell of the new edifice. If the possible home passes this test and the former snail owner has been accepted as not offensive, the next phase can start. The crab will begin to feel the shell with its claws and legs as if you would stroke a new piece of furniture and feel the upholstery. Is it to your liking Sir? Oh yes, yes this is very nice, and I see it has been constructed by one of my favorite architects, the King Crown snail. I previously lived in a Tulip snail shell and was hoping to upgrade into something a little more upscale. This should do nicely. Can I try it out? Absolutely Sir!

The hermit crab will quickly switch shells, tucking its fingerlike abdomen into the new one to get the feel of it. Do you like it? Yes, it feels very nice, so much roomier than my previous home, but I've grown sentimentally attached to my other house. I need to go back into the old one and think it over. And so it goes. The crab will switch back to the old shell, possibly thinking the deal over, all the ramifications of taking over a bigger house. Will it be too cumbersome to carry about? Will it snag up on other objects as I scuttle around? Most of all, will it protect me? All of these things are mulled over and deeply considered by the hermit crab. Nothing is taken lightly. At last the deal is finalized and our crustacean friend moves off with confidence and the pride of ownership of a new shell home.

A small seemingly insignificant occurrence in nature has great consequences for the life of the tiny hermit crab. In the scheme of life, some of the world's creatures have adapted to living off crumbs of insignificance, the proverbial chicken bones tossed off the table. An abandoned shell here, provides a home. Fur shed from the coat of a passing animal is woven into a nest which helps insulate it and maybe protect the young of an endangered bird. The discarded eggshells from the birds perhaps provide calcium for another animal that strengthens its bones or allows it to build a home.

In the warm ocean waters, a tiny creature called a coral polyp extracts calcium from the nutrient charged sea water, with which it in turn forms a coral skeleton. This skeleton provides a base on which more and still more are formed, creating a reef. The reef provides homes and sustenance for a volume of animals. Fish, mollusks, countless invertebrates, and even a few reptiles wander about the underwater caverns, valleys, gaps, and hills that comprise the coral forest. One of the most emblematic of the reef's tenants is certainly the parrot fish. These often dazzlingly colored swimmers with the parrot like beaks from which they get their name, diligently munch away at the coral, taking audibly crunching bites out of the hard skeletons to feed on the algae and polyps contained within it. The hard gritty meal is digested, and when this is complete, defecated as white coral sand. The white sand eventually forms a beach somewhere, to which interestingly enough considering one of the sand's sources, humans are attracted.

The mangrove forest is still another part of the natural web in which a seemingly insignificant event is the foundation for a critical relationship between the earth and its inhabitants. The act in this case is the shedding of leaves by the mangrove trees. The spent leaves fall from the tree and pass through the water's surface, fluttering their way downward through the aqueous brine solution and settle to the bottom. There they lay peacefully and eternally sleeping. Their job of feeding the tree over, the leaves appear to be nothing more than arboreal debris scattered on the ocean floor, but something is happening. Bacteria and fungi are beginning the process of decomposition. As the breakdown continues the leaf now becomes palatable food for tiny shrimp and other planktonic soup which continue the cycle to become food for small fish and then larger fish such as mangrove snapper, redfish and snook. In this way, these and many other animals are impacted by the small event of a tree shedding its leaves.

One of the largest areas of mangroves in Florida is known as the Ten Thousand Islands. Located on the southwest coast of the state, the area can be considered as one of the ecological crown jewels of Florida. The place is characterized by a tangled maze of mangrove islands, shell mounds, and isolated forest stands divided by weaving channels and dead end cuts. Names such as Shell Key, Turtle Key, White Horse Key, Fish Hawk Creek, and Dismal Key are well known reference points to the people who test these waters, which in centuries past was most likely pirates.

Florida's mangrove ecosystem consists of an estimated 400,000 to 500,000 acres of what can best be described as virtual food chain factories. If you have never seen a mangrove tree, the best way to visualize one is to take your hand and form a claw with it, as if one were gripping an orange. Holding the claw shape, next place your finger tips downward on a table with the back of your hand facing up. At this point you will have formed a kind of five legged structure, resembling some sort of walking animal. This is roughly what the base of a red mangrove tree looks like, except with many more fingers and without the order of the human hand. Each finger is more correctly known as a prop root. Now, picture if you will a green bush atop the prop root platform and you should be able to get an idea of what a mangrove tree looks like, but still we are not done with our description. The prop root base is either fully or partially submerged in the ocean, creating an underwater tangled maze that provides protection for all the fish and animal tenants that call the benevolent hand of the mangrove home.

At first sight a stand of mangroves can seem somewhat of a dark and mysterious place, but if you dare to strap on some dive gear and explore, one can't help but be changed by the experience.

After you slip on your snorkel gear, drop over the boat's side and quickly submerge, you at once will find yourself at the outer reaches of the forest in a sand channel that serves as an anchorage area. Here, there will usually be very little on the bottom, just the warm current slowly moving various pieces of plant debris by your dive mask. A loose fragment of sea grass passes by suspended in midwater looking like green cellophane tape, followed by a Red Mangrove seed pod somewhat resembling a cross between a green asparagus stalk and a cigar jettisoned from Fidel's island farther to the south. Swimming closer to our objective, we come to a darker area, we being the beneficiary of the trees above us with their shading aerial leaves. Then, coming into your underwater vision field, faint at first and then detailed, the ghostly submerged roots of the mangrove forest. Initially you are apprehensive and pause, taken aback by what seems to be only an eerie maze, but as your eyes adjust, you begin to perceive little rays of light from the sky above breaking their way through the cathedral like tangles, illuminating a spot here and another there. The warm water dissolves your apprehensions and then …, the fish start to visit. These aren't the massive schools one would encounter out on the coral reef, but the meeting is more pristine and individual. The fish here likely have not encountered a diver before. A large mangrove snapper wary in other venues, this time comes to admire his gray form reflected in your dive mask only inches away. Moving along, the silence of the area and warm bath like water take hold submerging you into a relaxing trance. Bolder now, we poke our head and entire body into various dark tangles, or sun soaked openings and sand patches scrutinizing fish of all variety, taking in the silence, all the while letting the current carry us along. But, too soon the end of the forest appears and you must reluctantly now head back to the boat. During your return, a group of barracuda swim by. They do not pay you any notice, unlike the more confrontational "cuda" of the coral reef, who like to give divers regular unexpected visits. Climbing the ladder back onto the boat, the body soaks up the welcome warmth of the sun after the initial chill that always accompanies a diver's emergence from the water. With the motors on a slow idle, we slowly pull away. You move to the bow where you sit and let the artificial breeze created by the crafts movement blow the water droplets off your body, where they eventually return to the balmy air atmosphere. You have experienced the mangroves.

5

EXODUS

Probably no man is more intimately aware of the essentiality of the mangrove tree to the Florida ecosystem than a marine biologist named Matt Finn. If someone was ever planning to put together a movie about the Florida mangrove forest, it would be necessary to create a character like Matt if he did not already exist, and a character indeed he is. A cross between a tobacco chewing southern backwoodsman, Jimmy Buffett, who he somewhat resembles, and the Crocodile Hunter by way of the bayou, is an apt description. A description that definitely does not fit the everyday notion of what a person with a PhD. in mangrove ecology would look like.

Originally from Maryland, Matt was always fascinated by plants and animals along with the interconnection of their existence. This interest led him to obtain a Bachelors degree in biology from Georgetown University, and that would have been the end of the story except for a twist of fate that led Matt to the Florida ecosystem. An odyssey that first started in North Carolina, then Arizona, and finally the Sunshine State. Along the way he had the urge to shove his face underwater and so he became a scuba diving instructor. These things kept him amused until his connection to Georgetown University, serendipitously led to him becoming captain of one of the Smithsonian Institute's research vessels. The scientists Matt chauffeured about soon took note of his amusing antics, along with his acute interest in all things biological, and encouraged him to go on and earn his doctorate, which he did in 1996.

Matt now makes his home in the small town of Goodland, Florida, which fronts onto the Ten Thousand Island area of the state, not far from Marco Island. For companionship, he lives with his wife Pam, who hails from Tomahawk, Wisconsin, a rustic fishing area surrounded by the Northwood's pine forests, whose aroma conjures up visions of Christmas during all months of the year. Matt and Pam's housemates include two dogs, one of them with three legs, and an ever changing menagerie of creatures that may at any time include seahorses, cats of various description, or even on occasion, a Diamondback Terrapin, a species of turtle that calls the mangroves home.

One "perk" of being a biologist is that an interest in living things, be it animal or plant, can be indulged on a daily basis through the guise of work. If one can draw a paycheck for bird watching, alligator wrestling, fishing, digging in the earth for worms, overturning rocks and stones to discover what creatures lay under them, poking around in forests, jungles, and swamps, keeping fish or turtles in aquariums, growing plants or gardening, so much the better. But, for the biologically inclined, if the truth be known, were forced to sell insurance, they would still continue to do the previously mentioned amusements without compensation. At the end of the day however, there is always compensation for the amateur biologist. It is the pure joy of discovery. The said discovery may not be new to the scientific world as a whole, but just as long as it is new to the first time observer, the reward is immeasurable. Who amongst us could not find fascination in the roller coaster flight pattern of an American Goldfinch and wonder why it chooses to fly in such an unordered way. Or why an alligator has such a bellowing voice. What purpose does it serve? What child is not hypnotized by a fishing bobber slowly twitching and then popping below the water's surface, attached to an unseen life form, or the lifting of a rock off of a damp resting spot to reveal the frantic dash of uncovered creatures below it. Many have found entertainment in the creation of the perfect colored mosaic of an elaborate flower garden, then silently watching the birds, insects, or other animal visitors that stop by without end. Forced inside, some find contentment in the observation of the miniature ocean diorama that an aquarium provides. It is from such stuff that all biologists are created, and in such a way, God created Matt Finn.

Matt's main research project and chief form of entertainment in July of 1998, was the gathering of data on a finny subject called a Jewfish. The fish scientifically known as Epinephelus itajara, is the largest member of the grouper family living in American waters, often weighing hundreds of pounds and capable of pulling spear fisherman who become accidentally attached to it to their watery deaths. Because of this large size, these fish provide a potential source for copious quantities of fish dinners, and this led to the grouper's over exploitation by fisherman with hooks and lures, or divers with spear guns. The story is not over however. The Jewfish has now been renamed the Goliath grouper for what can be termed politically correct reasons, although the renaming has not come without resistance from people on both sides of the religious fence. The name Goliath does bring up some interesting permutations involving Israel's King David and the Philistine Goliath, and just like Goliath, the Jewfish has the unfortunate habit of confronting invaders who have encroached on what it believes is its territory. If the intruder turns out to be a spear toting diver, the result is the same as in the pages of the Bible, the demise of Goliath ... grouper that is. Because of these reasons and personality shortcomings, the Jewfish was fished to near extinction. Now, the Goliath Grouper, a.k.a. Jewfish is protected throughout Florida's waters and is making an impressive comeback. But, just as with many other endangered or threatened species, little is known about the natural history or basic biology of this fish, and so in this way, Matt Finn became entwined with the grouper.

Discovery

It was a hot muggy day as was typical for the Ten Thousand Islands during July, and since this was the first day of the month it would not be getting any better until the cooler days of the fall, and this year, 1998, was no exception. A little over a year and a half from Y2K and all of its possible or imagined ramifications, Matt Finn, oblivious to what may or may not have lurked in the future, wandered down to the dock at the back of his house. The area looked something like a movie set from a story about life on the bayou with the hodgepodge stack of crab traps, tools, and other fishing paraphernalia. Without breaking stride he jumped aboard his twenty five foot mullet boat, a peculiar contraption with a hole in the center allowing the 115 horse motor to be mounted in the middle of the craft just ahead of the steering position. This enabled the boat to better operate and perform other net pulling chores in the dark shallow waters of the Ten Thousand Islands. A sweaty dampness covered everything so Matt took an old retired bath towel and wiped off the sky blue steering console and white 100 quart Igloo ice chest that served as his seat. He would get hot and perspire enough today, soaking his clothes without any help from a wet boat. Matt wanted to get a jump on his work before the sun got too high and so he cranked up the motor, and the resulting bass note of the pulsing throbbing exhaust told him the ignition had done its job and the inanimate motor had come to life. It was a good sound. Those who do not spend much time on the water cannot appreciate the song of a boat's motor, but to fisherman, divers and other such sort of sailors, it is the sound of impending adventure. The smell of these sea air, throb of the engine, the feel of the motor being put into gear, and the slice of the hull through the water with its accompanying washing bubbling serenade as the boat skims over the surface, make up a one of a kind poetry that men of the waters seek and live for.

Matt, a fair skinned blue eyed Irishman had donned his usual sun blocking garb, a thrown together Matt Finn designer collection of clothing that would not get him on the cover of G.Q. but served its purpose well and unpretentiously. Today his costume consisted of a Real Tree camouflage baseball cap, a dark navy blue tee shirt, weathered blue jeans with an assortment of holes that he rationalized provided extra ventilation, and of course, the ever-present polarized sun glasses. These would allow him to see through the ocean's surface and view any thing of interest laying below that air-water boundary. Matt munched on a piece of smoked mullet as the boat glided across the top of the water and the balmy air and smell of the sea began to envelope him. It swirled around like a narcotic smoke that would lull you into a sleepy trance if one allowed it. He never tired of the ocean and maze of islands he considered himself lucky to be working among, each one with its own individual mix of mangroves. The Red mangroves with their distinctive prop roots dominating the water's edge, followed slightly inland but not too far by the silvery tinged leaves and ghostly finger like pneumatophores of the Black mangrove, then still higher, the yellowish green leaves of the White mangrove. Flocks of bird dotted the air and foliage in a profusion of color squawking their language while various fish dimpled and disturbed the water. To complete the scene, even the occasional shark made an appearance, their dorsal fins giving away their location as they sliced frictionless through the water driven by the serpentine action of the fish's tail, perpetually on the move, forever looking for a target of opportunity.

Matt had to remind himself that he was out here to do some work as he pulled up to his first trap site and prepared to check the contents. His brain at once commenced to switch gears into its alert and inquisitive mode that is the earmark honed skill of a veteran biologist,. By observation, measurement, weighing, and gathering of empirical data, Matt would be able to determine the relative health of the Goliath grouper. What it is feeding on, how much does it weigh, how old is it, coloration, fin condition, external parasites, even the interior of the mouth would be checked for hitchhikers. The first trap however would answer none of these questions because it was empty and devoid of life. There is always anticipation when pulling up a trap. It is somewhat akin to checking the mailbox to see what treasure or trash has been left inside, and always a let down when empty. Not to worry though, there were many more to be checked. Matt rebaited the trap, threw it over the side of the boat and watched it sink out of sight, only a floating marker gave a clue to its presence. Drying his hands off with the bath towel, he put the motor in gear and continued on to the next site. This was the practiced routine that would be repeated many time throughout the day.

The second trap was more interesting. Still, no Jewfish, but a wondrous collection of tiny biological amusements poured out onto the deck. Crabs scuttled about and Matt shepherded them through the scuppers if the creatures were small enough, or in one sweep he caught them in a small bait net and flipped them overboard. There was a small moray eel in the trap which wiggled sinuously around until it too was netted and returned to its former home. A puffer fish frantically inflated itself with air instead of the usual water and when Matt threw it back, the fish comically floated on its back bobbing on the surface. Determining that it was once again safe, the puffer began deflating itself, letting out the air in a burst that sent it skittering across the water like a loosed balloon before it darted into the depths.

The old saying, "The third time's the charm", held true on the next trap. This time among the squirming, slithering contents, he spied a small, marbled, brown colored fish. The rounded tail confirmed its identity as a Goliath grouper, but for Matt this was only a formality in the fish ID book. He had seen so many of these fish that he knew what it was instantly. He methodically recorded the trap's location, and weighed the tiny two inch fish on a sensitive scale that could record its scant mass. The little grouper gave no indication now of the several hundred pounds that it might one day reach. Later back at home, Matt could fit the fish's weight and length into an equation that would be recorded in empirical data, indicating the grouper's relative condition.

And so it went on into the day. Move along, check a trap, record data, move along and do it again. A serene monotony that is only an elusive dream of attainment for most of the world. Matt was beginning to draw near to a place called Fish Hawk Creek, not far from another spot by the name of Dismal Key. He had been here countless times before. And then, there it was. In the peripheral limits of his vision, like a speck on his cornea, something out of place that shouldn't have been there. He didn't really see it at first, just sensed it. He continued to gaze across the water, digesting computer like the incoming information that his eyes, ears, and nose were sending his brain, and he began to hone in on a forlorn spot just at the tangled edge of the mangrove forest. He stood there in silence, sweat dripping off him, only the sound of the occasional bird punctuating the moment, then he once more put the motor in gear and advanced at a slow, no wake idle speed toward the area. An eerie feeling of death seemed to emanate from the spot as though something bad had happened here and the hair on the back of his neck began to stand up along with a feeling of unease which was not normal for a veteran of these waters like Matt.

Closer he drew to the spot, and then still closer. As the tangle of overhanging branches reached out at him, the detail of the area grew sharper. And then there it was again. A ghostly form, an oblong oval form, gently bobbing up and down in the wash of the wind driven lapping waves. What was it? All the information was now in place and then like some epiphany it clicked in. It was the lifeless battered shell of a sea turtle. Too bad!, he thought, "I wonder what happened to this guy?" Matt knew he should report this to the proper authorities. Sea turtles being an endangered species, the Florida Fish and Wildlife Conservation Commission, or FFWCC would want to know about this and record the information. Matt was in yards of the unlucky turtle now and he had to decide his plan of action. He prepared himself for the odor that he knew from past experience would accompany a closer approach. Things decayed quickly in the Florida sun and he also listened for the sickening buzz of flies, but strangely things were silent and the only smell was the usual soft musty aroma of the mangrove forest. Odd he thought, the poor guy must have died only a few hours ago. The boat slowed to a stop now and the turtle which Matt identified as a Green sea turtle, Chelonia mydas, was right along side. The wicked gash in the rear of the shell and emaciated body provided evidence that it was probably a boat strike victim. He prepared himself for the grisly task that he knew awaited him. Lying down in the boat, bracing himself with his chest partially over the gunwale, he reached outward to grasp the unlucky animal. What happened next caused Matt to lurch backward, recoiling with an unexpected start. The dead turtle let out a loud gasp as it inhaled a breath of air! It was not dead, but still alive, even if just barely. It still might have a chance if he could get it to the proper authorities quickly. Time was of the essence! He began to notice bubbling lesions on the animal's lower shell or plastron that indicated bacterial infection. Matt once again braced himself on the side of the boat and grabbed the turtle. It was very weak and did not struggle, as if sensing that this strange being might free him from his long ordeal. And then the warm comforting hands of Matt Finn, lifted the mangled but still alive Pete the Green sea turtle up into the air and gently laid him on the floor of the boat.

6

JOURNEY

Pete, who had never before been out of the water since the day of his hatching, was for the first time ever as he lay on the floor of the boat, feeling the full weight of his body. It is a feeling not unknown to snorkelers and scuba divers as they exit the water after a dive. It is a feeling of weight and clumsiness while you move about the deck and remove your dive gear returning to the pull of gravity. Pete weakly looked around moving only his eyes and focused on the sky blue interior enclosing him. It was a color he remembered from somewhere in his past. It had been many weeks since he had been struck, and now he could feel the vibration of the motor through the floor of this second boat in which he was now a passenger. In an ironic twist of fate, a boat not unlike one that had caused him so much pain, was now his vehicle of deliverance.

Matt gunned the motor and the craft moved off, the bow slowly lifting up and then just as slowly dropping again as it came up on plane carrying its strange cargo. What Pete could not know, now that Matt had rescued him and removed him from the water, was whether or not he would ever return to his ocean home or forever be in exile from it? At this point, all he could do being so weak and near death was to fall into a peaceful detachment from the world, and sleep, perhaps dreaming of better times on a safer ocean, an ocean he might never see again.

Somewhere between 9:30am and maybe 10:00 am on July 1, 1998, a phone began ringing in the office of Maura Krause, who was working in the Collier County Natural Resources Department in Naples, Florida. Maura, an environmental specialist in the Department's sea turtle protection program, was compiling and collating a mountainous load of data for the county's annual turtle status report. The phone rang a second time before she was able to mentally detach from the job at hand and pick it up just as it began a third ring beating the fourth that would have forwarded it to voice mail. "Natural Resources Department, Maura Krause", she answered. "Maura, this is Matt Finn over in Goodland", came the reply. "Hi Matt, what's up?", she responded. Already familiar with Matt Finn and his interesting adventures, she was at once paying attention, having instantly forgotten the paper work on her desk. "Maura, I've got a pretty banged up Green sea turtle in my boat. I picked him up this morning floating up in the mangroves. I thought it was dead but it still seems to be hanging in there. Looks like a boat strike. There's a crack in the rear of its shell and he's really emaciated."

Nothing more needed to be said between them. "I'm on my way Matt", Maura responded. Exiting the office, she first collected a sky blue plastic child's swimming pool and placed it in the back of the 1989 Chevy Blazer, a vehicle that was beginning to show that its better days were behind it. The little wading pool was covered inside and out with little cartoonish sea turtles frolicking on a beach somewhere.

Pulling out of the parking lot she started the trip south to Goodland, a distance of a little over twenty miles that should take between thirty and forty five minutes, depending on the traffic which was controlled by how many people were heading to and from the beach areas.

At the first point the traffic slowed down, she picked up her mobile phone and punched in the number of the Clearwater Marine Aquarium and asked to speak with a man named Glen. He was in charge of the aquarium's sea turtle rehabilitation and rescue program. A program in which sick, injured, or otherwise troubled turtles are rescued and treated with the hope of returning them back to the wild. "Glen, this is Maura Krauss. I'm on my way down to Goodland to check on an injured Green sea turtle. It's a possible boat strike. Once I get there I'll assess the situation. Be ready for a pick up!" "OK, no problem", Glen answered. "I'll be waiting to hear from you."

The miles continued to go by and finally Maura began to make her way over the bridge that connected the mainland to Marco Island, where the little town of Goodland was located. It would only be a few more minutes now. The road took on a more rural appearance with each passing mile and after a few turns here and there, she pulled up at the back of Matt's house. Parking the Blazer on a small strip of grass, she exited it then rang the bell on the fence. This quickly led to a barking greeting response from a three legged dog and his snow white side kick, an Eskimo Samoyed. The two dogs made for an odd combination. One, a friendly brown haired animal somewhat resembling a dingo but with only three legs, who seemed to be unaware that he was missing an appendage, or that he had ever needed it. At his side stood the Samoyed, who one would have thought should have certainly been more content attached to a dog sled in some northerly latitude, rather than patrolling the perimeters of a tropical compound that was the home of a marine biologist in some saltwater swamp.

Having been alerted by the dog's barking, Matt appeared from behind the house and spied Maura standing at the fence. "Hi Maura let me open the gate for you." He swung it open and she stepped into the yard. The two dogs recognized her scent and instantly accepted her as one of their own pack who had returned, then happily trotted along side, their tongues hanging roguishly over the sides of their mouths. The canine companions eagerly anticipated what amusements might be in store for them, which they always hoped would end up as something to eat, or at the very least, some malodorous object that they could shove their noses in and examine and consider at length. Matt and Maura made their way through the crab traps and assortment of essential fishing debris until they found themselves at the dock. Her eyes traveled over to one of the slips where the mullet boat and its cargo lay securely tied, silent and still, almost strangely so. Maura stepped closer and peered into the rear of the craft. Her eyes were met initially by the Igloo cooler turned boat seat. At first glance the deck appeared empty, but just as she was about to turn to Matt her eye caught some movement, and then the unmistakable outline of the front flipper of a sea turtle. A few steps more and there it was, a turtle looking lifeless and emaciated but still hanging on. She bent down to examine it more closely, her eyes running over the beautiful contours of its shell then coming to rest on the wicked gash in the rear. Almost certainly a boat strike she thought, the emaciation of its body giving testament to the weeks of suffering it must have endured. The toughness and survival instinct of these animals was legendary. Maura did not know if the turtle would survive over the long run, but it was still alive and so it was without question worth the effort to try and save it, and the effort would be made.

The first thing required was to fill out the official Sea Turtle Stranding and Salvage report as it was titled. Pulling a pen from her pocket she first filled in the date, July 1, 1998, followed by other pertinent information. Maura continued her way through the form next recording the species, CM was listed for Chelonia mydas, the Green sea turtle, location where found, mouth of Fish Hawk Creek west of Dismal Key, town of Goodland, latitude and longitude, condition of the turtle and shell measurements, straight width and length. Pete was 23 inches long by 18 inches wide. The condition of the turtle was listed using a numerical score card, which interestingly enough started at 0 for alive, followed by 1 for fresh dead, 2 for moderately decomposed, 3 for severely decomposed, 4 for dried carcass, and lastly 5 for skeleton, bones only. Maura entered a 0 in the blank. Pete was alive.

"OK", she said. "Let's get him out of the boat." As the dogs watched approvingly, Matt jumped aboard the docked watercraft, straddled the turtle, grabbed both sides of the shell and began to lift. He was always amazed by the weight of these animals, even in this emaciated state the turtle was still a handful. He lifted Pete about chest high, then slid him onto the dock while Maura helped and guided. The two dogs eagerly sniffed and licked their new found friend, inhaling all the wondrous odors that were emanating from the turtle. The groggy Pete scarcely moved through all this, just weakly looking around, wondering what this new obstacle would mean for him.

Matt held the turtle up so Maura could take a few pictures and she snapped a few. "That's good," she said. "Let's get him into the Blazer and out of here." Around from the back of the house the two carried the turtle, the dogs escorting them all the way. Then they laid Pete in the back of the vehicle, inside the kiddy pool with the cartoon turtle design. A damp towel was placed over his shell to keep it moist. It was in fact the exact towel that had served Matt Finn so well throughout that day.

"Thanks Matt," Maura said. "I'll get going then." "No problem", he answered. She started the vehicle, turned it around and slowly drove down the road, the dogs continuing to watch vigilantly. As the Blazer drove out of sight Matt too watched. Good luck, he thought, and then as if recalling something, he pivoted and returned to his world of mangrove forests and twisting water pathways. His dogs followed closely at his side, one with three legs seemingly handicapped, the other, snow white, seemingly out of place. Pete's journey had begun.

7

ARRIVAL

While the image of Matt Finn and his canine friends faded away in the Blazer's rear view mirror, Maura's thoughts were already returning to the job at hand. Once again the mobile phone was summoned and the call was placed to Glen at the Clearwater Aquarium. It was a call that he had been waiting for, a call that sadly too often failed to come. That meant that another turtle had succumbed to whatever trauma had been inflicted on it, and there would be no need for a pick up. But this time, the call did come. "Glen, this is Maura. I'm on my way. The turtle's banged up but still alive. I'll meet you at the usual spot, the Subway sandwich shop." "OK", Glen answered. "I'll see you there."

    Pulling into the first gas station available, Maura stopped to fuel up the vehicle. She found herself in the odd flux that on occasion people find themselves in. She was anxious to get to her destination, feeling an urgency to complete the job, but at the same time she was not in a hurry. Maura knew it would take Glen nearly three hours to drive down to Port Charlotte, the rendezvous point, which was triple the time it would take for her to drive north. While the fuel tank was being filled, Maura cleaned up the windows. As she did, she could see her turtle cargo in the back and reflected on the absurdity of the situation. Here she was, driving through Florida with an injured sea turtle for a traveling companion. On the other hand, she also thought how lucky she was to work in a job so unique and important. How many people in the world could say they had ever served as an ambulance driver for a turtle? Getting back into the vehicle, she looked over her shoulder to the cargo area where Pete was laying in the plastic pool then pulled out of the station and continued on her way.

    Meanwhile, in the back of the Blazer, Pete could feel the sensation of movement, but since he couldn't see out, all he could do was lay in his swimming pool bed and ride along in what had become somewhat of a magic carpet odyssey. Many weeks ago he had been a wild animal dealing with the whims of nature. Now, in less than a day he had traveled in a boat and now an automobile, a second form of transportation that few of his kind would ever experience. The boat had taken him from his natural home, now the auto was rapidly moving him northward along the Florida interstate network to an unknown destination.

Maura traveled first up highway 951 out of Goodland and Marco Island, then connected to Interstate 75 a few miles east of Naples. All the while Pete lay silent, barely moving at all. He remained in this state of torpor until after they had passed the Caloosahatchee River. As they traversed the span over it, Pete perked up and stirred a little. The tone of the Blazer's tires humming on pavement now changed to singing a different tune when they came to the bridge. Perhaps it was this change of sound or pitch due to the vehicle vibration, or the distant smell of the ocean beckoning him as its perfume wafted its way up the river and reached his nostrils, but for the first time on this journey Pete lifted up his head. He searched the air with some expectation of deliverance, but as the vehicle continued on, the ocean bouquet disappointingly faded, along with Pete's interest and hope of somehow returning to his home. His head slowly lowered until it came to rest on the floor of the plastic pool. He let out a breath as if sighing and once again returned to a state of fitful, dejected sleep.

Back up front, Maura continued her drive, deep in thought as the miles went by and scenery changed. The exit signs clicked by in rapid succession until one finally read, Exit 28. Her part of the trip was almost over. Putting on the turn signal, she pulled off the interstate and drove the short distance to the Subway shop and parked in front. Maura went inside to get a sandwich, ordering a turkey sub, all the while keeping an eye on the Blazer and turtle through the window, just as a dog owner might watch the car to monitor his friend outside. When she came out a few people tagged along with her, eager to examine and ooh and aww at the strange passenger in the back. "Is it going to be OK?", they asked Maura. "We hope so.", she answered. "It's going to get good care at the Clearwater Aquarium." She continued to talk with her small audience about sea turtles until they were all satisfied and the onlookers returned to the restaurant, eager to tell others and their families about all they had seen. Maura got back into the Blazer, looked back at her companion Pete, then started her lunch. While doing that, she also reviewed the the paperwork that had been filled out, and intermittently scanned the radio for news, music, or anything else that might help pass the time until Glen arrived. Various random thoughts traveled through her mind as they do when one is waiting for something and she periodically nodded off. Her head would slowly fall and then she would catch herself and quickly pop back to alertness, then do it again. After one of these tiny siestas her eyes awakened to focus on the sight of a white van pulling into the parking lot with the name Clearwater Marine Aquarium on its side. Help had arrived.

Glen pulled up along side her and got out. "Hi Maura, how's our friend doing?" "He's OK", she responded, "Let's get him into the van." The two walked to the back of the vehicle and Maura raised the rear door. It opened slowly, lifting up like a curtain rising on a stage revealing Pete laying in his swimming pool, bath towel covering his shell, silent and still. Glen gave the turtle a cursory exam. "Looks like you had a run in with a boat, Buddy", Glen said to the turtle in a one sided conversation in which no answer was expected. "Looking at the state your in, it must have been a while ago, pretty emaciated. OK, let's get him switched over to the van." The two of them slid the kiddie pool out a little, and then got a grip on the turtle, lifting him over to the waiting second vehicle, into still another plastic pool. The old bath towel was replaced with a new one from the aquarium and wet down with fresh water. The old one which had faithfully covered Pete's shattered body since he had left Goodland, was carefully and lovingly folded, then placed in the back of Maura's Blazer, now a souvenir to be remembered in the scrapbook of her mind.

"OK, thanks Maura. I'll let you no how it does," said Glen. Then he was off, vanishing as quickly as he had arrived. Maura watched the van pull away and fade in the distance. She sat in silence, filled with a sense of loneliness. She always felt an attachment to each of her rescued "babies", and it was always with a bittersweet feeling of joy and sadness when they departed. She would occasionally make a trip up to Clearwater to visit her previously rescued turtle friends, and felt pride in the fact that she had been an instrument in their survival. It was especially rewarding when a turtle she had delivered was fully rehabilitated and returned to the wild. Maura also had been lucky enough to participate in a few sea turtle releases, and it was a moving experience to witness a recovered one drop over the side of a boat back into the ocean, or carrying the turtle to the water's edge, watch the invigoration and what can only be described as elation when it feels the first caress of the sea, as if it had been reunited with a friend it had thought was lost forever, a relationship with its home resurrected at last. It swims outward, flippers driving with synchronicity, the lungs now filled with the energy of the ocean breeze as it soars through the water, ever farther, returning to the glory of its underwater heaven.

Maura knew sadly however, that since Pete was a boat strike turtle with probable spinal cord injuries, his chances of returning to the wild were slim. All that could be done now was to try and save him and provide the best possible life available.

As the hours passed, Pete continued sleeping in the back of his third vehicle in less than a day. He was oblivious to any possibilities that might come his way in the future. Perhaps the only force at work now was his instinct for survival, and sea turtles are remarkable survivors. He once again perked up as he felt the strange sensation of climbing along with another vibration and pitch change when the van began crossing the more than ten mile span of the Sunshine Skyway Bridge, crossing Tampa Bay. The scent of the ocean returned to him, this time stronger than ever. His throat expanded as he deeply inhaled the balmy air water elixir that rejuvenated and gave hope. He searched more intently this time. And then he slept again, more peacefully now. Perhaps the nearness of his ocean home draped around him like a wonderful security blanket caused this needed rest to come more easily. He slept so deeply that he never felt the van stop and the rear doors open. He had reached the Clearwater Marine Aquarium, his new home.

8

RESURRECTION

While Pete was deeply involved in his dreams as he slumbered in the rear of the van, things were starting to happen all around him. Perhaps it was the exhaustive nature of his long journey with its boat and multiple auto rides, or the cumulative weight of injuries and emaciation that weakened and sapped his strength that made him unaware of the small group of people who had converged upon the vehicle and were beginning the task at hand. The turtle was first gently slid out of the van and laid onto an awaiting cart and then escorted through the aquarium's doors. Pete, now awakened by the vibration of the cart's rotating wheels, started to take in the sights and smells surrounding him and wondered what this latest turn of events might mean. His long rehabilitation had begun. The first time one travels to the Clearwater Marine Aquarium your initial impression would be a feeling of peaceful isolation. This feeling is enhanced by the route you must travel to get there. Starting at let's say Tampa, you will head west on Highway 60, crossing the bay. Here, the Courtney Campbell Causeway Bridge takes the traveler on a low ride across the water for about ten miles. While you are traversing the bay, decorative palms planted here and there pass by accentuating the ocean which looks expansive and beautiful. The sea breeze here awakens something inside and it reminds one of the Florida of the Fifty's and early Sixties. You can almost look out over these shallow waters with their stretches of sea grass and recreate a mental picture of a time when sea horse "pushers" who in the past worked these waters with their distinctive push nets, would search for tiny dwarf seahorses to supply the aquarium trade. These little sea ponies might perhaps be destined for the fish tank of some young future biologist and provide hours of amusement for said person.

Eyes back on the road, we approach the end of the causeway, and in a short time find ourselves in the downtown area.

Clearwater is not a big town. It certainly does not have that feel about it. Still, at a little over 100,000 inhabitants it does at times provide a feeling of the city, but then again there is also a touch of the suburban. Continuing the drive, you take in the usual Florida sights, the ever present shopping districts, government buildings, some old and ornate, others concrete blocks of utilitarianism. Hotels and motels go by, the old, the new, those painfully past their prime. The stoplights also come and go. Then things start to thin out a bit to a span of less congestion where somewhere along this path you see a small sign with a still smaller arrow directing the traveler to the Clearwater Marine Aquarium. It is a sign whose location you can never remember until it is encountered again on the next trip, as though it materialized and dematerialized like some sort of ethereal mirage. You follow the road turning and veering according to instructions finally crossing another bridge, the Garden Memorial Causeway, which will take us across the harbor to the outer shoreline and onto a separate island north of what is known as Sand Key. We are now on a road called Windward Passage that brings us to the Clearwater Marine Aquarium. Here it sits, unexpectedly quiet and peaceful, not a large building, medium sized with a small cozy parking lot. The aquarium's blue aquamarine exterior is an unpretentious pure tone that relaxes the soul and mind.

    The building itself has the very humblest of beginnings. It began service as a wastewater treatment plant, certainly an ignoble start for a future aquarium. Things would have remained as such, except for the need of the city to upgrade its water treatment facility. At the same time as fate would have it, a popular exhibit called Fish-O-Rama was also in need of a larger home. So, in 1978, the City of Clearwater leased the building to the afore mentioned Fish-O-Rama for the sum of one dollar a year, and the Clearwater Marine Aquarium was born. That tiny investment would pay off many times over the next decades.

    It wasn't long before the aquarium's main objective became the rescue and rehabilitation of marine life, with emphasis on dolphins, otters, and of course sea turtles. Its record over the last twenty five years or so has in short been outstanding for such a small facility operating on a shoestring budget. It was into this oasis that Pete had been brought, and when one considered all the bad things that had come his way over the last several weeks, this was the one ray of hope shining in the dark that could maybe positively impact his life.

    Pete, still resting on the cart felt several pairs of warm hands gently but surely pick him up and place him onto an examination table, so the extent of his injuries could be evaluated. The warm lights illuminating him felt good on his shell and skin and reminded him of days gone by basking in the Florida sun. He awakened more and began to move his head, looking around at all the strange lights and people darting in and out of his field of vision. First, his shell was cleaned so that the wound the boat's propeller had made or any other problems would become more defined as they were cleared of algae or other ocean debris. The most obvious injury was a large gaping crack at the rear of his carapace as a turtle's top shell is properly called. Although the shell is oval in shape, if you picture the carapace as the face of a clock with Pete's head at the twelve o'clock position, the wound was located on the edge of the shell at about the 6:30 position and ran inward for about six or seven inches.

While Pete was being worked on, he was able to look around the room, and he saw that he was not alone. There were other turtles in the room, here, there, everywhere! They were of all kinds and sizes. Some were tiny hatchlings, perhaps cold stunned from a chill a few months earlier. Or maybe others like Pete's own nest mates had headed inland after hatching, lured by artificial lighting from homes along the beach, and gotten stranded in grass or other snags where they became spent and dehydrated. Found in the grass they had been rescued just in time.

There were other turtles, some medium sized like Pete, and some giants like the Loggerhead he had seen weeks ago. All species were represented, Hawksbills, Kemp's Ridley, Loggerhead, and Greens. Their injuries ranged from boat strikes like his, to monofilament fishing line or net entanglement that too often led to a slow amputation of one or more flippers as the line or net slowly tightens around them, cutting through flesh and bone. Shark bite victims were also represented with parts of their shells or flippers punctured or bitten off. Some turtles particularly Loggerheads, had intestinal impaction caused by eating ocean going debris such as plastic bags, balloons, surgical gloves, or fish hooks. Finally, there were also a great number of Green turtles with grotesque, warty, sponge like growths all over their shells, flippers, or heads. This was the disease called fibropapilloma.

Each of these animals would receive treatment as needed, through general care, surgery, or possibly laser surgery in the case of fibropapilloma, a regimen in which each tumor is carefully cut away and removed. After the laser has done its job, the turtle is allowed to recover to either undergo further surgery, or hopefully found disease free for one year, is tagged and returned to the wild. Some turtles suffering from fishing line or net entanglement would often need to have one or more flippers amputated. They too would be nursed back to health and if the damage was not too great, also be returned to the ocean minus a flipper here and there.

One Loggerhead turtle not far away from where Pete was located, a female named Arnold, had come in only two months earlier. She had been found not far from Clearwater, badly entangled in fishing line, stranded near a bridge. Arnold had lost seventy five percent of her front flippers and the aquarium was now her permanent home. Turtles with fibropapilloma, amputation, shark bites, cold stunned, or intestinal impaction, all had good hope of being released, even if not in every case. For Pete, it was a different story. The fact is and was that boat strike turtles are rarely if ever releasable. The reasons for this are usually twofold. First, the boat strike turtle due to spinal trauma frequently suffer from partial paralysis of one or more flippers, typically the rear, and there may even be some feeling in the flippers. This in itself would not rule out release, as shown by amputee turtles, but there is a second more insidious problem resulting from the injury. The victims are buoyant. In other words, they float, usually in a position reminiscent of a wheelbarrow, head down like the front wheel, rear flippers up like the handles. This swimming attitude in the water makes it difficult if not impossible to feed and in addition, increases the likelihood they will be struck by another boat and killed due to their proximity to the surface.

Whether Pete was releasable was only a point for debate. The main concern now was how to save this badly injured creature's life, and so the examination went on. Pete could feel a faint tingle as the needle from a syringe punctured his skin and withdrew blood from one of his flippers like a mechanical mosquito, and then again as the antibiotic, Baytril was injected inward. After a number of other procedures, he was placed in a small tub surrounded by shallow water. The liquid was only a few inches deep so his head was always out of it and no effort would be required to breathe. All that was asked of him at this time was to rest and heal.

The Road Back

It may have been days or it may have been weeks, but time did pass, and with it also began to pass some of the pain that had racked Pete's body for such a long period. For the first time since his last wonderful days floating on the ocean prior to the boat collision, he started to look around at his environment with a purpose instead of in a lethargic fog, and that purpose was clear and singular in its focus. He wanted sustenance, glorious food! His increased alertness was duly noted by workers at the aquarium, one of whom was his old friend Glen. "He looks a lot better. Let's get him into a deeper pool and then try some solid food.", Glen said.

Once again a small group of people were summoned and Pete was carried over to and placed in a deeper, silvery colored, plastic horse trough. The name Rubbermaid, was stamped or molded into its rim, but the manufacturer could never have imagined that the eventual use for their product would be a sea turtle recovery pool. The water in this new enclosure was only a few feet deep, so Pete could do little more than paddle in tiny pivoting circles, but this was of no concern. Everything at this moment in time and space was focused on his obtaining nourishment.

Being familiar with the idiosyncrasies of recovering sea turtles and guessing that Pete's increased activity meant he was finally considering food, Glen brought out a few pieces of squid. Its high protein content would be like a mega calorie milk shake intended to put pounds of weight back on the turtle's shrunken frame. Glen took a few squid in his hand and waved them in the water in front of Pete's nose where the oil and scent from it swirled around his head like the smoke from a shore lunch campfire. His eyes began to focus forward and zero in on the white tentacles waving seductively in front of him. His neck slowly extended and his nose touched the squid. It was not a smell or taste he was familiar with so he quickly retracted his head. Being a Green sea turtle, Pete's diet was mostly a vegetarian one, but still, the smell was of interest. Again his mouth and the tip of his nose caressed the undulating squid limbs that Glen was holding patiently in front of him. Once more he extended his neck, reaching outward, focusing intently on this strange target, the hunter stealthily eyeing its prey. Slowly closer, and then still closer the jaws came to the food. He was in range now. He paused, thinking it over, and then the snap came and he greedily wolfed down the prize. Good Lord it tasted wonderful! With relish he looked for more and Glen was eager to oblige. Two, three, four more pieces went down the reeducated and rejuvenated esophagus, then he worked his jaws with satisfaction and took an invigorating deep breath of air. It was a celebratory inhalation of a full stomach and the return of life.

These feeding sessions continued over the next several days which turned into weeks, then months. Pete's strength grew as the time progressed until it was time to move him still again to a bigger enclosure. His home now would be a much larger concrete tank with several feet of water in which his swimming and diving ability could better be evaluated. Sadly, the evaluation went as expected. Pete exhibited the positive buoyancy typical of other boat strike turtles, along with partial paralysis of his rear flippers. He was left with the trademark swimming style of his fellow victims. When he would dive downward and then stop actively working his front flippers, Pete would slowly float back up to the water's surface, kind of like a waterlogged cork, with a tail up head down attitude, a nose dive in reverse.

In the sport of scuba diving, there is a term known as neutral buoyancy that describes the diver's ability to move through the water at a chosen depth and attitude without floating upward or sinking to the bottom. The diver accomplishes this through regulating how much air is in his lungs and also with the use of something called a buoyancy compensator vest, better known amongst divers as a B.C.

Although it is not fully understood how they accomplish it, sea turtles also must maintain neutral buoyancy in order to feed and maneuver in the ocean. Pete, because of his injuries could no longer stay neutrally buoyant, and was left with a semi-floating, slightly struggling swimming style that would become his signature. Because of this, he was evaluated as permanently impaired, and could not be returned to his beloved ocean home.

He was accordingly placed on display in one of the aquarium's exhibits. A certificate was printed that told his story to the public. He was listed as a Green sea turtle, sex undetermined, and was given the name, "Pete", a name by which we have always known him.

9

YOU ARE MY FRIENDS

As the days turned into weeks, the weeks into months, and the months into years, Pete became accustomed to his new way of life. It was not like the home he had known in the sea, but the sea also held dangers, with its fast moving power boats, fishing line and net entanglements, sharks, and countless other hazards. Pete could no longer live there in any case. His handicaps were too great to permit that. What he needed most now was someone to love and care for him. He was not the independent free animal of the open ocean he had once been. Now he was dependent on the good will of others, and they were giving him the care he needed. Somewhere inside he searched for something that was slowly being washed from his memory like an outgoing tide. Futilely trying to understand life's cruel tests and the purpose for them, Pete swam around his enclosure and studied its finite dimensions. This became his daily routine.

Over the years his eyes and ears were witness to a passing array of sights and sounds. He became like one of the housekeeping staff at a hotel. New guests came and went. Pete was always there for the hello, and then goodbye to a various assortment of dolphins, otters, or turtles as they returned to the ocean, but he always stayed behind. All the while, more and more turtles, with clockwork regularity, continued arriving onto the doorstep of the aquarium with their various injuries and impediments. These too were patched and repaired as best they could be and sent on their way, but some like Pete could not be returned to the wild and they became his companions, all of them with sad stories to tell.

There was the female Loggerhead with the unsuitable moniker of Arnold. She had lost most of her front flippers to fishing line entanglement and had been at the aquarium when Pete arrived. Max was a Kemp's Ridley, a smaller variety of sea turtle. He had a debilitating head injury that made it necessary to hand feed him. Bailey was a Green sea turtle who had come in nearly nine years before Pete. Like him, she too was a boat strike turtle with buoyancy disorder as was George, a female Loggerhead from Georgia who came in two years later.

Not all of the injuries were man made however. Flip, was another Green turtle who had been found floating in the Gulf of Mexico, suffering from numerous shark bites to the head, shell, and flippers that permanently disabled him.

These turtles were the walking wounded, or rather swimming wounded who had already been in residence when Pete was brought in and they watched in silence as he was repaired. They all peered out from their various assortment of pools and tubs. On occasion a flipper might wave in the air, the turtle having lost its grip on the water in the tub, the appendage would then rise up over the rim. It was almost as if they were greeting one another, assuring Pete that everything would be all right, maybe looking for the latest news from the ocean. Was it still there? Was it as beautiful as ever? One could almost imagine them listening, eager to hear, always searching, never finding. In February of 1999, Sebastian joined the group; he too was a boat strike survivor, as was New Kid who came in during the month of May. Both were Green sea turtles and the first and second permanent residents to arrive after Pete.

Stubby, another Green, broke the continuous train of boat strike turtles when he came in a year later. He like Arnold had lost both of his front flippers to fishing line entanglement, forcing him to stay. Finally, Rob, a Kemps Ridley, showed up on September 3 of 2001, over three years after Pete. Part of his jaw was missing, most likely from another boat hit. This completed the coalition of the battered making up the group of lifers that were Pete's contemporaries at the Clearwater Marine Aquarium.

There were two other turtles however that were not injured, who nevertheless also claimed the aquarium as their home, oldest of all was the patriarch of the group named Mo. Big Mo, now a giant of a turtle, was picked up by someone walking on the beach in September of 1963 as a healthy Loggerhead hatchling and kept as a pet before that was illegal. Deprived of a natural life, he lived at the well known Pier 60 on Clearwater Beach for nearly twenty years before coming to the aquarium in 1982. Sixteen years later, Mo too watched as Pete, broken, shattered and pierced, was carried past him. Ironically, Mo also suffered from buoyancy disorder, although not as a result of any injury. It was from so many years of confinement in his original small pool at Pier 60. Sadly, Mo had lived his whole life just a few feet away from the sea, but unlike Pete he had never made it from the nest to the ocean, never knowing its taste, smell, or feel. He perhaps instinctively knew he belonged elsewhere, and may have spent part of his day looking for something intangible that never seemed to fully materialize. Undeterred, Mo's endless search went on, like a Papillonic goal he knew one day he would surely reach.

Last of the group but maybe the most important was Pinky, Pete's tank mate. Pinky was a leucistic Loggerhead, which meant she lacked normal pigmentation and looked as if she were an albino but without red eyes. She like Mo had lived her entire life in captivity. First hatching in Georgia, Pinky then went to live at the Norwalk Aquarium in Connecticut, followed by Clearwater, making her the nomad of the group. As tank mates, Pete and Pinky spent many hours paddling around and exploring their enclosure, occasionally looking up with possible amusement at the visitors who looked down at them. Sometimes, because it was an open exhibit, various objects or debris would come tumbling down and fall into the water where they would have to be retrieved or cleaned up. A paper cup, aquarium brochure, coin, or even the occasional camera would make a splash and catch Pete's attention especially, at least for the moment.

The high point of the day was always feeding time as it is for most turtles on sea or land, so Pete and Pinky would gather at the feeding spot like clockwork, greedily waiting for the greatly anticipated hand out. On one particular day, Pete was a little more hungry than usual and arrived a few minutes early at the small bridge that bisected his pool. He was not so patiently floating at this designated feeding area when a shiny object suddenly plopped into the water right in front of his nose. It fluttered enticingly like a small fish for a second before it was met by the snapping of Pete's jaws and then went down the hatch, at least partly anyway. It wasn't a taste he was familiar with but just then a keeper named Tammy arrived with a handful of his now beloved squid and before long his stomach was satisfied with more familiar fare.

And so the days past by. Pete was far from his old ocean haunts, but this home was a good one for an aquatically challenged survivor. He was getting the care he needed and would for years to come.

This Green sea turtle who had been given the name Pete, who had begun his life on some distant shore, struggling to reach the ocean, who had endured some of the worst trouble the world could throw his way, had overcome. He lived! Could anyone know what that might mean? Was there a purpose? …

> Perhaps I will stay with you awhile, or even spend the winter, so you can help me on my journey, wherever I go.
>
> —1 Corinthians 16:6.

10

ROTUNDA

Far to the north of Pete's home in sunny Clearwater, Florida, on the shores of a lake called Michigan, stands the City of Chicago. Unlike Florida which has two seasons, the warm season and the hot season, Chicago actually experiences four of them. There is spring, a time in which plants of all variety and size come back to life and flocks of birds return from warmer climates. After the spring we have summer, which to the surprise of many, is just as hot and humid as one would expect to find in Florida. Thirdly, there is the fall, a wonderful season. The air grows crisp with the return of cool Canadian breezes, while the trees take on their autumn color. The reds, yellows, and oranges that are displayed by the various deciduous artists cause you to stop, look and marvel at the beauty shown by nature's paint brush. There is one really bad thing about fall though. It precedes the winter!

You can spin it anyway you wish. One could say that the beautiful snowfall creates peaceful Currier and Ives like scenes. True. It is easier to heat a house than to cool it. Also true. The cold kills the mosquitoes. Can't deny that! These are all amusing rationalizations, but let's face it. The trees look gray and lifeless, like they were somehow inverted with their roots up in the sky. The grass, what there is of it, is dry and brown. Everything looks worn and haggard, including the people come about mid January. After the Super Bowl it's all down hill. You might as well dig a hole and live in a burrow. So why do people live in Chicago? Because it's a really neat place! We like the changing seasons. It makes you appreciate the good weather more. The City is full of all kinds of diverse neighborhoods and people, along with sports teams, restaurants and architecture.

First time travelers to Chicago are often surprised once they work their way past the massive sky scrapers like the Sears Tower and John Hancock buildings that contribute to the signature skyline to find that the City is indeed a port, a port on a massive lake. Expecting in their minds to see some sort of preconceived lakeside scenery, they are startled by the ocean like view with the infinite horizon and endless expanse they thought was reserved for the east or west coast, and this is an ocean you can drink. It's all freshwater! The boat slips, yacht anchorage, and beaches seem out of place in a Midwestern state best known for producing corn and livestock. Nevertheless, it does exist and on this same lakefront sits the graceful rotunda and long marble stairway approach to a building that has been one of Chicago's crown jewels since it opened in 1930, the John Graves Shedd Aquarium.

Where the Clearwater Marine Aquarium is a small building in a quiet setting, by comparison, the Shedd Aquarium is a massive structure that through its size, architectural appeal, and position of prominence right on the shore of Lake Michigan exudes energy with the promise of what must be inside its walls!

The building when first opened and for many years later exhibited its array of aquatic residents in a museum style of galleries positioned like spokes of a half wheel running from a central point axle located under the rotunda. The exterior and interior still exude a regal stateliness that must have caused travelers of the depression era who made the pilgrimage to the aquarium to gasp in awe while drinking in its beauty. As one walks up the thirty seven sweeping marble steps and approaches the Greek columned entranceway, you stop to look up at the eight sided rotunda that insistently and repeatedly compels your attention. When you do, you take notice that around the border of the dome's base runs a brocade trim of sea turtle and scallop shell figures. Wavelike support structures run up the side of the rotunda and converge at the apex of the dome, and here a trident points skyward. One would have to believe that if Neptune was not a mythical figure, this would certainly be his palace.

As you come into the building, the visitor finds himself in a large entranceway foyer surrounded by colonnades that draw eyes upward to the scallop shell trim, then downward to the marble walls whose grain was selected to suggest flowing and ebbing waters. The building's architectural features are in fact so intricate, that it really requires a guide with some degree of knowledge to point them all out. Even without the array of aquatic life it houses, the Shedd Aquarium would probably still be a point of interest for architects from around the world.

When the aquarium opened its doors to the public, the first exhibit that was in place was called the Swamp. A craterlike pit in the marble floor that was home to turtles and other creatures of the dampness, it took a position as the center axle in the half wheel and spoke gallery display. That exhibit and the rest of the aquarium were an instant hit, with lines of people weaving their way through the halls, stopping to look here and there, continually transfixed. That unbroken train has now continued for over seventy five years. This is in a large part due to the continued evolution of the exhibits which improve and change as technology and the skill of the keepers advance each year.

One of the first modifications to the Shedd's basic design began in the late nineteen sixties, when the oldest exhibit in the aquarium, the aforementioned Swamp, began a metamorphosis into of all things a Caribbean coral reef. Opening for the first time in the early nineteen seventies, the multi-sided 90,000 gallon circular exhibit took advantage of the vacated crater shaped moat in the floor left by the now departed Swamp. This circular hole was turned into a sandy ocean floor from which the surrounding tank rose about eight or nine feet higher. This allowed the viewer to look down, through, and up, into a dramatic simulation of a coral reef. With its elaborate illumination, replicated coral, gorgonians, sponges, and sea fans, over thirty years and some renovations later, the Caribbean Reef is still a thing of beauty that is the first thing most visitors come upon when touring the aquarium. With its glowing countenance directly under the rotunda, the Caribbean Reef is the Shedd's signature exhibit.

To really appreciate the mimicry of the coral community that is achieved by the Reef tank, one must have experienced first hand the wonder of diving a real ocean reef. Imagine yourself if you will, boarding the dive boat, where you instantly know you are in for adventure. As you take your seat and the craft starts its journey out to the reef, your blood pressure and heart rate rise as the boat rides up, over, down, and through the waves and breakers. Salt spray hits your face and some makes its way downward working through the lips and reaching the tongue where its briny ancestry reveals the fact that you are not on Lake Michigan.

Looking out to sea you spot the very distant reef marker off on the horizon,like some grave monument rising from the blue latitude. Traveling farther out to sea, the feeling of excitement continues to grow also now joined by one of intimidation and apprehension. This is because you are starting to grasp the fact that once you reach the reef, you are going to jump out of what appears to be a perfectly good boat and drop downward into an alien world. A world in which large creatures rule and engage in their trade as underwater predators and when you jump overboard, you are sure will all slowly turn and face in your direction wondering what treat has come their way! Still, when you reach the dive site and tie the boat off to a buoy, look over the side and down through the transparent ocean, you are greeted by a vision of coral and snow white sand in such profusion that your apprehensions melt away.

Slipping into the water we get our bearings and look down at the bottom. It's like floating in Treasure Island! The liquid we are in is so clear that the sun hitting the white coral sand bottom bounces back at us, causing us to squint behind our masks and actually feel the reflected heat. Our eyes focus on massive tan brain and elkhorn corals, one after the other, then fire coral in mustard tones followed by rhythmically swaying purple sea fans and brown fuzzy plumes straining the water for planktonic food. We notice the antennae of spiny lobsters poking out of every appropriate hiding place, continuing the theater. Before long, the fish arrive. Purple and blue toned schools of tangs mixed with brown surgeonfish in volume, swim past followed by a troop of multicolored parrotfish, twenty, forty, eighty in number, moving along to a predetermined destination, occasionally pausing at chosen spots to chew and crunch on the reef, their birdlike beaks incising the coral. Numerous barracuda watch us from an uncomfortable distance, always patrolling the perimeter of their domain, taking every opportunity to flash their dentition making it understood that you are not particularly welcome, just a tolerated interloper. There goal is intimidation. It works! We give them the room they desire. They leave us alone.

Suddenly, the sinuous movement of a large, brown sandpaper skinned nurse shark draws your attention away from the numerous barracuda as it materializes out of nowhere, always looking bigger than they really are. Eventually your eyes adjust their focus, downsizing onto the tiny fish flitting about the surface of the reef, darting in and out of each secret hiding place, dodging and swaying in the unseen breeze of the current. Neon gobies, damsel fish, wrasse, butterfly and angelfish, must have a copyright on all the colors ever created, but even silver fish like the school of Bermuda chub providing an escort as you swim about their home impress with the subtlety of their hue. Fighting the incoming tide has tired us so we head back to the boat. On the way we try to soak up as much of this world passing by as we can, trying to commit it to memory in case there is no return. We climb the ladder and it is finished.

While a manmade exhibit can never hope to capture the profusion of life that a wild reef holds, the Caribbean Reef at the Shedd does an admirable job nonetheless.

And this is why it continues to captivate its audience year after year as they enjoy its ocean mimicry.

As impressive as the exhibit is, it still needs people working behind the scenes to animate and bring life to its interior. They along with the animal inhabitants create the latticework that produces the intended picture. There was however one animal that for almost twenty five years was its signature performer. It was a Hawksbill sea turtle. His name was Hawkeye.

11

MESSENGER

Prior to beginning his reign as king of the Shedd's Caribbean Reef tank, Hawkeye the sea turtle was already an experienced world traveler, although not in the normal sense. He had not traveled the seven seas flying through underwater gardens and coral caverns, or soared between endless schools of glistening fish. Still, he did have a taste for the wild life as a youth, but it was just not enough for him. Certainly at an early age, his heart had a hold on a traveler's suitcase, or to be more accurate, a traveler's suitcase had a hold on him. You see, in 1977, Hawkeye was discovered hidden amongst the contents of a suitcase by the U.S. Customs Agency at O'Hare Airport in Chicago. Since by that time a sea turtle was already illegal contraband, he was seized as sure as a load of Cuban cigars and this gave him the opportunity he had secretly been waiting for. Hawkeye could now take his show on the road and fulfill a dream he had held for all of these eleven months of his life. He wanted to be a star!

Yes, it was a big dream for this little turtle, who at the time was less than two pounds and only five or six inches long, but he did have one thing going for him. He possessed a striking face! It was a face reminiscent of a celebrity! O.K., maybe that celebrity looked like Jimmy Durante or Karl Malden, but this big-nosed turtle had a certain pizzazz and panache.

Now according to the rules, any contraband sea turtles are supposed to be returned back to the wild, to the place where they came from. The problem was, nobody knew or were able to find out where indeed Hawkeye had come from, although years later, one might have suspected Barnum and Bailey. In fact, maybe, just maybe, no one had abducted him at all! Perhaps he had cleverly and stealthily crept into an unsuspecting tourist's open suitcase, all part of his master plan bent on hitting the big time! And so, he was brought to the Shedd Aquarium.

Unlike Green sea turtles which are vegetarians, or Loggerheads, indiscriminate omnivores in the most extreme sense, Hawksbill turtles like Hawkeye are much more specialized feeders, sort of gourmets if you will. It would in turn follow that because of their sophisticated tastes they would be more restricted in their habitats, and this is the case. Feeding to a great degree on sponges, Hawksbills are more often seen around coral reefs and other sponge friendly environs. Hawkeye having left the ocean at such a tender age most likely never partook of a sponge dinner and savored the taste of these aquatic "Twinkies", but once inside the walls of the Shedd's Caribbean Reef exhibit he became somewhat of a buffet freak, preferring the tastier squid, clams, shrimp and other food intended for the fish that shared the tank space he considered his turf.

Five times a day divers would descend into the artificial reef to feed its inhabitants, give lectures to the amused visitors and conduct question and answer sessions aided by an underwater microphone, all the while feeding the fish from a mesh basket. Hawkeye took the opportunity during these shows to perform his amusing antics for the onlooking and adoring audience, snapping up stray morsels that drifted his way and hovering around the various divers who made up his supporting cast. In fact, he made it his mission in life to consume as much food as possible. Unfortunately, just as with many other big stars, fame went to Hawkeye's head. If what he perceived as insufficient food homage was coming his way during the shows, he would begin to pester, harass, or even bite the chagrinned divers until they satisfied him just enough to get him out of the way. It finally came to the point were the divers in the tank could be divided into two groups, those who had been bitten by Hawkeye, and those who soon would be! Sadly, just as with many other over pampered stars, his over indulgence began to catch up with him and his weight ballooned up to one hundred fifty pounds, a far cry from the tiny stowaway that had arrived many years earlier. Despite his rotundness, Hawkeye still remained the star of the Caribbean Reef. His flamboyant nature and signature profile continued entertaining visitors numbering in the millions, who loved him despite his foibles.

Yes, Hawkeye was a star, but an aquarium or zoo is made up of much more than just one signature animal, and not far away from Hawkeye's realm, there is just a few yards down one of the Shedd's other galleries, another star, but this one is so sedate and unassuming that he frequently goes undetected and overlooked. He had been in residence over forty years already when Hawkeye first arrived. His name is Granddad. He is an Australian lungfish and when he arrived at the aquarium in 1933, he was already a full grown adult.

To appreciate the age and longevity of this fish which resembles a brown firehouse with paddle like fins, one would have to look back in time at the events occurring in the year Granddad came to Chicago. In 1933, President Franklin

Roosevelt was in the first of his four terms. Adolph Hitler was just coming into power. The biggest box office celebrities were Cary Grant and Mae West, and there swam Granddad. Eight years later, Pearl Harbor was attacked and World War II was on. Four years later that war was over until the Korean conflict started another one. Granddad saw the world walk by his window as John Kennedy was assassinated, the Vietnam War began and men landed on the moon. He was there for the resignation of a President, hostages seized in Iran, and the Challenger explosion. He continued his decades long swim during the Persian Gulf War, and the homeland tragedies of Oklahoma City, and September 11. All these events came and went while Granddad steadily swam, explored and reexplored his finite world, outlasting various changes to it and out distancing what must have been a long line of keepers and caregivers in charge of his well-being. How many must he have seen?

These people, the aquarists, trainers, keepers, and veterinarians, are inherently along with their charges, the true lifeblood of any zoo or aquarium, they are the battery that drives. Without them, there would be no fish to see. Hawkeye would not rule the Caribbean Reef, dolphins and beluga whales would not swim the inward passage. Penguins and otters would not dart about or play and even the venerable Granddad would languish.

All of the people that do this job must have a love for animals, but the absolute best of them are possessed of an unquenchable passion to be near and around them. They have a flame burning within that is ignited into a fire and then a full fledged conflagration when in the immediate proximity of fish, birds, dogs,cats,turtles or any other creature. When out of the company of their beloved menagerie, they tend to be quiet and introverted, avoiding crowds or social gatherings, feeling uncomfortable in such venues, preferring the company of the animal world to that of the human. They are often not well accepted by there own families who consider them eccentric or odd for not following the "normal" path. Public speaking is something to be avoided if possible, only relenting if the topic is a favorite fish, bird, or turtle, and then only when they become comfortable with the interviewer, accepting said person as one of their number. Once the guarded wall has been penetrated, a fascinating intelligence and multi-sided personality and background may be revealed, like some light shining through a previously dark prism, now showing its true makeup. Then they fade from view, retreating back to their personal island, to the home they have created amongst the furred, finned, feathered and scaled.

Their stories are diverse. Some have studied in small colleges or large universities. Some have come to their knowledge of animals through years of pursuit and observation, or close proximity. Some have lived in forests, deserts, jungles, and some on islands. One aquarist at the Shedd had indeed followed such a circuitous route and experienced the tropical isolation of a small island. This tiny land mass became famous out of all proportion to its size due to the fact that despite its lack of area, it still had the ability to accommodate an airstrip on which planes could land. The island was also home to flocks of birds affectionately known as "Goonies". Like Granddad the lungfish, these winged observers had also experienced times of war, but in this instance it was first hand. The "Goonies" lived on an island that became the objective in the most decisive battle of World War II. It was called Midway.

12

ISLANDS

To say that Midway Island is isolated is to define the word understatement! To understand this it is first necessary to grasp how remote the Hawaiian Islands, of which Midway is a part of really are. In the chain of small land masses that make up Hawaii, Midway is the farthest west, exceeded only by the equally minuscule Kure Island. If you have ever taken a flight or a cruise ship from the continental United States to this destination, you will soon realize by the time spent in the air or on the water that this place is really out there! The big island of Hawaii and its sisters to the west seem to be situated in the middle of nowhere, surrounded only by the blue waters of the tropical Pacific. They are disconnected from any other land mass by such an extent that they appear to be droplets of some solid material that fell out of a giant bucket on its way to the Philippines.

The Hawaiian Islands were first discovered by the famous Captain Cook in 1778. He apparently made such an impression on the local inhabitants that less than two years later they killed him. OK, now here is the kicker! Midway Island wasn't discovered until 1859, eighty one years later! Why? Because it is over one thousand miles to the northwest. To further illustrate what an outpost Midway is, consider this. If one were to take a flight from Honolulu to Midway by commercial airliner, let's say a 737 for example, it would take the same time as a flight from Chicago to Miami. I would bet that no one in Chicago considers Miami to be in their immediate proximity.

Midway Island would most certainly have disappeared into total unobserved anonymity, resuming it place as a hermit's dream if it hadn't been for one thing. In 1935, Pan American Airlines built an airstrip and refueling station there as a convenient stop for its sea planes. Six years later with the start of World War II and the attack on Pearl Harbor, the ability of Midway to accommodate an airstrip and its location thirteen hundred miles to the northwest of that Naval base, transformed it from a forgotten atoll to a particularly strategic base of operations. It was therefore fortified with U.S. Marines and its importance grew wildly out of proportion to its tiny size of less than one square mile. After Dolittle's raiders aboard their modified Mitchell B25 bombers carried out a daring low level raid on Tokyo from their secret base on Shangri La, better known as the aircraft carrier Hornet, the fact was not lost on the Japanese that Midway Island was an important objective. Taking it would give them a base from which to carry out attacks against Hawaii and threaten the American west coast, giving them an offensive upper hand. So, the Japanese developed a plan of attack for the invasion of Midway, operation MI as the imperial navy referred to it. The battle would also hopefully lure out the only U.S. carriers left in the area, Hornet and Enterprise. The Japanese had sunk the carrier Lexington at the Battle of the Coral Sea, and in addition severely damaged another one, the Yorktown, or so they believed

Unfortunately for the Japanese, the U.S. Navy's cryptanalysis or code breaking section had cracked important parts of the Japanese Navy code in which there was repeated reference to an "AF". Through a clever rouse involving a fake message concerning Midway's freshwater distillation system, the code breakers were able to discover that AF was Midway. The U.S. now had advance warning of the pending attack. What followed was certainly one of those battles in which almost everything that could go wrong for one side, in this case the Japanese, did go wrong. It started with an attempt by them to land a sea plane at French Frigate Shoals, which is situated about five hundred miles to the southeast of Midway. There they planned to refuel it via submarine and then fly over Pearl Harbor to check the whereabouts of the American aircraft carriers. If they were there, it would assure the Japanese that they had achieved surprise in their plans to attack Midway. However, when the sub arrived off French Frigate Shoals, they discovered it occupied by American forces, including PBY aircraft, a type of flying boat. As a result the seaplane mission had to be scrapped. The Japanese were now unaware of the fact that the U.S. carrier force had slipped undetected out of Pearl Harbor and were laying in wait northeast of Midway, anticipating the attack.

Also waiting, but not as well informed of the danger of the Japanese armada that was lurking out in the ocean to the northwest, were soldiers of the Marine Sixth Defense Battalion, numbering about four hundred men given the job of defending Midway. Among that group, one marine, PFC George Hire, working in communications, noticed increased activity for ten days proceeding the battle, with few idle periods. Most time was spent stringing wire and reinforcing the defenses, but never being told of the imminent attack or the massive invasion force that was heading their way. Mr. Hire would say many years later from his home in Melbourne, Florida, that he was happy he had not known what was waiting to overwelm them.

Suspiciously, a mess hall had been built only a few days earlier where there had never been one before, and the food did seem to Mr. Hire to be slightly better. Did the island command think this may be there last meal? One has to wonder if the soldiers on the island ever thought of supplementing their daily rations with fresh meat. Possibly unknown to the marines, or overlooked was the fact that Midway had swimming around its shorelines a source of food that was fair game back in the nineteen forties, Green sea turtles. So abundant are they around the area that three decades later and long after the battle, noted Hawaiian sea turtle biologist George Balazs working with the help of a scuba diving club called the Koral Kings, based on the island, were able to tag seventy percent of the entire Hawaiian Green sea turtle population in the surrounding waters. The group also discoveed that French Frigate Shoals was the nesting place for an estimated ninety percent of the total Hawaiian Green turtle population. Despite the staggering numbers of these animals in the area, the soldiers were apparently too preoccupied to notice this chance of expanding their culinary repertoire with turtle meat, and as far as we know never did.

As it turned out, the Battle of Midway Island due to many fortunate occurrences in favor of the U.S. Navy, the skill of a handful of naval aviators, and the bravery of countless others, turned into a rout. The U.S. carrier force sank all four of the attacking Japanese carriers that had been sent to the area. Without its planned air support, the Midway invasion fleet was given no alternative but to return home to Japan, and once again Midway Island commenced its journey back to isolation. Its main inhabitants now being sea turtles and Layson albatross, the fabled "Gooney Birds".

The island did nevertheless remain a military base for over a half century after the war, its surrounding waters working over the submerged relics of the 1942 conflict. A sunken barge here or perhaps a fighter plane laying in the sand were slowly cleansed of their former use by the tropical sea, transformed into homes for fish and coral, converted from instruments of death into havens for life.

About four decades after the battle, in the early nineteen eighties, Midway had almost returned to its roots. The birds flew the skies and nested on its scarred soil reclaiming their home. Colorful fish and invertebrates of all description inhabited any part of the reef not already occupied, and of course their were some human visitors. They unlike the animal life would only be transients, here today and tomorrow a memory. But one of them, a young sailor, embraced the natural beauty of this tiny atoll. Her name was Michelle.

Michelle was a lover of animals at an early age, and like other members of that tribe could spend hours observing and reading about the various creatures that came her way. Parents may or may not approve of their children's fascination and preferred association with members of the non-human species. The lucky child has one or both who will indulge this interest with perhaps the presentation of a pet, usually a small one. In this case, Michelle's mom bestowed upon her two pets, a pair of American Anoles, much more popularly though incorrectly known as chameleons.

Michelle was captivated by them, watching for long periods of time, amused as they would change color from green to brown and then back again to match their surroundings or as the spirit moved them. Their long delicate toes looked so fragile and the way they tilted their heads to look back at you through the terrarium glass, perched on a plant leaf, their eyes moving to examine you, was all absorbing. She named them Samson and Delilah.

Another hobby Michelle enjoyed was searching for fossils or anything that might crawl out from beneath the rocky areas they were found. Her favorite spot for this was around old strip mine spoil banks near Braidwood, Illinois.

As the years went by, she graduated high school and then enlisted in the Navy. This was followed by her being stationed on Midway Island. While some persons found this place to provide a dull existence, Michelle found it anything but that. Whenever she had some free time, beach combing was a favored activity. The waters edge, the littoral zone, was always a wonderful place to hunt for the unexpected. It was almost like searching for fossils again! There was an endless array of shipwrecked shells swaying back and forth in the tides wash, filling and then draining as the sea arrived and left, and arrived again. Occasionally some of the shells would get up and scuttle along on hairy legs as a hermit crab attempted to relocate his position on the wet beach, searching for new debris to pick through. The waves would come and the legs would snap back into the shell with a dull click only to quickly shoot out again once the ocean exited.

At times she would discover uprooted tree like gorgonians or sponges buried in the damp bubbling sand, the plantlike animals now disconnected from former aquatic habitats, their lives coming to an end unbeknownst to them. Michelle would often shuffle along at the water's edge with her feet submerged, feeling the joy of the surge and sand washing between her toes. Wiggling drove them down under the sand which resulted in a not unpleasant gritty massaging feeling. When walking in this area she always had to be careful not to step in the wrong spot and serendipitously discover the bad end of a stingray. The sun illuminated the ocean around her and schools of fish were revealed by their shadows darting and gliding over the white coral substrate. Looking out over the sea's horizon, feeling the warm water caress her feet, and listening to the ocean's sigh produced a supremely peaceful feeling. It worked its way into one's soul indelibly marking it. It is said that the sea hypnotizes and makes one long for more of it. Like a moth to a flame you must partake, you must return, you must experience it still again. Snorkeling was Michelle's next step, and mask and fins opened a new world. She was now on more even terms with the fish. She saw them and they saw her, their eyes scanning this possible new predator that had entered their world. Michelle could overturn rocks and look for unseen life forms living under them, perhaps a brittle starfish, sea urchin, or a colony of tiny hermit crabs. And still, this was not enough.

Finally, it was scuba diving that gave the best view of the ecosystem, and being in the Navy, there was always a good supply of potential instructors. But, it was the local dive club, the Koral Kings that answered the call of certification. This mission accomplished, Michelle could now swim out to the coral reef and observe it's profusion of creatures and plants. Hovering motionless, neutrally buoyant, she was able to stare into the holes and crevices at the aquatic jewelry that flitted about this lush submerged rainforest. You could easily exhuast a tank of air exploring even a small area of the reef. Most impressive were the schools of fish passing by only to be intersected by herds of other varieties of their finned counterparts, all traveling to some predetermined rendezvous. Invertebrates of various shapes and forms appeared unexpectedly with lobsters of several species being the most common characters discovered. If you were to return to the same location just a few minutes later, the show would always change, metamorphosing into a new scene with new players.

Then there were the turtles. Ever present, they would soar by in what seemed like slow motion, graceful and elegant, hauntingly disappearing to a place we cannot follow. There was a peaceful serenity about them that left her transfixed as she waited for them to return. They always did.

These dive adventures however, came to a close when Michelle's enlistment in the Navy ended. She returned to her home in the flatlands of Illinois, glad to be back, but never to forget her tour in her secret archipelago. This is how it is with islands. You may think you have had your fill of them, ready to move on to other parts of the world, but before long, the thoughts and visions retake their unbreakable hold, urging one to return. One thing Michelle was sure of, and that was that she wanted to further her education, perhaps making a career that in some way would involve animals and so, she enrolled at Southern Illinois University on the G.I. bill. Her major field of study was no surprise, biological sciences. After graduation she began her search for work and as with many who hold a bachelor's degree, had not really focused on one area of specialty. Competition can often be fierce among graduates, even for the lowest level jobs in the field of your choice, accordingly she deemed it wise to start building up her work experience portfolio by whatever means necessary. Even volunteer work became an option and one position in particular caught her eye. It was a non-paying situation for sure, but it would look good on that said portfolio. The volunteer position Michelle had decided on was working in the education department of a prestigious edifice located on the Chicago lake front. It sported an eight sided rotunda as its architectural trademark. Michelle would be working at the Shedd Aquarium.

13

I JUST HAD TO GO BACK TO THE ISLAND

Unlike many zoos, museums and the like, the Shedd Aquarium's volunteer positions for qualified individuals in the animal care field are quite different. In most other institutions of this sort, volunteers can expect their duties to include conducting tours, handing out brochures, assisting guests, or performing clerical work. The Shedd's positions in animal care in particular are generally nothing at all like that. In fact, some might call it a form of indentured servitude! This is because at the aquarium, volunteers perform most of the same work as the paid employees, cleaning fish tanks, scrubbing down exhibits, preparing food, assisting in animal transfers and medical procedures, even performing lab work and tests. For those with an interest in animals and aspiring to work with them this assignment is not without its reward and in fact, is an on the job training course, an extension of your college or high school education as it were, that often and frequently makes one eligible for hiring on as a regular employee, if the job is to your taste and a career at the aquarium is something you have decided would be of interest. In 1990, this was the program that Michelle found herself part of and it is as previously stated a stepping stone to regular employment at the Shedd. Unfortunately, the education department she was working in, while enjoyable, did not really offer enough hands on experience with the aquarium's finned and flippered inhabitants. Often when she found the time, Michelle would walk through the various galleries and peer through the rows of glass barriers into the miniature worlds each tank attempted to duplicate, her face almost touching the exhibit's clear boundary that separated her from the contents.

Fresh and saltwater fish from tropical and temperate waters swam about their artificial homes. Live coral and invertebrates made up miniature reefs reminiscent of those she had known on Midway, and clown fish in garish colors snuggled down into their stinging anemone blankets, then popping out and dancing enticingly. There were the dolphins and beluga whales, sea otters and penguins, octopus and sea stars. She could travel down the hall to Granddad's house and look at the ancient lungfish and his younger lungfish companions, and of course there was the Caribbean Reef exhibit. This was her favorite because she could watch Hawkeye, the tanks most famous inhabitant, still hamming it up for the crowds after all these years. The turtle seemed to want to catch her eye as if he noticed a greater degree of interest coming from this person on the other side of the glass. To Michelle it almost seemed like she was once again on Midway, watching the turtles hover over the sand and coral. But then she would snap back into reality with an almost caffeine like hit, the episode over.

Seeing and feeling these things made Michelle more determined than ever to reach the goal that so far had eluded her and so patiently and sometimes painfully she waited for an opportunity, an opening, a crack in the wall that would give her that chance. All good things come to those that wait, at least that is what's said, usually by those not waiting, but for those going through this test the stress on your will and body is often physically as well as emotionally draining.

The days went by and then weeks and months, along with peaks and valleys of determination. And then, one day the chance did come. There was an opening in Gallery Four, home to temperate freshwater fish like bass, walleye, and perch, the stuff of which a good fishing trip is made. These were not the residents of a tropical reef, but it was a start. So, she applied for the position and got it. The journey had begun.

For the next several years, Michelle worked this assignment, doing the designated chores and tasks. Preparing food for the animals, cleaning the never ending crop of algae from the viewing glass, carefully observing her charges for signs of ill health, doing water changes and general maintenance, all kept her busy. She enjoyed the work, and may have continued following that particular path if it weren't for an unexpected occurrence. As if mystically planned, another opportunity presented itself. This time strangely enough the job location was on an island, an island Michelle was very familiar with, Hawaii.

Now, with a much more impressive employment record, Michelle applied for the opening at Hawaii's Sea Life Park and shortly after, she was on her way, leaving her home again, returning to another.

Sea Life Park is a place that would be easy to fall in love with even if you were not employed there. Its beautiful collection of azure blue display pools, dolphin show theatre featuring a tall masted sailing ship back drop, and all of this overlooking a heart stopping Pacific Ocean panorama, made for a once in a lifetime experience. Fortune shined on Michelle while she was at the Park when she came under the tutelage of noted sea turtle expert, George Balazs. She was able to accompany him on several tagging expeditions where she witnessed the determined Balazs free dive down into various reef crevices and wrestle an assortment of sometimes very large turtles up to the surface and into the boat where data could be collected. Michelle was also able to participate in something called Sea Turtle Independence Day, a program in which captive bred turtles were grown and then released into the wild. She herself became so enamored with her shelled friends and so identified with them that her peers on the job started to refer to her as "Momma Turtle".

Often after a day of work at the park or sometimes after a tagging expedition out at sea, Michelle would return home and seek out a place of solitude on a beach somewhere. Walking the shore she would perhaps listen to the sounds of Hawaiian music, serenaded by the gentle voice of the late Israel Kamakawiwo'ole, IZ as his fans called him, or maybe she would mentally compose poetry as she crossed the sand. If she were to look up at the Hawaiian sky with all its clarity, and hear the wash and hiss of the tide could she be looking at the same view as the inhabitants of Midway Island, far, far, out to the northwest?

Unfortunately, this idyllic life was about to come to an abrupt end. After about three years, the park started to have financial troubles and was forced to make layoffs, one of which was Michelle. "Momma Turtle", was no more. Perhaps heartbroken, disappointed, bitter, or all three, she left Sea Life Park quickly, literally here today and gone tomorrow. Maybe like pulling a bandage off a wound she felt it was better to get it over with, just short fast and painful. But this wound had not healed, and maybe never would?

As if fleeing from some broken love affair, she distanced herself as far as possible from her beloved islands and now landed half an ocean and a full continent width away. Her new positions followed one after the other starting at the Mystic Aquarium in Mystic Connecticut. Next came the New York Aquarium and finally back home to Illinois and a job at a Chicago pet store called Old Town Aquarium where she took a job as an aquarium maintenance technician.

While she foundered around and tried to reestablish course, her passion for animals continued. Turtles, fish, cats, anything that walked, swam, or crawled might and usually did get her fond and close attention. Over the years she still had her collection of pets, but perhaps most beloved of all was a dog that had been given to her by a friend. It was a black dog, a Labrador mix, she was Michelle's friend just like Samson and Delilah the lizards had been in times past. She loved the dog and it loved her, she named her Nickel

For those who have not known the love of a dog and loved one in return, you are only to be pitied for your loss. Dogs are happy, frolicking, pleasure seeking, self indulging pirates with tongues that flop out of the sides of their mouths when happy. They will join in anything that they percieve as pleasurable, especially with their master. They sleep when we sleep, happy at our feet or at the foot of the bed, sometimes on the bed itself, greedily hogging the choicest mattress spot, dreaming and twitching when deeply involved in a good siesta. Sometimes serving as a pillow or we theirs.

Eating is of course Nirvana and is something to be anticipated at all hours of the day. They are always alert for the sound of a crumpling candy bar wrapper, popcorn popping or anything cooking, ever eager to join in the feast. Dogs smell everything! The more powerful the odor, the more the source is coveted. Day old socks, half rotted animals in the yard, garlic, dirty underwear, perfume, flowers, all lead to an LSD like experience in the dogs world.

They are sad when we are sad, watching us closely with head on paws, eyes fixed on us for signs as to why. We are their heroes, holding the highest position of esteem and they our constant companions following everywhere, exploring with us, helping to select just the right tool when we are doing projects around the house, or tagging along as we take out the garbage. But sadly they age too fast and grow old so soon. They become not as eager to follow, sleeping more and deeper, lost in the arms of Morpheus, harder to arouse. The young spunky companion that we knew so well, has changed unnoticed. They may need help up the stairs or just to get up. This bothers them and makes them grow despondent, for they feel they are there to serve and protect us, not you them. Their muzzle grows grey and their eyes start seeing less with each day.

Then one minute they are gone, gone way too soon, and we are left with a no longer needed bowl placed on a closet shelf or a collar now empty, no longer jingling to greet us, perhaps draped around a bed post next to their master's pillow watching over him as he sleeps. There is an empty spot at the foot of the bed that matches the empty spot in our hearts and we say we will not get another because there could not be one like this again. Then one day we see a puppy, maybe by design, maybe by accident. Are we looking, or is it destiny? The young dog's eyes make contact with ours and the tail begins to wag. They have won our heart and the cycle starts once more.

Perhaps it was Nickel that helped heal Michelle's heart, or maybe it was just that time had passed since leaving Hawaii. She was ready to move on. Incredibly, she now came full circle, as if some master plan were starting to be worked out. Once again, she applied to the Shedd Aquarium, and now with an impressive if curiously well traveled work record, she was hired. This time though it was not Gallery Four with its fisherman's delights she was to care for, but instead it would be at the Caribbean Reef. This was the home of the only sea turtle at the Shedd. It was the domain of Hawkeye. Hawkeye, now somewhat of a senior citizen was grossly overweight. Too many years of high living and no natural threats to flee from had caused him to push the scales at 150 pounds, but Michelle took care of him as did chief diver and Caribbean Reef aquarist Keith Pamper who was in charge of the exhibit.

Interestingly, there was another pet Michelle acquired after she had been working at the aquarium for a few months. It was a stray cat that had taken to roaming around the aquarium's loading dock. The feline was your typical alley cat, perhaps jettisoned by some uncaring owner, but somewhere down the line it had the good fortune to catch Michelle's eye, who then decided it needed a home. Unfortunately, the cat did not entirely agree, at first anyway. Not to be defeated, Michelle patiently began to feed and coax the cat to draw her near. Weeks went by before she was able to befriend the animal and win its trust. The hardest part came next because it required that same trust she had worked so hard to gain to now be betrayed. The unsuspecting cat had to be trapped in a fish landing net and then transferred to a cage.

Hissing and scratching in its portable jail, Michelle took the cat home and released the tiny tornado into her apartment. This was not unlike releasing the Tasmanian Devil of Bugs Bunny fame into your living area, with the cat flying in every direction ever created. Michelle just let it run out of gas, and then after several days she again worked her magic, winning the skeptical cat over for the second time. She had a new friend. Michelle named the cat Minnow, a good name for a feline from an aquarium she thought. This little animal also served another purpose. It would fill an empty space in her life. A few weeks earlier her faithful dog pal Nickel had died. Her picture now was attached to Michelle's workstation cubicle wall right above her desk, where the dog could watch over her. The year was now 2002.

Inside the walls of the Shedd Aquarium are many people like Michelle. There are animals like Granddad and Hawkeye, and fish from the earth's four corners. For over seventy five years the aquarium has entertained millions year after year. Perhaps when visitors look at the various exhibits and stop at the Caribbean Reef they might pause a little longer to peer inside. They most likely don't know the stories of the animals and people like Michelle who make it tick. Neither are they likely to know that the Reef rose from the previous Swamp exhibit that had been there way back in 1929. But even more obscure would be the fact that the whole thing got its start with a shipment of sea water destined for the Shedd Aquarium's saltwater tanks. In 1929, the water was carried in one hundred fifty railroad tank cars coming from a far away place at the time. The rail shipper was named the Florida East Coast Railroad, also known as the "Railroad that went to Sea". That railroad was built back in the early nineteen hundreds by a man named Henry Flagler, and it came from a place called the Florida Keys

14

CHAINLINK

The Florida Keys are certainly at the top of any list rating interesting spots to visit or live in. Strange might be a better description than interesting, although in this case the two terms are not mutually exclusive. The place is without a doubt a cul-de-sac for eccentricity, where the unconventional is not only tolerated but encouraged.

An argument could be made in favor of placing a monument at the entrance to the Keys that would mimic the Statue of Liberty, but instead of the inscription on the national version that reads, "Give me your tired, your poor, your huddled masses yearning to breathe free", the Keys version might go something like this: "Give me your odd, your non-conformists, your serenely unmotivated, your huddled masses yearning to sleep on the doorsteps of Key West between street performances. Give me your social outcasts, artists and writers yearning to work for free, for they will find unqualified acceptance here."

People who call the Florida Keys home live a fragile existence, surviving on a string of surprisingly tiny islands that resemble mounds of sand more than islands in many cases. This may be the reason for their live for today non-judgmental view of the world. Any hurricane, even a level one storm, has the potential to devastate and wipe the residents away from their precarious perches on this archipelago. But, they still stay! Why? It is because the Keys are a unique and different place, maybe not to the Caribbean area as a whole, but certainly to the United States. They come as an unexpected pleasure to those seeking peace and tranquility from the hustle and bustle of nearby Miami. They provide an ever changing panorama of sights, smells and tastes.

Case in point, there are forty two bridges from the beginning of the Keys to the town of Key West, the southernmost point in the continental U.S. and the terminus to the connected string of islands and sand spits that make up the area which starts in the Everglades south of Homestead and stretches out into the ocean about one hundred twenty miles from the mainland. The view from any and all of these mostly low lying bridges can at times present visions of maritime beauty, as perhaps a string of sailboats mark a far away horizon, looking like distant lighthouses, masts jutting into the sky taking in the wind that gives them life.

At the next bridge maybe you will be treated to a view of a spectacular sunrise over the ocean or sunset over the gulf. Much of the way, the bridges traveled over are paralleled by other much older bridges, some intact, others reduced to fragments. These are relics from the washed out right of way of the Florida East Coast Railroad, destroyed by the Labor Day hurricane of 1935, the same railroad that brought the first shipment of seawater up to the Shedd Aquarium in 1929. The old trestles and spans are persistent reminders of the ingenuity and ruggedness of turn of the century engineers and builders. Names such as Long Key Bridge, Seven Mile Bridge, or Bahia Honda Bridge have become landmarks to those traveling up and down Highway 1, the main drag that runs the length of the Keys. The auxiliary bridges old and new that run along side the road are continually populated by a colony of sun baked, darkly tanned fisherman whose inventiveness in reaching far out coveted spots on these platforms is remarkable. These choice fishing destinations on the piers can be reached by foot, bicycle, grocery cart, rickshaw, scooter, or whatever other form of transportation might be commandeered. Once there, a sun cover of some sort may or may not be erected. Blue plastic tarps, umbrellas, or even actual pop up tents can serve these anglers as shade providers. Then the patient wait known to all fisherman begins. A radio may be employed to pass the time or conversation with a fellow fisherman. The point of all this you see, is not so much to catch fish, as just TO fish. Being many feet above the water one always has to wonder how the hopeful anglers are able to land their catch, which once subdued must make a long vertical trip up and out of the water to the weathered, dirty fingernailed hands waiting to grab them. They apparently manage somehow.

As we travel down the highway, other islands come into view, hundreds of them, in all shapes and sizes, not connected to the concrete artery you are rolling down. They all seem mysterious, sitting out on the ocean as they do, fading out to the limits of your vision, out of reach and silent, waiting to be explored.

Most auto excursions to the Florida Keys begin by taking a trip through the Everglades south of the formerly Hurricane Andrew ravaged town of Homestead, on a span of road called the 18 Mile Stretch. At that point, the highway runs through the brown grass fields of the bird infested glades, looking not particularly Florida-like to northern travelers, and often more reminiscent of the brush surrounded roads of northern Minnesota. You half expect a moose to come lumbering out of the underbrush, but these bushes are mangrove trees, mostly a mixture of the red and black variety.

No ocean view is easily seen here because it is blocked by the profusion of vegetation. There are some big spans of water but they look somewhat lake like and swampy. One of these spots named Lake Surprise because it was discovered by accident during construction of the railroad, is home and sanctuary of the American Crocodile, a seldom seen, less common cousin to the Alligator. Eventually you will arrive at a place called Jewfish Creek. Here a drawbridge sits to block the progress on occasion of Keys travelers coming or going. This spot is by most, generally regarded as the entrance to the Florida Keys proper and shortly after crossing it you will find yourself in Key Largo. Key Largo, most famous for its connection to the old Humphrey Bogart movie of the same name, is indeed home to what must surely be one of if not the most revered Bogart artifacts, a boat called the African Queen. To the cinema fan's delight, next to the Key Largo Holiday Inn moored up to the dock or suspended by davits above the water sits the actual steam driven boat used in the movie, The African Queen. Looking down at her, she looks just as she did in the film. One can clearly picture Bogart and Katherine Hepburn seated inside traveling down the river in Africa, Bogey pulling the boat with a rope through a steamy swamp, then emerging from the water covered with actual live leeches. Interestingly enough, you can even charter the African Queen today as she is for hire and those interested can take their own excursion on her once the boat builds up steam.

Off the ocean side of Key Largo and out at sea lays John Pennekamp Coral Reef State Park, America's first underwater park. The reef is home to arguably the most famous dive sight in the world, the Christ of the Abyss statue, also known as Christ of the Deep.

The first time I ever visited and dove this spot was in the month of October, not a peak dive time, and I was fortunate enough to be one of only five divers on the spot, which is known as the Dry Rocks. The statue is truly magnificent to view. The Christ figure which stands in a sand based pocket in the coral, is posed reaching up to heaven and is usually wreathed by a school of silver oval shaped fish called Bermuda Chub, which sounds like a tropical clothing line for overweight people.

If you make the mistake of diving the site in the summer, unlike the fall you will find the statue wreathed with people rather than fish. At times the numbers of snorkelers and divers can exceed one hundred individuals, making the experience more akin to a swim at a Y.M.C.A. pool rather than a coral reef!

Returning to shore after the dive we get back into the car, leaving the windows down to help dry our saltwater frazzled hair as we continue the journey down Highway 1. There is a feeling of traveling south when driving down the Keys road but in fact, you are usually heading southwest or due west depending on how far along the way one is. Conversely, when on route back to Miami, the direction is due east or northeast. Everything in the Keys is usually located by what they call, "mile markers". For example, you might say that your restaurant is located at mile marker 88, or a resort at mile marker 58. The post office might be at marker 83. These markers start north of Key Largo at about 120 and end in Key West at 0, so the lower the number the closer you are to Key West. This invariably results in confusion for rookie Keys visitors, who having read the travel guides expect to see a series of concrete markers or some such thing that say marker 99 or 77. Surprise, surprise! No such thing exists, at least not in the profusion or form expected. Only the usual and occasional green mile marker signs found anywhere else in the U.S. are provided. This is of course just another one of the quirks that make this corner of the world unique.

Rolling along, we next come to a series of islands known as Tavernier. Here we find the usual collection of dive shops, marinas, and small restaurants. More importantly it is here that we first get an occasional unrestricted view of the ocean. One of Tavernier's more famous residents is Jimmy Johnson, former coach of the Dallas Cowboys and Miami Dolphins. He lives here in quiet seclusion surrounded by his saltwater aquarium collection, a favorite hobby. As we cross the Snake Creek drawbridge and advance from there to Whale Harbor Channel, we can look out to the ocean side again and watch the fleet of fishing boats that are lined up like a herd of circus elephants, following perfectly the channel markers out to the fishing grounds, seeking dolphin, sailfish, wahoo, or shark.

Somewhere along the way you become increasingly aware of just how small and narrow most of the islands you are traveling over really are, many times there being only a few feet separating the Atlantic Ocean from the Gulf of Mexico. This must be a real sweet place to be during a hurricane!

The fleet of fishing boats we saw earlier signals that we have now arrived at another grouping of islands, the most prominent among them being Upper and Lower Matecumbe Keys. This area is known collectively as Islamorada, which translates in Spanish as "purple island". Islamorada still retains much of the "Old Keys" flavor, with several historic sites like the Hurricane Monument from the late 1930's. Beneath it lay the remains of several hundred victims of the Labor Day hurricane that ripped through the Keys back in 1935.

Not far from the monument was a building that survived the same storm. It was a gas station at the time and later a restaurant called Sid and Roxie's Green Turtle Inn. The place was somewhat oddly positioned between two roads and one could easily visualize its former use as a filling station and where the pumps must have been. Inside, the eatery had a rustic charm accented by the old wood paneling whose look and smell generated a feeling of age and nostalgia. You might have expected to look up from your meal to see Ted Williams or Ernest Hemingway seated at the bar. Add to this, lounge music from the fifties that was always being played and you really had entered a time warp. Sometime during your meal you came to the realization that Dean Martin music is impossible not to smile to. Looking down at the glass covered table you were seated at, one could view hundreds of business cards slid under that same transparent cover, each with a story behind it. The wooden walls were adorned with old photos from the forties and fifties, showing proud fisherman from a half century ago, now only a memory. Sadly, the original Green Turtle Inn is now also a memory. What the 1935 hurricane couldn't do, time, termites, and other storms did. It has now been replaced by a newer version. Maybe another set of memories are in the making?

Since Islamorada is the self proclaimed sport fishing capital of the world, most restaurants in the area feature fresh sea food and "catch of the day" specials. Many of these eateries sport what seems to be an obligatory picture of George Bush, Sr. and his wife Barbara, who are long time frequent visitors to Islamorada. The couple usually stay somewhere in or around Cheeca Lodge. The former President is an avid fisherman who prefers backcountry fly fishing. Should you decide to have breakfast at the lodge, you might catch site of Sam, a large white wading bird, either an egret or heron, who likes to comically stride in from the outside into the dining room on his long spindly legs in search of a piece of pork sausage handed to him from his server friends.

Later in the day, you might want to try a bowl of conch chowder, a signature dish of the Florida Keys. The stuff is sort of a cross between Manhattan clam chowder and chili and can vary between restaurants from mild to decidedly hot and peppery. For many people, conch chowder can become an addiction.

The other Keys favorite is of course, key lime pie. Here again, just as with conch chowder, key lime pie seems to be a cross between two dishes. In this instance, lemon cream pie with lime substituted for lemon, and cheese cake with graham cracker crust. While many people enjoy key lime pie, it is very rich and can be an acquired taste. Someone who did find the pie to his liking was one of Islamorada's most celebrated residents, Ted Williams. Before his death, Ted would fish the open ocean and back country flats for all manner of game fish with the same passion he exhibited when hitting a baseball. His former home sits sadly quiet and unviewable now behind high walls on the well hidden, Ted Williams Way.

Across the road and not far from the Hurricane Monument, you may find the post hurricane Red Cross constructed house of Bernard Russell, one of the few survivors of that 1935 storm that hit the Keys with such force, it is considered by many to be one of the most devastating hurricanes in history. Fossilized bones from some of the victims are still discovered today on some of the more remote islands in the Keys. Bernard Russell lost around forty members of his family to the storm. Sadly, he recently passed away himself, but his name still appears on his white house that seems something of a monument also.

Unfortunately, much of the Florida Key's rich history is passing away on an almost daily basis. Few travelers are aware anymore of the presence of a fleet of Spanish treasure galleons that were sunk just off shore. In the late forties and throughout the fifties, one time famous treasure diver Art Mckee, made a living bringing up an assortment of fabulous finds from various forgotten and newly discovered shipwrecks, mostly from what is referred to as the 1733 Plate Fleet, that went down in still another hurricane.

Silver bars, doubloons, cannon, and an array of other recovered artifacts were put on display in a edifice called the Treasure Museum. After that closed down the buildings housed a variety of retail shops out front of which is now located a giant replica of a spiny lobster, around which tourists crowd for photos. The stores were renamed Treasure Village, but looking up at the castle like structure that makes up the buildings most prominent architectural feature, you still get a strong feeling of the museum it once was. The ballast stone posts and anchor chain fence along with the rusting away cannon testify like ghosts from the past with stories to those interested. Oddly, the doors to the various shops were propped open by ship's ballast stones, now doorstops, that were laboriously brought up from their ancient resting places on the ocean floor by forgotten adventurers. The building complex has now finally become a school, and perhaps a new generation will be taught of the history that lays on the bottom of the ocean just a short distance out to sea.

Staying in Islamorada and moving up and down the road, we pass on the ocean side again, a water park called Theatre of the Sea, that features dolphins, seals, sharks, fish, birds, and turtles. All these are displayed in a surprisingly tranquil and tropical setting. This could be considered unusual since the park itself sits on and makes use of an old quarry that supplied stone and aggregate for the railroad's construction when Henry Flagler was Lord of the Keys. Flagler, a railroad magnate and former partner of John D. Rockefeller, is credited with opening up and developing the east coast of Florida by continually extending his railroad line southward. He never really stopped until reaching Key West, then died shortly thereafter.

It's starting to get dark now so we better get something to eat before everything closes. In this part of the Keys even Burger King and McDonald's are shut down by ten o'clock!

The next morning we arise early in order to catch the sun coming up over the ocean and enjoy the slowly developing illumination of the vacant horizon. Poking along the beach we search for what oddities have washed up overnight and pick through the beached rafts of Sargassum weed and mangrove pods, looking for biotreasure. Walking out on a dock always tends to hypnotize as you focus your eyes on the various shapes and shades in the water, trying to separate the inanimate from the animate. Schools of mojarra along with a few juvenile barracuda lurking in the shadows, and scuttling horseshoe crabs can amuse you too long. It is time for us to leave and we slowly and haltingly walk back from our wooden peninsula to the beach from which it arises.

The journey is resumed as we continue on, still in the Islamorada chain of cayos. At mile marker 78, just between the diminutive Indian Key, the tiny island that was the former and unlikely seat of Dade County in the mid eighteen hundreds, and Lignumvitae Key, named for the "Ironwood" trees that grow there, sits a classic, old time, Key's marina called Robbie's.

The attraction here is not the tropical shack like building right out of Gilligan's Island that welcomes visitors. No. Instead it is the giant tarpon, a species of silver sport fish that looks very much like an oversized shiner minnow and is affectionately known by anglers as "Silver King", because of its spectacular leaps. The fish live around the dock and can weigh 100 pounds or more, sometimes way more.

A small fee paid to the motley crew that runs the place gets you access to the pier, and another buck or two buys a bucket of dead bait fish that can be fed to the waiting tarpon. Seeing these massive fish suck down your offerings, or a school of jacks that also live here, run down a tossed fish and intercept it just as it hit's the water, leaves a lasting impression even for experienced fisherman and provides cheap amusement.

Watch out for the pelicans on the dock! These ungainly birds with their comical looks will try to steal your bucket of fish when you aren't looking. They seem to study you, waiting for just the right opportunity to make their covert thieving move. There is a border collie who now calls the dock home that makes it his mission in life to chase away the offending birds from his turf. His trembling intensity and single minded pursuit of the pelicans who remain unharmed, adds to the theatre.

On we go, crossing bridge after bridge, always cognizant of the ocean surrounding us. Almost all the spans are low to the water due to the shallow sea depth below them, exception being the soon to be crossed Channel 5 Bridge, which climbs higher to allow boat passage in the coral free water below.

The current flow under the various bridges can be wicked at times which in turn will attract feeding tarpon in the slack water behind the pillars and supports. This in turn brings in hammerhead sharks who feed on the tarpon. Many an angler has hooked into a trophy one hundred pound plus "Silver King" only to reel in half a fish, the other fifty pounds or more now being in the stomach of a large hopefully satiated shark.

All the while we are traveling, you are continually reminded through the presence of the old bridges running along side parts of the highway, what it was like for the first railroad passengers as they glided along the track at about fifteen miles an hour, sliding over these structures with only blue ocean on either side, the rails below invisible. It must have seemed to them that they were suspended in air as they gazed out the open windows at the surrounding and overpowering blueness that was everywhere. Looking into the passing transparent waters, visions of the submerged detail of the sea grass beds, schools of fish, leaping rays, or even a sea turtle here and there must have provided unending entertainment as the miles clicked by. Considering that this was a time before World War I, it must have been heady stuff.

Back in our modern day auto we pass through Duck Key and Grassy Key, then after a little while we start to approach the outskirts of Marathon, another collection of islands which outside of Key West is the largest strip of commercial enterprise in the Keys. The town consists of the familiar grouping of chain stores, charter boats, dive shops and restaurants you would expect.

Approaching the area from the east, we pass a rare stoplight at the side road to Coco Plum Beach and continue straight on into Marathon. The town sort of begins with a souvenir shop on the ocean side called the Shell Man and on the right, the Island Tiki Bar. A few miles down from there in the central area, we find the little used but surprisingly appealing and tropical Marathon Airport, now called the Florida Keys Airport. This place has never really caught on with travelers who seem to prefer flying into the much more utilized Key West Airport. That is a shame and the more relaxed Marathon destination remains a gem yet to be discovered.

A little west of the center of town, we next come upon Crane Point Hammock, a collection of nature museums that offer us a chance to walk through a Florida Keys hardwood forest, hammock being the Keys name for forest. When you enter the park, get ready to be greeted by a rather large iguana who occasionally patrols the wooden ramp leading to the starting point. The walking trail will take you past butterfly laden glens and near pristine ocean panoramas that give hikers a grasp of what this land originally must have been like.

The walk takes about a half hour if you want to work up a sweat, or longer if you don't. Early on along the trail, we pause to explore an original Keys settler's house. Looking inside and out you can see what a hard life the occupants must have endured on this isolated spot, pestered by swarms of mosquitoes and sapped by the tropical heat. This was perhaps balanced by the tranquility and beauty the location offered up. The latter must have outweighed the former because the settlers stayed.

Continuing our stroll down the hammock path, we stop and pick up some fallen Red mangrove pods and examine them before passing the injured bird rehabilitation center with its battered tenants on the mend. Our spirits rise again when we look into the water below a foot bridge at the end of the trail and spot a school of rainbow parrotfish with their birdlike beaks. They always resemble some sort of piscine-avian experiment in progress. Taking advantage of the added height of the bridge, we look seaward and are treated to a now elevated ocean scene surrounded by the tropical stillness

The walk completed, we are perhaps, depending on our pace, somewhat or a great deal hot and sticky. Getting back into the car we proceed on, hoping to cool off with a swim at Sombrero Beach, or maybe take one of the catamarans out to the reef itself and snorkel the fish laden waters around the Sombrero Reef Lighthouse. This structure dates back to pre-Civil War days, and interestingly, was actually constructed under the supervision of George Mead, who would later go on to lead the Federal Army at the Battle of Gettysburg. The tranquility of the lighthouse must have been a stark contrast to the bloody scene he would witnessed a few years later.

In a few more miles, we will be approaching arguably the most famous spot in the Florida Keys, the emblematic Seven Mile Bridge. As the town of Marathon dwindles, the speed limit drops from 45 to 35 miles an hour, and while we begin to slow down a brown and beige sign subtly catches the eye. If we hadn't already been looking to the right we certainly would not have noticed it. The sign reads,

Hidden Harbor Motel. Next to it is another building that sports block lettering on the exterior wall spelling, The Turtle Hospital, in front of which is parked facing out, as if on alert, an orange and white van emblazoned with the words, Turtle Ambulance. We make a mental note to definitely check this place out some time!

Passing the quaint and tropical looking 7 Mile Grill with its outdoor dining patrons seated at the counter and plastic tables, we are nearing the eastward limit of the old and new Seven Mile Bridge. Getting closer, we become aware of a malodorous sulfur smell wafting up to greet us, emanating from the rotting vegetation blown up by the tide and current and deposited at the base of the bridge. The stink is occasionally encountered in various spots in the Keys depending on wind and tides. Caused by the anaerobic decay of plant material, this aroma could never be mistaken for Chanel No.5 perfume. Perhaps a new scent has been born? This one more aptly called, Channel No.5. Before crossing the bridge we decide to take a sharp left turn and visit the Pigeon Key tourist center, which is housed in a converted Pullman railroad car. This piece of stationary rolling stock is one of the last examples of railroad equipment left from the heyday of the Florida East Coast Railroad. While browsing through the gifts and souvenirs inside the railroad car, we become intrigued and purchase a ticket to visit Pigeon Key itself, which is located just a few miles away, accessed only by boat or the old Seven Mile Bridge.

The ticket we have bought takes us by the landlubber's route across the bridge. We will be driving over its long span in a jeep converted to look like an old steam engine. The faux jeep steam engine has been christened "Henry", after Henry Flagler, the builder of the railroad.

The view from the old bridge is alone worth the few dollars admission, as we are treated to a scene that was first experienced by travelers of a century past. What must have been going through their minds when they took in this scenery? We are rolling along the same bridge they once were. Now, in a way, we have become connected with them.

Arriving at our destination, the faithful Henry descends on a rickety wooden bridge that seems uncomfortably near collapse. Ironically, the more than hundred year old Seven Mile Bridge seems wildly more sturdy. Reaching sand, our miniature train pulls up a few yards and stops in the center of a tropical island. This is Pigeon Key. Pigeon Key was a work camp active during construction of the Key West extension of the Florida East Coast Railroad. Peaceful, tropical, and charming, the place gives you a feeling of having stepped back in time, along with a sense of escape as you visually survey the assortment of old work camp buildings. A short film is available for watching chronicling the life of Henry Flagler and the railroad's construction. It is shown in a tiny air conditioned room which is a cooling treat, followed by a tour either with a guide or on your own. Our guide today is ironically not from Florida, but Cicero, Illinois. His knowledge of Flagler and the Keys however is impressive.

Having brought snorkel gear with us, we decide after exploring the island, to test the waters off the tiny Pigeon Key beach and check out what might be under the dock. It turns out to be a pretty good beach dive, not comparable to the reef, but surprising for the variety of fish close in to the shore. Today it is mostly French grunts and snapper, along with a stray jackknife fish here and there, fluttering around isolated rocks with there tall dorsal fins looking like tiny masts on gossamer sailboats. They flit, hover, and shimmy, and thoroughly captivate. The coral growth on the dock pilings themselves is also unexpectedly profuse and diverse in various spots, providing macro photography opportunities. Underwater visibility here is not the greatest as is usually the case with any inshore dive, but overall the swim was a good experience.

Trudging out of the water, we quickly kick off our fins and head for a nearby picnic bench to sit down, rest, and dry off, thanks to the accommodating tropical sea breeze. After a period of time the solitude is broken by the clanging of a bell, signaling the departure of Henry back to the tourist center. Once again, now even more relaxed and a little fatigued because of our beach dive we enjoy the return trip over the historic bridge and ultimately back to the parking lot where our little train deposits us. Returning to our auto, we see another group of tourists board the engine and head out, and we soon follow them out of the lot and out onto Highway 1.

Now we are driving down the new Seven Mile Bridge, which parallels the old one for much of its length and before long we get an aerial view of Pigeon Key as we pass from our higher vantage point. The little island looks even more quaint from this angle with the omnipresent ocean stretching in all directions. This surrounding sea panorama is one we will enjoy for the approximate ten minutes it takes to cross the long span, but of course as with any travel in the Keys this depends on traffic.

As the bridge terminates we are once again driving over dry land, a situation which never lasts for long anywhere down here. It isn't too far before we are next taking in the scenery of Bahia Honda Key, home to what is considered to be one of the most beautiful natural beaches in the United States by the people who have the time to rate those sort of things. There is a nice park here and as we come to its westward limit, once again one is bombarded with more railroad memories.

This time it's the Bahia Honda Bridge, which looks like the remains of a giant old Erector set, a favorite toy of the nineteen fifties. You get the feeling the engineers who built this bridge must have entertained themselves with such a toy or inspired the actual Erector set itself. Passing through some of the lesser known islands like the very Caribbean sounding Spanish Harbor Key, our drive continues. Opening the windows to let the sea breeze fill the car makes us feel like we are in a boat of some sort rather than an auto. In a few minutes our wheeled vessel cruises to the outskirts of Big Pine Key, probably the most rural of the developed islands. The main reason for this, in fact the primary reason is that this Key is the home to the tiny and endangered Key deer, a much smaller and secretive version of the white tail deer. Newborn fawns are reputed to be so small that their hooves are the size of a human's thumbnail! Catching sight of these dwarf antelope is not likely unless you travel through the area at dawn or dusk, or take one of the lesser traveled side roads.

Rolling through the heart of Big Pine, we stop at a rare traffic light and adjust the car radio to get the marine report and any fishing information available. We have to navigate the radio channels around the never ending salsa music that seems to be available twenty four hours a day. All salsa, all the time! I'm beginning to wish for Dean Martin again.

The light changes and we proceed over the Little Torch Key Bridge landing of course as you might expect on Little Torch Key. Off on the ocean side and out on the horizon is the exclusive Little Palm Island, known for its tiki hut accommodations, resident chef, and no road access, it is reached only by vintage motor launch. Way beyond Little Palm out in a solitary spot in the ocean you might be able to spot a small reef marker. This tower poses like a silent sentinel, standing watch over one of the most beautiful reefs in the Florida Keys, Looe (pronounced loo) Key National Marine Sanctuary. Even after a severe hit from Hurricane Georges in 1998, it is still rated by many divers as the best there is down here.

The reserve gets its name from the H.M.S. Looe, that ran aground here in the seventeen hundreds. One has to wonder if aboard this ill fated English vessel the word looe had the same meaning if not spelling as it does in England today. Picture yourself as a disgruntled sailor aboard the H.M.S. Toilet!

Starting to get fatigued at this point having traveled nearly one hundred miles or more since the beginning of the trip with an average speed of 40 to 45 miles an hour, and also having made numerous side stops along the way, we arrive not a moment too soon at the oddly named Saddle Bunch Keys. Here next to a dilapidated trailer like building is the home of the also unusually named Baby's Coffee, the Key's version of Starbuck's. Baby's logo is a kind of bloodshot eyeball looking thing and you can't help notice that cars are pulling off the road with great regularity, like bees returning to a hive waiting to refuel. Heading inside for a cup, we our greeted to a counter with a bunch of "pump-a-drink" type thermos decanters lined up with an assortment of Baby's roast coffee concoctions. Names like "Killer Joe", "Death by Coffee", Baby's Private Buzz", and "Voodoo Queen" jump from the labels on the decanters. We choose a cup of "Hemingway's Hair of the Dog", along with a slice of key lime pie which seems like an appropriate selection.

Happy and now "wired", we continue the journey past the Boca Chica Naval Air Station, where the Navy "Cats" roar overhead on training exercises high above "Fat Albert", a white blimp like balloon tethered in the sky, whose mission has never been fully disclosed.

The scenery becomes more urban with each mile until finally we arrive at a stoplight at a fork in the road at which both choices lead to the same spot. We have reached Key West. Lord help us!

15

CAROLINE STREET

If the Florida Keys can be considered as a singularly unique place, an apex of oddity, Key West would certainly win hands down as the capital. Still, this in itself is an anomaly because Key West is really not representative of the Keys as a whole. The remainder of the island chain outside of the southernmost city is almost rural and rather quiet for the most part.

Key West itself is a city of contrasts. It is more lively than the rest of the area but still decidedly laid back. It has a subtle quietness and glorious seediness about its well preserved nineteenth century homes which are usually surrounded by dense tropical foliage that makes the houses seem even more tightly spaced. These dwellings of mostly wood construction are in fact so close together that law requires them to have tin roofs in order to prevent the spread of fire.

Turn the corner on any given street and the subtle quiet might instantly metamorphose into an intrusive grotesqueness with a passing parade of oddness. Rickety old cars, now adorned with painted flowers or inlaid with costume jewelry right out of a sixties acid trip and dubbed "Conch Cruisers", might be seen in front of a cigar making factory. Those cigars could next appear jutting from the mouth of a weathered old Caribbean woman as she sits on the porch of a shack like Bahamian house, puffing away contentedly.

Down at the dock, cruise ships disgorge their tourist cargo, who eagerly board 'Conch Trains" that scurry off into the maze of thoroughfares and alleys sprouting off Duval Street, the main drag that makes up the center of what is called Old Town.

The city has a one of a kind charm that intrigues and amuses, and then after awhile makes you want to flee it. Key West is divided into two distinct areas, New Town, that takes in most of the beaches and what people consider "normal" hotels, chain stores, and fast food restaurants, and Old Town, which includes Duval Street running from Mallory Square, home of the Sunset Celebration, to the famous Southernmost Point, 90 miles from Cuba at the other end.

The name Key West itself has a probable three pronged origin. Most obviously it is the westernmost significantly populated island in the chain, thus Key West. In Spanish the area would be called Cayo Oeste, or little island to the west, but to the English ear this too may have sounded like Key West. Finally and most telling, legend has it that when the Spanish first arrived on the island, they were shocked to discover countless numbers of bones scattered all over the shore, beaches and inland forests, from past Indian wars. They named the place Cayo Hueso, or bone island. The word bone in Spanish, hueso, is pronounced phonetically HWAY-so, which again sounds possibly like the English, west, as does oeste, but here's the interesting part. To this day, even on television and radio, Spanish speaking stations refer to Key West as Cayo Hueso, not Cayo Oeste, which lends credence and tradition to the bone island theory.

However the name arose, Key West undisputedly draws its life and pulse from the Old Town area. This section is made up of a long expanse of stores, vintage homes, open air restaurant, saloons once frequented by the likes of Ernest Hemingway and Jimmy Buffett, museums, and marinas. The latter giving harbor to dive boats, cruise ships, glass bottom boats, and tall sailing ships. These all leave with clockwork regularity for exotic adventures in such places as the Marquesas, Quick Sands, or the Dry Tortugas. If you have never been out to sea aboard a ship under sail, put it on your life's "to do" list. It is stirring to experience the silence of sailing, broken only by the rattle and hiss of the sails in the wind and a phosphorescent bow wale splitting the ocean's surface.

While Key West is at all points tied to the sea, which virtually surrounds it and has over its history isolated it and held it captive from the rest of the world. There is more to find than nautical entertainment. Ernest Hemingway made his home here while he worked on several novels, narrowly dodging the Labor Day hurricane of 1935 that leveled Islamorada and destroyed forever the overseas railroad, before he a few years later fled to Cuba for more anonymity.

His home on Whitehead Street has been a point of pilgrimage for his fans for many years as has favorite watering holes Sloppy Joe's Bar, and Captain Tony's Saloon, the original site of Sloppy Joe Russell's tavern. Papa's house is home to a colony of cats that are descendants of those kept by the writer himself and are famous for their extra toes or polydactylness that makes the cat's front feet somewhat reminiscent of a catcher's mitt. In fact, most of Key West seems to be home to a large population of cats, and in addition oddly enough an equally voluminous flock of chickens and some very vocal roosters. One of the island's hometown experiences is being awakened in the black of morning by the raucous serenade of hundreds of the crowing birds.

Perhaps this barnyard alarm clock was one of the charms that attracted President Harry Truman, once a farmer himself, to this island retreat. Truman lived here at the old Navy base, not far from where Hemingway docked his famous boat the Pilar. The President spent off and on almost an entire year in Key West during the course of his presidency. The building where he stayed is called the Little White House, now a museum well worth the visit. Inside you will get a feeling of intimacy with the man and a grasp of the no frills humanist that was Harry Truman.

In this day and age, Key West's most famous figure and off and on again resident would undoubtedly be none other than the flamboyant Jimmy Buffett. Parrotheads, as Buffett fans are known, also make the pilgrimage to this city, as do Hemingway fans, but in this case they are in search of the tropical lifestyle portrayed in his famous songs. Jimmy patrolled the bars and saloons here, singing and purveying his ballads and lyrical tapestries until he made the big time. It is interesting to look at some of the old Jimmy Buffett album covers and see his smiling face and beach bum hippy look right out of the sixties. He fit right in!

One cannot come to the Florida Keys or Key West without becoming a Buffett aficionado. His music is so emblematic of the Caribbean, and his lyrics so ornate and descriptive that you just couldn't imagine the place would ever have been what it is if he hadn't existed. The Chamber of Commerce would have been forced to invent him! Jimmy Buffett is to the Keys what Babe Ruth is to baseball. He doesn't overshadow this place, but he did help to make it what it is. The fan-performer love affair his music has created has made him one of the most successful money making performers of all time which comes as a surprise to non-fans who see a man that until recently had only one big hit song, but then they arrive at this place of sea, sand, and sun, and before long they are Parrotheads too. He often records part of his albums at his secret location in the Keys. Perhaps if you are lucky you might sometime catch sight of him at the Margaritaville Restaurant.

Jimmy is known also for his love affair with airplanes and flying. Perhaps the fact that Pan American Airlines had a base here in the late nineteen twenties as well as the one later on Midway Island intrigued him at some point. Midway Island and Key West, Pan Am did get around didn't they.

While Key West is thought by many to be the westernmost island, this is really not the case. Farther to the west are the Marquesas, a sprinkling of small land masses that were the resting place of Mel Fisher's Spanish treasure galleon, Nuestra Senora de Atocha, which lies in a place called the Quick Sands. Still farther out we find the Dry Tortugas, another small grouping of islands. Tortuga being the Spanish word for turtle. The Dry Tortugas can be reached by only two means, a boat, or the Jimmy Buffett way, a seaplane. Today, a Monday in July that has dawned sunny, clear and hot, I have chosen the quicker air route, which will take about 45 minutes instead of the two hours or more by boat. This half day excursion will give me a chance to sample the Tortugas and still be back in Key West in time for other diversions.

If you should one day ever find yourself at a floatplane base north of the border in let's say Ontario, you will notice all the planes, Cessnas, Beechcraft, and the workhorse Dehaviland Beaver are lashed to the dock, floating on the liquid support of a pine tree and granite bordered lake, waiting like bobbing Canada geese for the signal to take off. In contrast if you fly on a seaplane in Key West, boarding is at the airport, which despite the surrounding ocean is totally on dry land. As a veteran Northwood's fisherman of literally hundreds of floatplane flights, I wondered where the water was that this thing was going to take off from. I asked a fellow passenger this question, to which he answered, "The runway I guess.", looking at me kind of oddly. It was then that I took more notice of the small wheels sticking out of the bottom of the plane's floats. In Canada, those wheels were only used to pull the plane in and out of the water in order to make repairs. Here, they would be used for take-off and landing. Hmm, this duck's got wheels!

A runway take-off in a seaplane, this could be tricky I thought. Boarding the plane with my usual load of dive gear and underwater cameras after I had surrendered my complimentary cooler of soda and or water, I climbed the ladder after giving the pilot/flight attendant, my boarding pass, a plastic coated piece of paper that said, "Chuck", our pilot's name. I guess that's so if you get airsick, you will know that it was "Chuck" who caused it, and you could then rename him, "UpChuck". Chuck looks at all my gear and scowls, audibly wondering if I'm planning to camp out there. I just ignore it, being used to the authoritarian nature of floatplane pilots who are usually and thankfully, men of few words. I discover the plane is air conditioned, a nice feature never found on the Canadian versions, sit down in the co-pilot's seat and harness myself in. All the while, Chuck watching me so I won't "screw up". I am touched by his courteous nature!

The takeoff is surprisingly smooth and effortless compared to the teeth rattling, engine roaring water exit of a Canadian Beaver. We climb quickly, the resulting aerial view of Key West reveals how small a world it really is. The beaches, marinas, Duval Street, Mallory Square, and even Hemingway's home are all easily identified from the air and I watch as they all disappear from view and fade into the horizon.

Lone Sailor

Not long after leaving the airport, Chuck began to inform us of various sites we would be passing over, shipwrecks being the most prominent, and their ghostly maudlin outlines were clearly defined under the water due to our high vantage point. He also cautioned us to be on the lookout for an assortment of wildlife near the ocean's surface, most likely dolphin, shark, stingrays, and the occasional sea turtle.

During any low level flight in which a passenger is able to observe meaningful and discernable scenery, it usually takes awhile for the eyes to adjust to the scale and size of objects being searched for in a backdrop of blue sea and breaking waves. One tends to become mesmerized by just the movement of ocean currents and foam trails only visible from the air, that tease the eyes by throwing flickering shadows and elusive shapes at them. Here one instance and gone the next. Eyelids become half closed as if you were under the influence of a relaxing massage, causing submergence into a semi-coherent state of consciousness.

And then, something caught my eye. At first I wasn't sure what I was seeing, if anything! It was there, and in the next instance gone, dematerializing into the apexes and troughs of the waves. It seemed to have some solid form about it even though its shape was elusive and transient. My brain at once reawakened to a state of useful alertness, and my eyes strained to regain the image I was certain had been there. Maybe I was wrong? Maybe it had just been waves and shadows? Unconvinced, I kept intensely scanning the teal colored ocean, looking, looking, looking, and then there it was again!

It was an object on the ocean's surface that from my position far above appeared to be circular to oval in shape and it contracted and expanded in size as it bobbed up and down on the pulsing, foaming waves. Its color was milky brown or maybe the color of sand at times. I couldn't look away! My eyes remained transfixed on this one solitary object on the surface of the blank sea below. My brain trying to make sense of the information my eyes were sending its way. What could it be? Maybe just a piece of wood or oddly colored Sargasso weed.

Then as if a curtain had been lifted to now make all things clear, I saw the slow, steady, rhythmic stroke of the long front flippers, the smaller rear ones steering and guiding the path, and then the weathered head, glistening in the sun, break the water's surface and inhale the morning air. It was nature's lonely sailor, a sea turtle, unmistakable, bobbing up and down in magnificent solitude. The singular tranquility of that vision and moment was from that time on, forever fixed in my mind, that certainly and quickly. Never to be forgotten on this side of existence. The gallant mariner, alone, tranquil, purposeful in its swimming motion, heading to a place where we cannot follow, riding the currents and waves for days, months, years, and decades, eternally and faithfully.

The vision made me wish I could leap out of the plane as if I myself could fly and soar down to become closer to the scene, now unforgettable but fading fast in the aircraft's wake. I kept looking backward at the turtle until my angle of view out the window brought the encounter to an end.

There would be others sighted along the way, especially now that I knew what to look for, but none would have the impact of that first one, although each new turtle spotted was a singular delight. I became so absorbed in my search for others that I was unaware we had reached our destination, Fort Jefferson and the Dry Tortugas was just out the window.

The seaplane made one circuit of the Fort for photographic purposes and then quickly lost altitude as it slowed its airspeed and made the landing approach, drawing near to the element for which it was intended. I watched the ocean's surface rise up to touch the plane, the pilot who had been slowing the aircrafts speed now accelerated momentarily to overcome the drag of the water against the pontoon floats while we made the swift transition from air to water. The steel bird made a staccato chopping sound as we rapidly cut through the waves and I felt the familiar sensation of the seaplane bobbing up and down. We had become a boat with wings.

The plane coasted into the shore and gently beached itself on the sand where our group quickly departed the faithful air taxi. All but one of the nine passengers headed to the Fort's tourist center to begin a tour of the more than century and a half old Civil War era structure. They were all eager to learn more about its most famous past resident, Dr. Samuel Mudd, who was imprisoned here for unwittingly setting the broken leg of a fleeing John Wilkes Booth. I alone am here to dive the waters around the Fort, only myself, like the turtle on his voyage that still stuck in my mind and would not leave. The walk over to the isolated beach takes about ten minutes due to my heavy bag of dive gear and a decade of back trouble, the gritty coral sand filling my weathered old gym shoes as I proceed. Once I reach the edge of the ocean, I take out a beach towel that carries the image of a dog, a small terrier having his foot bandaged by someone's caring hand, below which are the words, "Anti Cruelty Society of Chicago", and lay it out on the white sugar sand. Sitting down, I begin to assemble my cameras and dive equipment, trying futilely to keep grit out of my gear, and start to feel the heat of the July morning and the excitement of this unshared adventure as beads of perspiration run down my face. Solo diving is generally considered by those in the know as unwise, but in my life I have discovered that if you don't want to dive alone, you won't be diving much. It's either dive alone or not at all. One thing I have discovered about diving by yourself, it puts you in touch with your senses very quickly.

Plodding down to the water with all my cameras and gear, I move like an ungainly crippled duck. Sitting in the bathwater warm sea, I strap on my fins and mask. Twisting around to lay flat in the water with my chest on the sand, head under water, inhaling air rhythmically through the snorkel, I face forward, push off, and leave the Earth!, a lone astronaut exploring inner space.

Aiming towards the Fort's submerged outermost wall that I have been told is the spot of choice, I approach it, my heart beating strongly along the way in anticipation of what might be encountered. The sand is white, and sparkles on the ocean floor, reflecting the sunlight back to my squinting eyes until relief comes as a shade line appears when I come under the influence of the moat walls.

There is nothing much to see of note at first, just a few stray fish here and there skittering across the bottom, until a small cylindrical pipe of some sort comes into view and I slowly raise my camera. I am rewarded when a green head begins to poke its way out of the hideaway, tentatively at first but then more boldly. I am being greeted by a small green moray eel, who although possessed of terrible eyesight seems to be welcoming me in a rather cordial manner to his aqueous world. Snapping a few photos while he takes the time to pose for me, I then swim off watching as his tiny head pivots to follow, surely wishing me an enjoyable swim, then he contracts back into his drainpipe hotel.

The wall is coming into sharp view now with soft and hard corals starting to appear into my vision field. Sparse at first, the treelike gorgonians, colored sponges, and fissured brain corals in their burnt sienna coloration become more and more profuse as I advance onward, the minutes flying by until the corals blend together into a full fledged reef environment.

I have arrived at the initial outside corner of the submerged six sided moat wall and make the first turn. I am truly alone now, no longer visible to anyone on shore, but nonetheless lured on by the still unfolding underwater theatre. I can't turn back now even though my heart rate is rising. In the back of my mind I am aware of the potential presence of large sharks in the area, having recently read a copy of the Keynoter newspaper that displayed a picture of a happy angler with a 400 lb. bull shark he had recently battled. Under the picture was the caption," Location of catch: Dry Tortugas". I put that thought out of my mind, continuing to swim along, mentally cataloging the various fish I was seeing. There were four eyed butterfly fish who get their name from a false diversionary eyespot on the rear of the body, gaudy queen angels adorned in canary yellow and brilliant electric blue darting out of coral crevices to examine me pensively at first and then more boldly before disappearing into the living forest that is the reef. I come to a hole in the wall that is wreathed by a school of mangrove snapper who are bolder than I would have expected. I keep going on and on, farther from my beach landing pad until I look at my dive watch and find that I must turn back soon in order to exit the water, dry off, and walk back to the plane. Executing a 180 degree turn, I retrace my fin steps and get a slightly different perspective, this time off my left shoulder as I now swim counter clockwise back to the beach. Periodically I look back to see if anything is following, a habit I have developed. When I do this, I often catch sight of my own swim fins as I kick through the water. They are the split variety which provide maximum thrust with low effort that I find compensates for my back trouble. The fins fold and unfold in the water slowly and delicately as though I too have become a fish. I wonder how anything with such a graceful motion could be attached to me. Approaching the beach, I again come upon the tiny foot long discarded drainage pipe, now home to the little green eel who bids me farewell. Maybe I will see him again someday, and then there I am in the hot shallow water of the tropical ocean shore. Standing up, I let the saltwater drain from my head, face, and wetsuit, which on a cooler day gives a sensation not unlike urinating on oneself, as water warmed by your body inside the suit drains down your legs. I feel heavy now and no longer graceful as I return to gravity and sit down on my beach towel. I repack my dive gear and cameras in preparation for the plane's return trip. and slowly walk, more fatigued now, back to the waiting aircraft. Passing along the old Fort wall, I wonder what the rest of the group has seen on their dry land tour, but since they are all family groups and I am alone, they do not include me in their conversation or ask me about my dive. Maybe next time?

I make some small talk with the pilot before again taking my seat. We get underway quickly, the seaplane's growling engine pulls us out and away from the beach. We taxi over the water's surface, building speed, getting lighter and lighter, finally bursting from the suction of the ocean and becoming airborne. We do not circle the Fort this time but instead head straight out in order not to disturb nesting birds. We are on a bee line back to Key West. The ferry boats are just now arriving. We leave them behind in the distance. My thoughts return to the little eel, my friend on the ocean floor and I wonder if I will ever see him again.

Fighting off sleep by mentally planning the rest of my trip, I scan the surface of the sea below, searching once again for a fellow lone sailor and before long there they are, seemingly more numerous than on the trip out. I can now differentiate Loggerheads from Green sea turtles, my eyes having become more trained and honed to the task. The deliberate stride of the front flippers and water washing over their shells again produce indelible visions, but little by little they become less numerous until I sight Key West on the horizon followed by the airport, where we return to earth and the adventure is over. Gathering up my gear bags, I return to my car which greets me with a blast of hot air from its enclosed interior. I am reenergized for no good reason now and start driving down Duval Street, taking in the colorful crowd as I go, passing Margaritaville, and Sloppy Joe's, along with the Conch Trains going the opposite direction. I turn right on Caroline Street made famous by our friend Jimmy Buffett, pass Curry Mansion and other classic old vintage homes representative of the tropical "Old South", before turning left on Margaret Street. I park the car across from the historic Flagler Station where the saltwater for the Shedd Aquarium was loaded back in 1929.

I walk down to the dock which is bordered by some restaurants including one called the Turtle Kraals Restaurant that features turtle races with box turtles a few times a week. I might eat there later or perhaps take a trip on the glass bottom boat Discovery, moored further down the dock. But first, I am destined to visit out near the end of the pier, an old, weathered, wood framed building once owned by Charles Thompson, one of Hemingway's pals back in the day, and also a place where sea turtles were brought in and slaughtered for market. It is now called the Turtle Kraals Museum, and inside you will find an historical display depicting the now extinct sea turtle industry along with other educational information about them.

As I enter the open air door my eyes travel to the right where there is a round aqua colored horse trough that holds a small rehabilitating sea turtle recovering from an injury. Off to my left is a sales counter, behind which is standing a petite woman who has the incongruous occupation of fishing boat captain. She greets me with a smile. "Hi Jim", she says.

This person is Tina Brown. She came to the Keys over twenty years ago and her life has never been the same since. She lived in Marathon in the center of the islands with a man named Richard Moretti and together they unexpectedly were drawn into a project that changed everything for them. Together, they started The Turtle Hospital.

16

TINA AND THE TARPON

The tale of The Turtle Hospital begins strangely enough with a fish story, and like all fish stories, at least the really good ones, there is an unexpected ending.

 Tina Brown has loved fishing all her life. While it is not unusual for the occasional woman to enjoy angling, most merely dabble in the sport, possibly intrigued a little at first or simply using it as a means to get close to, or spend time with a male prospect, never really showing a passion for the sport that men do. Tina would be the exception to this, now the captain of her own charter sport fishing boat as well as founder and manager of the Turtle Kraals Museum. Her pursuit of game fish does indeed rise to a level on par with that of any man. Really good fishermen not only like to catch fish, they want to be in their company. They enjoy looking at fish, swimming amongst fish, reading about fish, eating fish, and keeping fish as pets!

 Back in 1983, in the heart of the Florida Keys, Marathon to be exact, there existed an old rundown 21 unit motel named the Buena Vista, that had fallen into foreclosure. In fact, there was not too much Buena in this particular Vista. The place had certainly seen better days, and those better days had passed a long time ago, but to the discerning eye the property was not without a certain hidden charm with its little enclosed harbor and quiet setting.

 Tina Brown and her friend, Richard Moretti, a newly affluent owner of a succesful Orlando, Florida based Volkswagen restoration business, made up somewhat of an odd couple. Ritchie is a pony tailed, Johnny Appleseed type with a mercurial personality. He has a reverse curve posture that makes him appear as though he is leaning back to look up at something, perhaps the result of years of working under cars.

 Tina on the other hand is a quiet type, reserved, one who patiently observes, gathers facts from this, and then reacts, in other words an ideal fisherman. In Ritchie's world everything must happen yesterday, today at the latest, lead, follow, or get out of the way! This attitude led to the expected health problems for him and the resulting search for a new life style.

Over the years, Tina's interest in fishing had rubbed off on Ritchie, who had now been infected with somewhat of a fishing Jones himself. They decided a change was in order for them, so as fate would have it, they became aware of a certain dive of a motel called the Buena Vista, a fixer upper by any stretch of imagination, which by the way to add to its marketability was located next to a seedy strip joint named Fanny's. Certainly a nice piece of property by anyone's standards … maybe that is, after just getting out of prison.

For whatever reason, they decided they must have the place, which they proceeded to rehabilitate into an appealing neat as a pin establishment, which they renamed the Hidden Harbor Motel. While cleaning up and rejuvenating the property they also made sure there was always time set aside for fishing. And, of course, since they were just a few minutes boat ride from the Seven Mile Bridge, a tarpon hot spot in the spring, they would take the occasional night off to test the waters and currents running through the bridge supports for a "Silver King".

On one fateful balmy evening, the weather was just right, there was a nice gentle sea breeze and the moon would be full in the sky, all good things if you are a tarpon angler looking to connect. So out they went. Tina and Ritchie boarded the boat whose live well had been stocked with fresh live mullet, the bait of choice for tarpon. In fact it is tarpon candy!

Reaching the bridge they got the boat in position, the bow facing the current. They then secured their spot by dropping anchor and tying the line off to a red beach ball like float before attaching the float's line in turn to a boat cleat. The reason for this maneuver is in case of a hook up with a fish, you can quickly shed your anchor without pulling it up, chase the fish with your boat, and after hopefully landing it, you return to the beach ball float and recover said anchor.

This is the practiced routine that was in place that evening as Tina baited the rods with the mullet and cast them out into the current, the water making a trickling washing sound as it ran under the boat. The wait had begun.

Time waiting for a fish to strike is usually passed taking about fishing, the weather, or all things nautical, while all the time you keep your eyes fixed on the rods and water. You watch your bait's movement and the tension in the line, periodically changing position from one foot to the other, sitting, standing, pacing, talking, not talking, restless, but relaxed.

This all came to an abrupt end when the reel's drag sang out a high pitched whine, as line began to explosively peel off guitar string tight, and the rod loaded up with weight and bent over in a tortured semicircular C pattern. As if the boat had burst into flame, everyone sprung into action into a rehearsed response that would be the envy of any fire engine crew. The motor was started, anchor line disengaged, and engine thrown in reverse as the boat burst from under the bridge, rapidly backing up to gain clear fighting space, like a race horse breaking from the starting gate.

Tina quickly picked up the rod that now felt like it had been connected to a maniacal force on the other end and pulled back to put maximum pressure on the fish and make it pay for every foot of line it burned from the reel as the demonic silver apparition headed for Cuba, spitting fire all the way.

The battle was now joined as Tina pumped the rod up and then on the downward stroke cranked the reel as rapidly as possible to gain line on the powerful fish. Sometimes it would answer with a demoralizing fast burst of speed that would take back all the line that she had fought so hard to recover. Her forearms and upper legs began to ache as she rested the rod in the fighting belt she had clamped on so she could flex and unflex her cramping hands. Periodically the rod would angrily undulate up and down as the tarpon on the other end vehemently protested its situation.

Slowly, little by little, and painstakingly surely, Tina began to gain line as Ritchie skillfully maneuvered and manipulated the boat, setting her up in the most advantageous position to deliver the best counter punch to the streaking animal. Suddenly the tarpon erupted from the ocean like a volcano spitting hot lava and cleared the water completely, frozen in mid air, the fading sunlight glaring off its silver scales, gill covers rattling like a man shaking his fist at you, water spraying everywhere,. "How dare you hook me!", the fish seemed to be seething.

The time passed and still Tina and Ritchie kept working patiently wearing the creature down, sapping its strength as they too became drained. The struggle continued until little by little, yard by yard, foot by foot, and inch by inch the now exhausted fish was alongside the boat.

Some fishermen will tell you they fish for sport, enjoying the search and the fight, or the exaltation that comes with the conclusion of a successful encounter, but there is another group, these are the chosen ones who do it because of love of the outdoors and all things natural. They have an undeniable bond and respect for their quarry, the fish. So it was this day. Tina observed the animal she had battled for so long, now subdued, floating on its side next to the boat, no longer the powerful swimmer traveling along ocean pathways, through reefs, bays or under bridges, testing the parameters of the abyss, instead now reduced to a paralytic immobility, floating on the surface of the sea, buoyant, unable to submerge, its powerful rear caudal fin motionless and spent.

Perhaps a oneness or empathy with the helpless tarpon kicked in a this point, for Tina Brown saw a fellow ocean traveler that needed help. She must save this fish! In this day and age keeping a tarpon is not legal without the angler having purchased a special tarpon stamp with their fishing license. Since the tarpon is not considered table fare, few fishermen these days opt to keep one, instead releasing it after the fight. In 1984 however the custom was to keep the fish for pictures, display purposes, possibly the occasional taxidermy mount which was very expensive, but the end result was the death of the tarpon.

As she continued to look at the big silver fish, now lying still on the floor of the boat defeated and dying, Tina decided to act, and it was an action that would change everything. She told Ritchie to start the motor and run full speed back to the motel only a few minutes away. When they reached the dock they quickly enlisted the help of some rather surprised motel employees to carry the hundred pound fish to of all places, the motel's large saltwater swimming pool.

Grabbing hold of the tarpon like pallbearers of some strange silver finned casket, the group rapidly in lock step shuffled the silent fish over to the concrete pond and dropped it into the water. Then they stepped back from the pool's side to see what would happen next. The fish responded by slowly rolling over on its side like a capsized ship, the tarpon's gills barely moving. Fish CPR was in order and urgently needed.

Jumping into the pool, Ritchie and Tina took hold of the animal, hands supporting its sides, and held it in the correct upright position, then began to walk it around the shallow end of the pool. This action forced oxygenated water over the stunned fish's gills. On and on the strange procession went, it began to seem like a long time until finally the life giving water flow though the fish's mouth and over the gills started to at last have its effect. They could feel through their hands the powerful muscles of the tarpon start to flex and contract and flex again as life returned to the fish.

Gradually they loosened their grip on the slowly reviving animal and watched to see if it would remain upright and start breathing on its own. Totally unsupported by Ritchie and Tina, the fish was watched by everyone in the motel audience each one holding their breath and waiting to see what would happen, but with no big fanfare the tarpon calmly swam off as if nothing had occurred and began to explore the limits of its new world.

As time passed, the new "pet" tarpon, who had been christened the "Big Guy" became the star attraction at the Hidden Harbor swimming pool now turned aquarium, and little by little more fish of various species were added to the collection. There was by the way, another addition to the motel, a new freshwater swimming pool, built this time for the exclusive use of the motel's customers. There would be no fish in this one!

Somewhere down the line, Tina began to feel that their miniature ocean was just not complete. It lacked something and she knew what that was. She talked to Ritchie and he agreed. They inquired to the State of Florida about the possibility of getting a sea turtle.

The hitch was, that sea turtles were a protected species, so getting even one for the motel was out of the question ... that was unless the motel was willing to become a sea turtle rehabilitation center for sick and injured turtles, and oh by the way pay for it all themselves.

The State of Florida powers that be at this point probably went off chuckling, thinking that this was the last they would see of these two "crackpots". This may have been one of the grandest examples of underestimation in the history of mankind, well at least in Florida anyway, because to Tina and Ritchie this of course sounded like a great idea. Rehabilitate sea turtles? Why not? So, the couple set to the task of learning all they could about the care and husbandry of sick, injured or for that matter healthy turtles.

They read, they talked to people, and then read some more, acquiring over time an impressive knowledge of the subject, until the State authorities probably much to their chagrin were compelled to certify the Hidden Harbor Motel as a sea turtle rehabilitation center.

In 1986, the motel got its' first patients, but they were not injured or sick. They were a pair of Green sea turtles who had been arranged by a man named Ross Witham. Ross was a survivor of sorts himself, but in his case it was of the attack on Pearl Harbor that rocked the Hawaiian islands in 1941, whose effect was felt all the way from the Navy base on Oahu, to the marine barracks on far away Midway Island.

The two turtles were brought as a breeding experiment to see if they would mature and nest on the little sand beach that had now been created adjacent to the swimming pool and leading into its waters. While this experiment was waiting to come to possible fruition, the first injured sea turtles began to arrive from fishermen, boaters, and even the Coast Guard.

They came in sick with intestinal blockage from ingesting garbage and fish hooks, suffering shark bites, fishing line entanglement, and of course there were the boat strike turtles. Sad victims of collisions with an assortment of watercraft, their cracked shells were filled with paraffin and covered with epoxy or fiberglass in what must have seemed to Ritchie like a revisitation to auto body work. Tina would prepare nutritious feed for the turtles, helping them to lay down new bone and heal the gaps in their broken shells as time passed, but too often even after the shells healed, the turtles were left semi-buoyant "floaters" unable to dive down without floating back to the water's surface, rear flippers silent and the spinal chord injury they were believed to be suffering from remaining a frustrating puzzle.

As the years passed the reputation of the Hidden Harbor Environmental Project as it was properly known continued to grow. Turtles suffering from all kinds of maladies were brought in. Probably most prominent of all, and alarmingly so, was a strange affliction called fibropapilloma, a suspected viral disease whose cause and cure would remain elusive. Sea turtles with the sickness are characterized by the presence of sponge like tumors on almost any part of the body including internally. FP as it is called, in advanced stages leads to the death of the turtle. Even in preliminary stages, if the tumors are located around or on the eyes, the disease can cause blindness, resulting in an inability to feed, leading to a slow death.

To help find a cure for this troubling malady that was occurring in sea turtles world wide, Tina and Ritchie brought in a veterinarian from the University of Florida to do research named Dr. Elliot Jacobsen. Eventually another gifted veterinary surgeon, Douglas Mader, who had a passion for reptiles, would pioneer laser surgery as a means of removing FP tumors.

Sadly Tina Brown and Ritchie Moretti eventually would go their separate ways, the differing personalities becoming less and less compatible. Ritchie's fame continued to grow world wide as he became more and more a fixture in the world of sea turtle rehabilitation and a familiar face on animal oriented TV shows. He hosts an annual sea turtle rehabilitation symposium at the motel which has recently opened its doors to tour groups.

Tina Brown went on to become a skilled sport fishing charter boat captain, her love of fishing still burning strong. She also founded and runs the Turtle Kraals Museum in Key West, sea turtles still being in her blood. Before she left the hospital Tina had brought in a volunteer to assist in the growing work load. Her name was Sue Schaf, a University of Florida graduate with a passion for reptiles, particularly snakes and mud turtles which she would collect during summers spent in Wisconsin. Later Corinne Rose, a Canadian from the land of maple leaves and float planes who also had caught sea turtle fever came on board along with a continuing flow of other able bodied turtle fans.

Certainly a strange and wonderful story! A ramshackle motel rehabilitated by two people rehabilitating their own lives, who rehabilitated a tarpon, that led to the rehabilitation of sea turtles; and it all started with the catching of a fish, but there was still another wonderful story yet to come. Several people who had never met one another, leading parallel paths, heretofore disconnected, would have their lives knotted together forever by one particular Green sea turtle, who himself had overcome the odds to just perhaps fulfill a special purpose.

17

SAVE-A-TURTLE

After Tina and Ritchie had acquired the motel, revitalized it, then gotten into the sea turtle repair business, early on they had been put in contact with a certain park ranger who was assigned to Lignumvitae Key, located not far from the rustic Robbie's Marina and its tarpon feeding dock. The island could in fact be seen from that position quite easily, laying out in the ocean mist, low in the water, off on the nearby horizon. The ranger who worked there was named Pat Wells, and the three of them had been brought together for the purpose of getting the motel certified as a turtle rehab facility. Tina and Ritchie were also interested in finding out if Pat might know something about the fibropapilloma disease that seemed to be plaguing the sea turtles in increasing numbers. In Pat, Tina and Ritchie had found a kindred spirit. The ranger's hometown was Leesburg, Florida, located in the central part of the state, an area known mostly for its number of freshwater fishing lakes that held quantities of trophy sized largemouth bass. As a kid Pat had loved poking around the woods and waters looking for creatures large and small that might be just around the next corner of forest. He could lose himself in this environment for countless hours as it provided a never ending theatre of biological delights, snakes, lizards, turtles and tortoises, birds and fish. Each living find was carefully examined and then gently returned to its place on the forest floor. When not pursuing this line, the only other thing that vied for his attention was sports, football in particular. As a matter of fact, as his college years overtook him, he could not resist the opportunity to play that sport for the University of West Virginia while he attended there. What he soon discovered was that the difference between high school and college sports was like day and night. Playing football began to take its toll and he was becoming physically and mentally drained by it. Choosing a major field of study had also become a task and he floated in indecision between math or biology. Even worse, he found himself with less time to pursue his wilderness walks.

Pat realized that he would have to make a choice sooner rather than later, and this he did in a decisively radical way. He left football, the University of West Virginia, returned to his home and the University of Florida, and decided on a major in biological sciences.

As it turned out, being in your home state surrounded by woodland haunts was a mixed blessing. There was always a conflict that had to be overcome. It was a choice between sitting in a room or library, reading books on chemistry, physics, and genetics, or taking to the field and interacting with the natural world just outside the door and down the road. Pat was just too easily called away, so the battle of books and nature was continually won by the latter. This caused him to once again change his major, now to the lifesaver for all college students, business management, which also resulted in graduation.

Well, there he was, free at last, out in the world, ready to make a living in the field of his choosing, which in the tough post Vietnam job market turned out to be running a Goodyear tire store. This was not how he had envisioned his life working out! The smell of the tire rubber, sound of pneumatic tools, and the feel of axle grease oozing between his fingers was a far cry from the earthy clean smell of the forest, the quiet of the morning sun climbing over the woodland canopy, or the thrill of a flock of birds thunderously taking flight from a blue lake and bolting into the cloud punctuated sky. After about a year of selling his allotment of automotive rubber doughnuts, Pat was beginning to reach his limit, and ever a man to change course, he decided again to return to his roots, but what could he do? Well, he did have a degree in business didn't he? Why not start one up himself, but this time it had to be outdoors, no more side tracks and dead ends! A tree service seemed to be the answer, and so he embarked on that trail. At last he hit the jackpot, pruning, planting, removing trees, all played right into his woodsman skills and also honed them. He loved it! However, his journey was not yet complete. As luck would have it, often, during the course of some of these jobs, Pat had the occasion to come in contact with various personnel from the Florida Park Service. One thing led to another and one day he found himself filling out an application for the position of ranger. It was accepted, and finally his circuitous job search odyssey had come to an end. He could now do what he loved most and get paid for it.

He was first stationed at Little Talbot Island near Jacksonville, a stint that lasted two and a half years, after that, he was able to transfer to the exotic and remote Lignumvitae Key. Although he had some exposure to sea turtles at Little Talbot Island, once Pat arrived in the Keys, things along those lines started to get serious. He quickly found out from residents that there were plenty of turtles down in these islands but no nesting taking place. Pat didn't take much note of this or pay any heed to it one way or another, until in his travels around the area he began to notice a few turtle crawls, the telltale tracks left in the sand that are indicative of sea turtle nesting activity. Since there were a large amount of raccoons in the area, the chance of nest predation was extremely high.

Because of this, Pat started to regularly patrol the various beaches in his area looking for more turtle nests in order to protect and monitor them. It didn't take long before he realized that he could not cover so much area by himself. He needed some help. The answer he thought was to create interest in beach patrols by local volunteers,so he attempted to do that, but without much success.

A short time after this first failure, Pat was patrolling Long Key and ran into a camper named Larry Lawrence. Larry was a biologist who had also been discovering turtle crawls with some amount of regularity and he too understood the need to develop a network of volunteers to carry out the needed beach patrols and nest monitoring. It was at that point that a germ of an idea came to them. Why not start some sort of charitable organization or club composed of beach combers or other types of Keys inhabitants! Larry and Pat could use their connections with the State of Florida to obtain the necessary authorization, then connect with the media and get the ball rolling.

The result was that in 1985 a little group of people came together and something called Save-A-Turtle was born. Its initial mission statement was, "the preservation, protection, and enhancement of rare and endangered sea turtles in the Florida Keys", as its purpose. To meet this end, the first volunteers were trained and granted permits to carry out beach patrols in search of turtle crawls and nests, or to recover stranded and injured sea turtles. This included on any given occasion, assisting, and sometimes this involved a solo effort; in the recovery of stranded turtles at sea or even highly decayed dead ones anywhere else. Over the years Save-A-Turtle expanded into funding for fibropapilloma research, contributing to the ongoing study for a cause and cure.

It has now been over twenty years since Pat Wells and Larry Lawrence created their little "club". During this span the group has included some colorful characters, each one contributing to the cause in their own way. Some have moved on. Some still roam the beaches of the Florida Keys, perhaps even as we speak!

Caroline Street Patty

Patty Anthony has been a Floridian all her life, and a resident of Key West for more than twenty years. Like many people in the state, lifelong resident or not, the longer you are down here, and this includes northern transplants, the less tolerant one becomes of cold weather in any shape or form.

The quest for warmer climes led Patty to move from her home in Jacksonville up in the northern part of Florida, to Miami, and finally after a particularly cold snap, at least to her southern point of view, Key West. This was as far as she could walk the plank in order to escape the pirate of cold weather and his chilling saber and still remain in the U.S.

She was already familiar with that part of the world, having stayed there as a young girl. Her family owned a home on Caroline Street, which at the time was an unpaved dirt road, but even with this lack of modernity, she had developed a taste for Keys living. So in the nineteen eighties, this is where she found herself.

Early on, Patty was pulled in by the diversity of terrestrial, avian, and aquatic wildlife that made their home on the island chain. This fascination led her to join the local Audubon Society as a volunteer. While serving in this capacity, an opportunity arose to work in the bookstore located at Fort Jefferson in the Dry Tortugas. It would be a rather large commitment of time due to the fact that accepting the position would entail taking a trip out to the remote islands by boat launch, then spending a ten day tour of duty at the isolated site, which by the way was reported to be haunted! Patty, a determined person decided she would partake of this adventure.

During her tenure on the Tortugas, Patty was witness to many an odd occurrence. On one occasion she was crossing a bridge near the fort after the park had closed. As she did, she passed a man wearing a Civil War era uniform standing on the overpass. Figuring he must be a tour guide, Patty paid little attention to the man. When she mentioned it to someone, they told her that no one like that was employed by the park, and all the tourists had already left for the day. Certainly an odd experience that might give anyone second thoughts, couple this with the constant raucous din of nesting birds, and you could say that the fort was an eerie place at times.

While all these things did provide entertainment, Patty took them in stride, after all, she did live in Key West where strange was the norm. One morning however something did happen, and this time, it would have an impact on her life.

On that special day she was walking along the sandy beach on one of the adjacent islands to the fort when she noticed something crawling across the sand, heading towards the ocean, flip flop hopping along. She focused in on the tiny creature thinking it must be a crab of some sort, but as she moved closer she made out the tiny flippers and green scaled shell that unmistakably identified it as a sea turtle! It was a newborn hatchling scrambling to reach the ocean. While she was looking at the miniature turtle and admiring the determination it showed, some other movement not far away caught her attention and she discovered this little guy was not alone. In fact, she was surrounded by a Lilliputian army of miniscule sea turtles adorned in their olive drab shell uniforms marching toward the ocean objective. They seemed to be everywhere! All around her she began to see more and more turtles erupting from the sand like bubbles in a boiling pot of conch chowder. It was as if some timer gun had unleashed them on a reptilian marathon race.

Patty had unwittingly stepped right into the middle of an impressive nest hatching. She thought this was one of the most wonderful sights she had ever seen! From that point on she was hooked. Soon after returning to Key West she became aware of something called Save-A-Turtle and became a member of that new organization.

The Bernetts

Herb and Yea Bernett like Patty Anthony also came to the Keys from up North, but in this case it was not from northern Florida but Pennsylvania. The City of Pittsburgh would be the antithesis of anything one could think of as tropical, but that in a way is how people from colder more temperate climates become attracted by and to the State of Florida, particularly the unique Caribbean island at times almost third world feel of the Florida Keys.

Herb had worked for one of the steel companies and Yea as a nurse. Then they took their first trip to this land of sea, islands, and sand, and they knew then they had found the place to retire.

As is the case with many hard working people, the retired life provided perhaps too much leisure time and often the couple would look for new things to keep themselves occupied. One day as luck would have it, they witnessed a stranded sea turtle recovery on Summerland Key. They became fascinated by the operation and in short order decided to become members of Save-A-Turtle. Not ones to sit on their hands, they took things a step further when they signed up for beach patrol training. Once certified they would be expected to get up early in the morning and walk several miles of beach in search of turtle nesting activity or crawls.

During the nesting season which normally ran from April to September, Herb and Yea would arise somewhere around five o'clock a.m. so they would be able to start the patrol no later than six. Throughout the course of any given nesting year, they could expect to discover between twenty to twenty five nests. One season, a special nest in particular, was lucky to have the Bernetts watching over it.

When they first came upon it, the nest was already in the process of hatching. Yea and Herb stood over the little sand crater and proceeded to watch the show. One by one the little turtles popped from the gravel until the nest had emptied the contents. The hatching now completed, the couple turned and started to walk away, resuming the patrol, but then something happened. A sound caught Yea's ear and then Herb began to hear it too. It was a weak peeping sound not unlike that of a baby chick, but softer and of less volume. The peeps seemed to be coming from the sand where the nest had been. All the turtles were gone, no new ones anywhere. The old ones had already reached the ocean and were swimming out to sea. Intuitively they both began to dig down into the sand where the old nest had been. Their hands and fingers probed through the shifting porous grit searching in vain for the source of the whispering call. Just as they were about to give up, all of a sudden there it was, the feeling of life, struggling life, searching for the first light of day from a sun they had never seen but knew must be there. The nest was not yet empty!

Herb and Yea began to dig up each tiny turtle and then place the now freed but weak babies one by one into a plastic container. The peeping had finally stopped, still, to make sure, they dug a little deeper. No, there were no more! Picking up the box they headed back to the car, then on to The Turtle Hospital in Marathon, to the waiting arms of Tina Brown and Ritchie Morretti. There, over time, they were carefully nurtured back to health and finally released on an unknown weed line, somewhere out at sea under an early morning sunrise.

Without the help of Herb and Yea Bernett, today there would be a few less turtles swimming in the open expanses of ocean to points unknown and enriching our lives. It was in this way that two people from an unlikely place, a place of snow and cold, that had never known sea turtles, truly lived up to the name of the organization they were now joined with, Save-A-Turtle.

Tropical Mike

Tropical Mike Hall as he calls himself is a Florida Keys jack of all trades, and master of many. As a matter of fact he is a master in the literal sense of the word, a dive master to be exact, teaching the sport of scuba diving to a variety of Keys residents and tourists. He also has a love of animals and creatures of the wild, particularly the aquatic forms such as, fish, crustaceans, and as you would expect sea turtles. The latter interest in turtles could be easily predicted if one is familiar with his pedigree, you see his mother is Patty Anthony.

Mike's interest in the sea turtles began to peak when one day in 1986 he was teaching one of his diving classes out at sea and away from the confines of a swimming pool. There the group encountered one rather large Loggerhead turtle swimming along the coral sand bottom. Mike and the class followed it and were treated to a one of a kind experience of watching the two hundred fifty pound animal feeding on queen conch, the football sized, rock hard shelled snail that gives the Keys the other name by which they are known, "The Conch Republic".

The turtle would move from one unlucky gastropod to the next as if it were connecting the dots in an underwater puzzle and at each point crushing the dense conch shell into oblivion, swallowing the exposed snail meat, then moving on to another, duplicating the powerful viselike bite time and again with the same results. The group of following divers could hear the crunch and feel through the water the vibrations coming from the pulverizing grinding of the thick shell. This show went on for about thirty minutes.

Mike was in awe of the sheer power of the docile looking animal with the lethal bite and the experience became burned into his memory along with another that occurred on a reef not far away. This time it was a Hawksbill turtle. It seemed to be begging for attention and followed Mike around like a loyal puppy for the whole dive, perhaps looking for more out of life, or a moment in the limelight like another turtle from some other time and place.

Mike on other dive excursions was also beginning to notice something that disturbed him. A third species of turtle, the Green sea turtle was showing increasing presence of the tumors indicative of the fibropapilloma disease. He became concerned and wanted to do something if he could. As fate would have it, Mike was reading the local paper and spied an add asking for volunteers to work beach patrols and turtle rescue for Save-A-Turtle. He decided to enroll in one of the classes at Saint Peter's Church in Big Pine Key, where he was certified as a beach patroller by a man named Pat Wells. Over the following years, Mike's sea turtle encounters continued, but there was one in particular that he never forgot. It was the sight of a Leatherback turtle entangled in three lobster traps but still able to tow them along. The fact that the turtle was that badly encumbered and still exhibit such a feat of strength left a lasting impression and a feeling of awe and respect for these animals he never forgot. Something that left an even better memory souvenir was the fact that he was able to catch the Leatherback, remove the traps. And then watch the fortunate leviathan, now freed of the burden, slowly disappear into the ocean depths.

Tropical Mike Hall had other adventures in store for him. He would go on to Captain the glass bottom tour boat, Discovery, now located in Key West, having relocated from Key Largo. During the day he chauffeurs land lubbers and all manner of non divers out to the reefs, giving them a glimpse of what lays just off shore and out on the horizon. Mike would also through the years rise through the ranks of Save-A-Turtle to become President, serving for three years. What he could not have known was that during his final year, the organization he served would reach out to touch the lives of some people and a creature he had never met.

The Jensens

Long time Florida residents Don and Margie Jensen, like so many others who have come to the state, soon fell under the spell of turtle worship and were then drawn to Save-A-Turtle, joining the group early on. Making their home in the Islamorada string of islands, they too have experienced a distinct collection of sea turtle adventures. As active S.A.T. members, it wasn't long before they signed on for stranding, recovery, and rescue work.

One of the tasks that would fall under this job description was picking up and transferring to a safe haven, usually The Turtle Hospital, turtles who had gotten themselves entangled or entrapped in an assortment of precarious predicaments. Sometimes the animals are alive, sometimes they are dead.... Way dead!! This would seem a thankless task by some measures, but not theirs.

Margie has an impish sense of humor and must have enjoyed her husband Don's tale of the recovery of one rather large Loggerhead turtle. This big guy, nearly 250 pounds, just did fit into the bed of his compact pickup truck. After being shoved and shoe horned into that space, Don watched as the truck springs sagged under the weight of the sea turtle before clicking shut the rear lift gate. He had as usual been given instructions to run it down to The Turtle Hospital in Marathon.

The Loggerhead himself had long since decided that wheeled transportation was not to his liking, so he proceeded to attempt to climb out of the fast moving vehicle and make good on an escape, extricating himself from some unknown fate. With wind blowing in his scaled hair, he took matters into his own hands, or flippers as it were. Imagine if you will, the expressions on the faces of the drivers following Don's truck, who witnessed a strange, alien, brownish, flipper like appendage, attached to who knows what sort of life form, waving at them over the back of the tailgate. Traffic began to build up forming a strange procession with Don in the lead, sweating it out all the way. He breathed a sigh of relief when at last he deposited the shell covered behemoth at the hospital, safe and sound. Just another normal day in the life of a S.A.T. volunteer! When not rescuing turtles, one of Margie's diversions was entertaining herself with the occasional game of Scrabble at the home of a friend named Edna Bier who lived a few islands to the west. Edna's son was an architect with a taste for the island life and sailboats. His name was Mike, and he also loved sea turtles. Boy, did he love sea turtles!

Island Mike

Island Mike Bier, an architect from Lower Matecumbe Key, like many of the other stalwarts, joined Save-A-Turtle in the early years. He has a love for sailing and this sometime vies with his interest in the natural history of the Keys for first place. Sometimes the sailboat wins, sometimes the turtles. Mostly the turtles! The first impression of Mike would be that of a tropical leprechaun, well tanned and weathered. He seems to be in on a joke that no one else is aware of and is waiting for the punch line to be played out, or like a base runner who knows the pitcher's pick off move and with confident larceny in his heart, steals the next base.

Mike like his contemporaries, fell under the spell of the sea turtle and soon became a hands on volunteer. As luck would have it, one of his first assignments was the recovery of a dead turtle that had washed up on the beach of a nearby resident's home and had become an unwelcome visitor. Upon arrival, Mike confidently told the occupants of the property not to worry, he would gather up the remains of the cadaverous animal and transport it to the appropriate authority.

And this he did. Placing the turtle in the back of his car, he exited the area satisfied with a job well done, patting himself on the back, and started his drive. Then it hit him! At first it was only a faint tap on the shoulder of his nostrils, a whiff of smoke per se, some fragrance of a distant shore. Mike's nose started to process the incoming data. Yes, there it was again! There was no denying it, a strange odor was beginning to work through the car and was rapidly gaining strength!

As if the scent had a life of its own, it continued to grow like a too ripe tomato until it erupted like a spewing volcano of unadulterated stink. It was not just any stink, but one of epic proportions like rotten eggs, dirty socks, and a hot garbage truck on an August day all rolled into the "Mother of all Stenches", leaking from the putrid entrails of the departed turtle! Mike couldn't get to his destination soon enough. Once there he hastily escaped his vehicle and painfully removed the acrid smelling carcass from its cargo area, but not before it had deposited some vile juice into the upholstery that caused the car to stink for weeks.

That lesson learned, Island Mike became useful as an example of how not to handle exceedingly dead sea turtles, and as the unwitting subject of future training lectures conducted by S.A.T. founder, Pat Wells. Mike and Pat in the future often found themselves working together in other ways. On one such occasion their task was the extraction of another large Loggerhead turtle from an Islamorada swimming pool. Arriving at poolside, the pair discovered that removing the sea turtle would require Pat getting into the water, grabbing the animal's shell, and then steer swimming it out of the enclosure, an enclosure that the turtle seemed to be coming more fond of by the minute. That phase of the rescue did however come off without a hitch, that was until Pat had to go back to the truck and get a tape measure to record the animal's dimensions and dry off a bit. Accordingly, he instructed Mike to hold the turtle in place until he returned. This is where things started to deviate somewhat from the plan.

At some point known only to him, the big Loggerhead decided he had experienced enough of the good life for that day and proceeded to make a bee line for the beach, dragging Mike behind like a piece of trailing toilet paper stuck to a shoe. Not being a person of large stature or weight, he tried every trick in the book to impede the stubborn turtles advance until as a last resort, Mike crawled up on the turtle's back. Undeterred in the least, the Loggerhead kept on going even with Mike on board.

When Pat eventually returned, he was treated to the sight of the pair marching toward the ocean with Mike on top in what one could call a compromising position. Let's just say it looked like Mike REALLY loved turtles!

In the scheme of things, perhaps it could be said that Mike Bier's most memorable adventure was yet to come. In a few years he would make a phone call at the request of fellow Save-A-Turtle member Margie Jensen. That call produced some results that neither person on either end of the conversation could ever have imagined, and also for an animal who was waiting patiently, on the west coast of Florida, waiting for those he knew would find him.

The tangled channels of the Ten Thousand Islands.

Pete's final resting place in the Ten Thousand Islands.

The dock. Pete's arrival point at Matt Finn's.

Pete and Matt Finn. July 1, 1998.

"Pete" 11/19/02

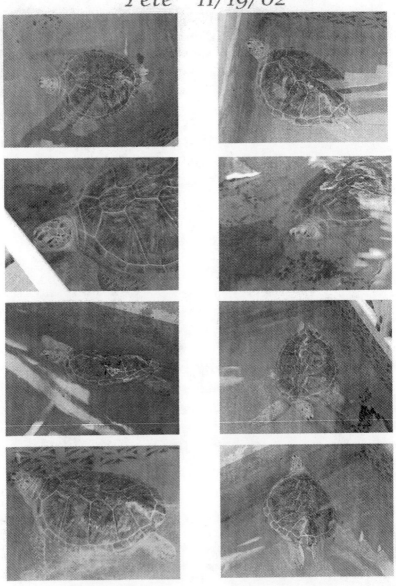

Pete's portfolio sent from the Clearwater Marine Aquarium to the Shedd Aquarium.

Pete's pool at the Clearwater Marine Aquarium.

I visit a friendly manatee at Crystal River, Florida.

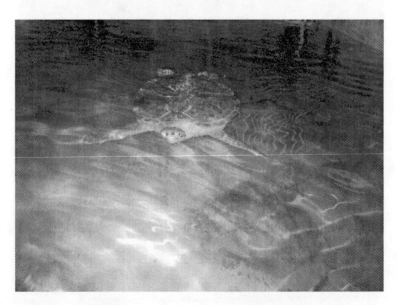

Pete greets me at the Clearwater Marine Aquarium.

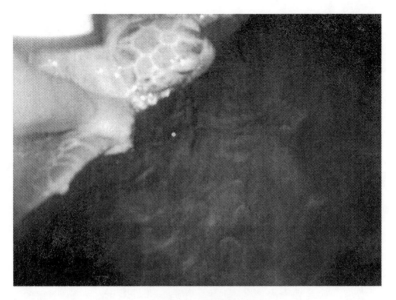

I make contact with Pete.

Sue Schaf feeds some patients at The Turtle Hospital.

Coasty and friends at The Turtle Hospital.

Hidden Harbor Motel.

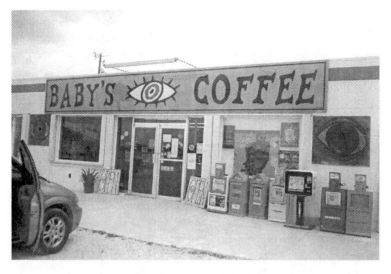

Baby's Coffee, the Keys' version of Starbucks.

The Turtle Kraals Museum, Key West, Florida.

Tina Brown, co-founder of The Turtle Hospital,
at her Turtle Kraals Museum.

Choppy, the pug, waits for my return.

Barney, the Newf. (Photo Credit: Carol Flisak)

Pete in his shipping crate at O'Hare International Airport. April 23, 2003.

Nickel shortly after his release into the Caribbean Reef. July 22, 2003.
(Photo Credit: Carol Flisak)

Michelle gets acquainted with Nickel. (Photo Credit: Carol Flisak)

Michelle "tickles" Nickel. (Photo Credit: Carol Flisak)

Nickel's "head down-tail up" swimming style.
(Photo Credit: Carol Flisak)

Relaxing under the coral in the Caribbean Reef.
(Photo Credit: Carol Flisak)

Nickel, star performer. (Photo Credit: Ann Lyssenko)

I meet Matt Finn. December 2003.

18

FISH STORY

With me, it was always fish. I was drawn to them from the beginning, as if it had always been planned that way. Even to this day, I can't define what it is about them that attracts or interests me. Possibly it's the grace and frictionless ease with which they move about and through their fluid world, or perhaps the endless variety and colors presented to the eye by each individual species? Could it be the array of locomotion displayed as they swim, walk, slither, or crawl about the streams, lakes, and oceans of the world? Or maybe it was imprinting, like a baby duck that at first sight of an object, then identifies it as its mother, whether it be another duck, dog, human, or anything else, even inanimate.

The reason I suspect imprinting arises from a story told to me by my mother. She would often relate to me a tale of how when I was a small child of no more than two years old, she could shop all around the grocery store and leave the cart, with me in it, in front of the frozen fish section, where I would sit quietly, mesmerized by the iced display of finned creatures laid out before me. Since this was the early nineteen fifties, the fish were usually sitting in the butcher's case in whole, unpackaged glory, but then again I may have been to old to have been imprinted at that point.

My mother was divorced when I was about two or three years old and I saw my father very little from that point on, no more than a half dozen days or so until his death from a heart attack when I was a teen. One of the only memories I have of him is going fishing at a lake somewhere near Burlington, Wisconsin, which is the town where we lived. I don't know where the lake was or its name, but I do remember my brother catching bullheads, a species of small catfish, and then dropping them into a bucket of water. The little creatures captivated me, and I would spend the whole time looking into the container watching the whiskered fish swim about inside, they looked somewhat like brown tadpoles.

I recall an early memory of my Mom and I going to visit a married couple, who were friends of hers. They were moderately wealthy by the standards of the day and running along the stairway going down into the recreation room, they had a good sized aquarium that one could look right through, serving as sort of a room divider. The man took out some fish food and carefully poured a small amount on the rim of the tank, he then told me to push it into the water a little at a time. This I did just as instructed, and for the next two hours I was treated to the sight of an assortment of tiny tropical fish, happily picking at the sinking flakes of food floating down. I never moved from my vantage point on the steps the whole time we were there. I don't remember a single detail of the house or the people, but five decades later, I still remember that aquarium and the fish swimming in that wondrous miniature world.

When I was in elementary school in the first grade, my teacher, Miss Pearson, who was a friend of our family and already knew of my predilection for those sort of things, would always send the class's pet fish home with me during holiday vacations, or if she was off sick, there would be a chalk message on the blackboard from the school's principal instructing the substitute teacher that I would take care of the fish.

My fish loving reputation always preceded me with every grade advancement from then on, each new teacher being grateful that they had someone to take care of the aquarium and to pawn the fish off on at the end of the year.

In the seventh grade, I remember one particular instance when my teacher quietly came up to my desk and told me my sixth grade teacher from the previous year was out in the hall and would like to talk with me. A rush of fear went through me as I went out into the quiet void wondering what I could have possibly done. As it turned out, my former teacher had some questions on how to keep some fish in an aquarium he had just purchased. This was quite an honor for an eleven year old, and was one of the few instances of positive reinforcement I would get when it came to my fish hobby.

After my mother was divorced, we went to live in Berwyn, Illinois, a suburb west of Chicago, residing in a house owned by my grandmother and great aunt. My mother went to work at a local retail drapery store for fifty cents an hour, leaving my grandmother in charge of my older brother and my great aunt of me, they each became our individual substitute mothers.

My memory of my grandmother who we always called "Gram", was that of a hardworking, no frills homemaker, whose motto could have been, "Save your money in case you have to buy underwear". She cooked almost all of our meals, along with a lot of baking which often featured a Bohemian, sweet, bread like coffeecake, called hoska. In fact some people started calling her the "hoska lady". She had a bitterness about her, most likely caused by the loss of her husband from a heart attack while in his fifties, which led to the loss of her house. This forced her to move back to her childhood home and live with my great aunt who was my grandmother's half sister. To further rub salt into her wounds, her own full sister who was closer to my great aunt, ended up marrying a man who later became the C.E.O. of Johnson and Johnson Pharmaceuticals, then living in a New Jersey mansion with maids, servants and horse stables.

You could not say I was the apple of my grandmother's eye. She took every opportunity to criticize me and would eagerly point out anything she perceived as a fault. She also looked on my interest in fish as one step above alcoholism, praising me only on occasion. I think she was a good person despite this, who many people liked, so this made her constant fault finding hurt even more, causing me to withdraw into my underwater world with my silent finned companions.

There was, one positive note in those early years, that was constant, faithful, caring, and always supportive,…. My great aunt Margaret. When I first met her I was about three or four years old and she was already in her sixties, retired from her job at a telephone assembly factory.

I would like to say that she was one of the finest, most decent people I have ever known in my life, but that would not do her justice. She was not one of the best, but THE best person I have yet to know.

She always encouraged me in my interests, especially Civil War history, all animals, and fish. My aunt would tell me stories about World War I, the horse named "Dolly" and the electric car they had when she was young, the Titanic, or read to me over and over from any book I chose. I particularly liked a book on dogs. It had black and white drawings of any number of breeds but a picture of one dog stayed with me the rest of my life.

The drawing was set on a seashore somewhere and there was a lighthouse off in the distance. At the center of the picture sat a beautiful large black dog, silent, vigilantly looking out to sea. He had an undeniable appearance of dignity with his heavy ebony black coat, large domed head, and massive paws. The dog seemed almost bear like. I learned that the breed was called a Newfoundland, and that it was the national dog of Canada. I never forgot him.

The phone company where my aunt had worked was active in the assembly of the new RADAR, as it was called during World War II, and it wasn't long before I became interested in that segment of history also. Particularly one naval and air battle at a place called Midway Island, but fish were still the main interest in my life.

On countless occasions my aunt and I would walk together the three quarters of a mile distance to the only pet shop in the area, where she would let me pick out some fish for my small aquarium that sat on top of our black and white TV set.

I remember that fish tank very well because after all these years, I still have it. The aquarium was plastic with a matching pink hood and light. The store had been out of blue. It held a scant three gallons of water and had an air pump that buzzed annoyingly, but I thought it was wonderful! My Mom had given it to me for Christmas and I guess I still have it because it was the best present I have ever received.

My aunt Margaret was a deeply religious person. I remember falling asleep night after night as she sat on the edge of the bed reading from her prayer book, faithfully reciting her prayers, lips moving silently while she turned the well worn gold edged pages. If any person deserved to have prayers answered, it was her.

When my mother remarried I was in the fifth grade. We moved to another house and from that point on, I would see my aunt less and less until she fell and broke her hip, and had to be placed in a nursing home, never walking again. This was ironic because she was an avid walker all her life. It was not unusual for her to walk three, four, five, or six miles on any given day. I know because I was often along side. This caught on, because I would walk for pleasure or as a relief from stress the rest of my life.

When I said we moved to another house, I meant my mother and I. My brother elected to stay with our grandmother who had become his mother figure due to our mom having to work.

My new stepfather took up right where my grandmother had left off, criticizing my every move and what was worse, I had to get rid of my aquarium. In addition he had a volatile temper which would frighten me to wits end until I became accustomed to his frequent outbursts and accepted them as part of my daily life, quite a contrast to my serene aunt. It was an unhappy existence, separated from her, my brother, and even my grandmother, who seemed warm and caring compared to my substitute father. One thing always kept me going, my extreme interest in animals and of course fish.

Several years before the move, I had seen a TV show that I would never miss, it was called Sea Hunt, starring Lloyd Bridges, who played a scuba diver. Each week for a half hour in black and white, there would be a new underwater adventure. It was like he himself had become a fish!

I wanted to be a scuba diver, just like the guy on the TV. Since this was not in the sphere of possibility for someone in the first grade, I did the next best thing. I pretended. Taking an old shoe box my aunt had provided, I strapped it to my back scuba tank style and would creep around and through our dining room table and chairs that served as a make believe coral reef.

I think this is something missing in today's children, the ability to improvise, pretend, or make believe, in other words create entertainment where none appears to exist. Today they would get on the computer and do a virtual scuba dive, maybe never having the desire afterward to try the real thing.

First Visit

I have never forgotten my first visit to the Shedd Aquarium in 1957. It seemed like this massive building to me, which was enhanced by its stately appearance and position, standing alone and iconic on the edge of the freshwater ocean that was and is Lake Michigan. I recall climbing the thirty seven steps that slowly elevated you to the intimidating portal, then passing through into the rotunda interior where the feeling was that of having entered some ornate cathedral where the religion was fish.

Up and down the rows I went, slowly sliding my hands along the wooden railing running along the front of the exhibits, and peering into each individual aquarium at the collection of creatures inhabiting each one. The sheer volume of aquatic life was overwhelming and I cannot remember with great detail any of the fish tanks as standing out, with the exception of two exhibits that for whatever reason always stayed with me. One had a brown fish in it that didn't look like a fish at all. It was eel like with fluid paddle shaped fins. It seemed lethargic in its movement but the odd shape and appearance caught my eye. It was called an Australian lungfish. I learned from the sign in front of the tank that it had been there twenty four years.

I also cannot forget arriving at a circular railing that surrounded a round craterlike pit in the center of the rotunda floor. I looked downward into the bowl shaped depression that was home to freshwater turtles and other creatures of the "Swamp", as the exhibit was called. It all appeared very green, jungle like, and tropical.

The years went by, one by one, grammar school, high school, and then college. I attended the University of Illinois at Chicago, which at the time was called Chicago Circle. It was a rather unattractive place to look at, a monotone gray monument to concrete construction that seemed to have sprouted from the nearby Eisenhower Expressway. Despite this somewhat dull appearance, it was populated by some excellent and academically challenging professors.

I majored in biology and even was able to go on the occasional field trip to the nearby Shedd Aquarium during my Ichthyology class, entering behind the scenes and above the newly constructed Caribbean Reef, whose floor was made from the old Swamp exhibit that I had looked down into sixteen years before. It had been converted into a 90,000 gallon coral reef. The few of us in our class who decided to attend this special tour were escorted through a brass entrance door and then climbed some stairs to overlook the top of the reef. From above it was the ultimate aquarium, a tropical reef as I always imagined it would look!

During that same year I was introduced to and became interested in another field of biology, Herpetology, the study of reptiles and amphibians. That particular class may have been my first exposure to that group of animals at an academic level but it was certainly not my initial experience with them.

Many years before during one of my weekly visits to the pet shop with my aunt, I had spied a low sided enclosure with a pile of rocks in the middle surrounded by water. On top of the rocks and swimming in the circular pond were hundreds of half dollar sized tiny green turtles called Red Eared Sliders. Their little bean shaped heads streaked with red at the sides, variegated emerald green shells and tiny feet and toenails produced an altogether appealing effect, and I instantly wanted one.

My goodhearted aunt was always happy to oblige and at fifty cents apiece, before long we were walking out of the store with two of the miniature turtles in a cardboard Chinese food container, along with a new home for my pets. It was a circular plastic bowl with a preformed basking area in the center from which had apparently sprouted some plastic palm trees.

This was the standard way these baby turtles were kept back then and along with the packaged turtle food which consisted of dried flys and ant eggs, led to these poor little animal's early exit from the planet. I wouldn't accept this scenario, so I supplemented their diet with pieces of hamburger, lettuce, and worms. In that way, I improved their quality of life as best I could on my no income budget.

When we had brought the turtles home my grandmother of course acted like I had just purchased a pair of hippos!! She took an immediate dislike to them, sure that they would somehow escape and menace her in bed at night. Ah yes, ... more points for me with Gram

During the course of my college studies I made friends with a graduate student named Carl. A true eccentric like myself, Carl was a pipe smoking, professorial looking type who had been wounded in Vietnam. He was a turtle fanatic, just as I was with fish. He had a pond located in his backyard just for his pet turtles.

His house in Lake Zurich, Illinois was also home to various species of tortoises. I think more of his interest in turtles rubbed off on me than was the opposite case, because I never saw Carl with a tank of fish but I started my own turtle collection.

One of the perks of being in the Ichthyology/Herpetology class was a weekend trip to Southern Illinois University's outdoor lab and the Shawnee National Forest for a fish and reptile collecting trip. Since I had already been exposed extensively to fish collecting with it's pulling of nets and seines on many occasions, I took the opportunity to try something different and go "herping" with Carl in search of the box turtles, salamanders, and snakes that populated the forest.

Little by little I became more interested in turtles and under the tutelage of Carl my collection of them started to grow along side my fish tanks which I had reacquired in greater and greater number. Since keeping them at my own house was out of the question, my grandmother who was now living alone, allowed me to keep the fish in her basement, and oh by the way, she still hated turtles. So why did she let me keep them in her house? She never new they were there! I would covertly smuggle them inside via a gym bag stuffed with school books, and because she was too old and unsteady on her feet to climb down the old wooden stairs that led to the lower level zoo, she was never aware of the legion of shelled houseguests that shared her living space just one floor below her bed. What nightmares she missed out on, perhaps running down the street with a herd of turtles in hot pursuit!

My turtle companions quickly became focused on two varieties, the Diamondback Terrapin, and the American Box Turtle. I first became aware of the terrapins when I came across a photo of one. It showed a striking animal with a gray shell, whose each individual scale was adorned with concentric patterns that loosely resembled diamond shapes. It had bluish gray skin dappled with black spots and lines. To top it all off it sported a white mustache on it's face. It was described as having an outgoing personality, which I discovered was the case. I began to add one after the other of them to my turtle colony until I had five subspecies of Diamondback Terrapin, a few of which made their homes in the mangrove forests of South Florida, and somewhere called the Keys.

Box turtles became an interest after I had graduated from the U of I and enrolled at Southern Illinois University for post graduate studies in fisheries biology. Since I was still friends with Carl and would go visit him frequently back up north, he asked me if I had seen any box turtles while hiking through the woods. I told him I had, so he asked me if I could bring some specimens back for his collection. Thus inspired I became quite the box turtle hunter, able to spot them at great distances along the edge of roads and highways, thanks in part to the car I owned.

The auto that I was the proud owner of was a turtle green Rambler American. It was ten years old with 100,000 miles on it. I had purchased it from a Lutheran minister who I am sure bestowed the last rights on it after I paid the two hundred dollar asking price. Against all odds it served me well for the next year, transporting me safely each weekend from Carbondale to Chicago, covering the six hundred mile round trip like a faithful horse.

The reason the car helped me with my turtle hunting was that it had one headlight, the right one, that no longer shined straight ahead but toward the side of the road. Ever the optimist, I did not see this as a handicap but an asset, because the light would illuminate the roadside during my after dark forays into the forest. The cockeyed headlight would reveal turtles and even the odd venomous Copperhead snake, which once discovered would slither off into the tall dried grass with me following on foot, plunging into the darkness with my homemade snake stick in hand. Catching sight of and pursuing a viper in its natural habitat in the dark of night, even one as even tempered as a Copperhead, made me consider the possibility that possibly my sails were not cut from the same canvas as everybody else. For the first time in my life I was beginning to appreciate that fact.

My nightly adventure over, I would return to my dorm room, sit at my desk and study my fisheries books, just me and my pet chameleon Roy, who lived in a small cage on my table. Roy was named after one of my professors who had the habit of showing up for class still wearing his chest waders. I would feed my lizard a mouthwatering assortment of bugs I had caught for him during my forest hikes, along with the occasional cockroach that crawled out of the sink. Roy eagerly pounced on all my offerings and I enjoyed watching the relish with which he crunched them up.

The underwater world still held first place in my heart despite my journey into the reptilian realm, so during my second year at the U of I, I had become a certified scuba diver. Once at SIU, I would attend pool dives with the schools dive club along with a fellow student who was a member, or dive in the nearby Devil's Kitchen Lake. My goal however was still the same as it had always been, to dive a coral reef, just as I had seen on that TV show so many years before, and later spurred on also by Jacques Cousteau and his undersea world specials. I also pursued another passion whenever the opportunity arose, a sport I had been introduced to back in Burlington, Wisconsin as a little boy, fishing.

So, these were the forces that drove me and often sustained me throughout my young life, fish, fishing, diving, and turtles. They provided the course I followed not knowing where it would lead. A letter my brother sent me while he was in the Army may have provided a clue. He suggested that when he got home we should take a trip down to Florida to a place where we could fish and I could dive. It was a string of islands that jutted out into the ocean that was seemingly disconnected from that state and the rest of the world, the Florida Keys.

19

CHANGE OF PLANS

Fishing was a hobby that took me everywhere. It provided inspiration each morning as I thought about where the next angling adventure might lead. The destination could be Wisconsin one week, and the next Florida or Canada. I traveled constantly, in fact, during one particularly busy year, I was licensed to fish in nine different states and one Canadian province. Fishing provided welcome relief from the world when things were not going well.

The urge to fish seemed to have always been there. It was innate, instinctive, and ever present, just waiting for the chance to be unleashed and reveal itself. I guess my first serious exposure to fishing as a sport came during weekend trips to reclaimed strip mine lakes near Braidwood, Illinois. I was about six years old at the time and we would travel the fifty miles or so to the lake area about every other week, riding in my mom's 1955 Chevy Belaire.

These trips were always greatly anticipated by me because I could paddle around the beach and practice to be a scuba diver, sometimes I would even see some fish. My aunt had bought me a dive mask and my mother a pair of swim fins that looked like Donald Duck feet. These helped propel me through the water as I honed my self taught swimming maneuvers. No one ever taught me to swim, I just picked it up on my own, like a sea turtle hatchling getting it's first feel of the ocean. A friend's father had told me the basic moves to make, "Kick with your feet and drive with your arms", but when I entered the water, it was always alone. I was often afraid at first, but the urge to travel underwater and see or be with fish was stronger than fear and little by little I got the hang of it.

During these outings I would also do some freshwater beachcombing, walking along the shoreline spotting schools of bluegill sunfish or the occasional largemouth bass swimming in the transparent water through crisp green weeds or hovering motionless over sunken brown logs. I could see the fine detail of their translucent fins, watch their eyes rotate and move in the sockets, and study the subtleties of their disruptive coloration. What really fascinated me was watching my brother's friend angling for, and then catching these same fish. He also had a tackle box full of colorful fishing lures that had names like Hula Popper, River Runt, and Lazy Ike. This of course all had a deep effect on me because here was a way to see fish up close, hold them in your hand and possess them. This was something I had to do! Again my Aunt came to my aid, buying me a small, two foot, plastic rod and reel. Since it didn't come with line or hooks, I took some bakery string and a bent safety pin as a substitute. I was in business, and so with my trusty fishing pole, I started my angling career.

Fishing stayed along side me as a faithful companion in those early days, then throughout grammar school, high school, into college, as a young man, and continues even now. The big turning point in the sport for me came when I was twenty five years old and was introduced to my grandmother's life insurance salesman, a man named Stan, who at the time was fifty years old.

Stan was an avid fisherman, his wife and daughter were not. So when he found out from my grandmother that she had a fisheries biologist for a grandson, he jumped at the opportunity to invite me on a fishing trip to Northwest Ontario and a place called Green Island Lodge. Since my angling excursions at that point consisted of trips to Braidwood, southern Illinois, and the scenic little towns of Tomahawk and Minocqua Wisconsin, I eagerly agreed to this trip across the border.

I loved the Canadian land instantly. I fell under the spell of the beautiful vast wilderness. The pristine views, endless panorama of lakes, trees, white clouded blue skies that were punctuated with just the right amount of red highlights in the evenings, and the lake that vanished off into horizon, was like a religious experience. The place seemed to have no boundaries or end to the forest. I was thrilled to ride aboard the vintage float aircraft with their big radial engines that bellowed bass notes when running. The sound would bounce off the granite outcroppings and rock walls that surrounded these lakes of the Canadian shield, then breaking the surface suction the plane would blast off from the water with audacity and authority. That is how I spent my vacation time, three times a year for the next twenty two years, heading always north on a compass heading, straight to the land of the maple leafed flag.

During those next two decades, my fishing career took on a new face, that of professionalism. I was pursuing the sport with such passion that I was becoming more and more successful at it and began to notice I was catching fish when no one else was. About that time a friend suggested that I should consider writing articles telling the less fortunate how to catch fish for a magazine he worked for called Midwest Outdoors. He introduced me to the managing editor and owner of the publication Gene Laulunen, and shortly afterward I became a field editor, starting in 1983.

For the next fifteen years I advanced through the fishing ranks, catching large trophy fish with regularity, all on the light tackle that had become my trademark angle for my magazine articles. My association with Midwest Outdoors grew with their entry into television and radio, where I was often one of many regular guests, and I was also appearing on a local cable TV show called, Jim Kapsa's Pro Sport Report. During those years I was still able to spend time on the water and was lucky enough to land four line class world record fish in the process. Fishing certainly seemed to be working out for me. It appeared I was on my way, but something that had been set in motion while I was still in grammar school, would bring my hopes for a career in pro angling tumbling down, this however would result in something unforeseen, a special purpose in life yet undiscovered.

Stumbling

I was in third grade at the time and it was during one of the class's gym periods that I first seriously hurt my back. We were running a kind of variance of a three legged race. In this one you would hop on one leg while holding the other one behind you with one of your hands. I was hopping along with the other kids, having a good time, when suddenly a severe pain like hot lightning shot up my back nearly forcing the air from my lungs. When I finished I quietly headed to the back of the relay line, barely able to straighten up and only able to walk with excruciating pain. I knew I had hurt myself badly but I didn't say anything to anyone or my teacher. I was afraid I would be sent home from school and get in trouble with my grandmother, so I just toughed it out, like a wounded animal covering its injury.

Every time I stood up after sitting or walked, it felt as if my body was out of alignment and breathing was difficult. A few of the other kids were starting to notice something was wrong with me but fortunately my young body healed itself. Thirty years later, I would feel that exact all too familiar pain again. This time I went to the doctor. The diagnosis was a herniated disc in my lower back.

During the many years between the playground accident and the herniated disc diagnosis I had made a career out of abusing my back. As a child I used to get a kick out of jumping off the side of our front porch, for whatever reason I don't know! Maybe I was pretending to be a paratrooper? After executing this eight foot drop, I would land stiff legged on the neighbors concrete driveway. In high school I played some football and while practicing would often smash into blocking sleds, getting a crushing jolt to my lower back in the process. While in Canada, I would backpack gear that weighed fifty pounds or more on uneven rocky ground. It just continued this way for years. The piper was soon to be paid.

In my mid thirties I started to notice I was having difficulty sitting in a boat for any extended period of time, or after a long drive I had trouble straightening up. Fishing was becoming something I looked on more and more as work because of fatiguing back pain. My career in the sport was starting to suffer. I began to prefer the company of my dog, a one hundred forty pound Newfoundland named Salty; the same breed of dog I had seen depicted in the book read to me by my aunt; the dog on the beach; the one in front of the lighthouse looking out to sea. I would take him on fishing trips rather than people. I could stop fishing whenever I wanted. Salty never asked questions or whined about going in early. Instead I would take him swimming at a small pond near Land'O'Lakes Wisconsin named Merrill Lake. I watched him endlessly retrieve his favorite water toy, a foam rubber retrieving dummy given to him by the friendly motel owner, Bruce Renc, a fan of Newfoundlands.

Watching a "Newfie" as they are affectionately called, swim, is a pleasure known only to owners of this breed of dog.

Newfoundlands are a large working dog weighing in at about one hundred twenty, to one hundred sixty pounds or more. They resemble a sort of black Saint Bernard, which people unfamiliar with these canine giants often mistake them for. Newfs come in a few colors, chiefly, black, brown, gray, and black and white, which is called Landseer, after an artist who showed a preference for painting that color variety. Traditional black is the signature shade for this national dog of Canada, and is the most commonly seen. Newfoundlands have become famous for their heroic water rescue efforts, pulling stressed swimmers from life threatening situations. These gentle giants have mild, loving, temperaments, but they feel swimming is a sport reserved for them, often pulling swimmers who are not in peril out of the water anyway. They apparently feel these ungainly humans should not be risking their lives in an element that is so clearly to the dog not proper for people.

The Newfoundland's swimming stroke can best be described in one word, power ... unfailing consistent power! They do not have the flash of the more sporty Labrador or Chesapeake Bay retrievers, who speed through the water like unleashed PT boats. The Newfie's freestyle in contrast is slow and steady with a purpose of mind, like a furry battleship with massive bear like webbed paws, driving forward, not to be resisted or stopped on his mission until everyone is safe. A Newfoundland aboard the Titanic, swam through the frigid waters of the North

Atlantic, searching for his master, who was one of the ships crew, the dog saved other passengers in the process. The Newf swam for over three hours, looking in vain. He survived unscathed, … except for the broken heart from the loss of his friend. Salty was my beloved friend and companion and he too watched silently from the front of my boat, looking back at his master, who was fishing less and less.

The straw that broke the camel's back came finally in August of 1990. I had just arrived home and opened the door when the phone started to ring. I had an odd, strange feeling that I should not answer it, but I did anyway. It was my neighbor calling from a few houses away. She told me that she thought there might be some raccoons up in her attic that had gotten in somehow and asked if I could come over and let them out. Usually when there was some sort of distasteful animal job in the neighborhood I would get the call, and while I was apprehensive about it, I said I would come over since she was an elderly widow.

When I arrived at her house I went into the dining room and climbed the ladder up into the attic. I stuck my head through the trapdoor and slowly looked around the dimly lit space like a prairie dog sticking his head out of a burrow. I looked to the right, forward, and then to the left. When I stared in the last direction, my gaze was returned many times over by not one, but several pairs of eyes peering out from behind their Lone Ranger masks!

My raccoon audience looked at me quizzically with no particular fear or aggression, just simple amusement, as if I were some sort of entertainment brought to perform in a floor show they were attending, waiting for it to start, and now the curtain had just gone up. They made little cooing sounds as if they were enjoying my amusing antics and even though I knew they could be dangerous, I couldn't help but smile.

The lady waiting pensively downstairs asked if indeed there was a raccoon up there?, to which I responded that there was not "a" raccoon, but five of them. This was followed by a distinct shrieking noise emanating from below. Her next request was for me to make my way to the rear of the attic and open the window so that the furry intruders might make good on an escape. At this point I began to question my sanity and that of the lady!

In any event I pulled myself up through the trapdoor and slowly started to advance toward the window, which under the circumstances seemed rather far off. I was sure at any minute I would be descended upon by a troop of angry raccoons sinking their rabies covered teeth into my neck, legs, and back in unison and squirting out little raccoon "turds" all over me once they discovered their evening entertainment was making a getaway! I soon found out the danger would not come from the ambivalent raccoon family, but from another source.

Continuing my advance toward the window I carefully stepped from one crisscross ceiling support beam to another. I was just about there, the goal of the window latch seemed within my reach when the nearly imperceptible but distinct crunching sound of slowly cracking wood caught my ears. Before I knew what happened, the beam beneath me totally fractured in half like a parched sun dried piece of driftwood and I found myself falling through the ceiling not unlike a condemned man's fall from the gallows floor after the trapdoor has been sprung.

The plunge was sudden and hard, but I did not fall through completely, instead my lower back slammed against another crisscross beam which abruptly arrested my rapid decent. I hung there dangling for no more than a minute while I waited for the air that had been knocked out of my lungs to return. Then I contemplated my next move. The tendency at that point was to lay there and wait for help but I knew none would come. I heard a voice in my head telling me to "Get Up!, Get Up! No ones going to help you anyway!" So that is what I did. Pulling myself back up through the hole, I could hear the lady below asking if I was all right. Even though I knew that I had hurt my back, I said I was OK, being more concerned about her newly ventilated ceiling than myself at that point.

All this time the raccoons had not moved from their front row seats, seemingly enjoying the show. Within a week they were gone. Seven months later my back was still bothering me.

I eventually went to the doctor, more out of curiosity to find out what might be wrong with me than from necessity. He did a cursory exam and then referred me to an orthopedic specialist, who later performed further tests. The finding was that I had a very deteriorated back, equivalent to that of a seventy year old man, which at the time was almost twice my age. There was a bulging disc and another one that was badly herniated. The recommendation was surgery or physical therapy to possibly avoid the former route. I, as I'm sure most people would, chose physical therapy first. If you have ever experienced sciatic nerve pain resulting from back problems, I am sure you are familiar with the discomfort that goes along with it. The pain can best be described as a throbbing tooth ache running down the leg. Standing, sitting, driving, and eating at home or at a restaurant, all become a collection of torturous acts that bring sweat to the brow and depression to the soul. Relief only comes when you give in and swallow still another pain killer that too soon looses its effect, or lay down with a pillow under your knees and wait for the drugs to take hold. The occasional stint on a traction bed also brought an escape and once strapped into the paratroopers harness, produced a feeling not unlike having your pants slowly pulled down.

I worked with an excellent group of "PTs", but after eight months my condition had only deteriorated. I now had to manually lift my leg out of my truck. In addition, when I went back to the doctor, he checked my leg for reflex action with the standard rubber hammer to the knee routine. Nothing happened! No kick, no jerk, zero! I thought to myself, "This can't be good!!" The doctors facial expression mirrored my own. "This isn't going well", he said stating the obvious.

My next move was to find a doctor who I trusted to do the surgery. A few months passed before I found one, a younger surgeon who seemed to be on top of his game. I also acquired a new personal physician who interestingly enough owned a Newfoundland and liked to fish.

The surgeon also told me that I would not be able to continue in my current job because the physical requirements would be too much for my deteriorated back, even after the surgery.

A few weeks later as I lay in the hospital awaiting my trip down to the operating room, I contemplated my life and wondered what I would do now for a living. I knew things would be changing drastically. What would the future now bring? My back operation came off without a hitch. Next came the post operative physical therapy to restrengthen my muscles. The pain was now gone most of the time, but my back remained fragile and almost any movement might trigger unexpected spasms. I would have to be careful about testing it for the rest of my days. During the time I spent recovering I started to consider new means of employment. One thing that came to mind was possibly finding a job at the nearby Brookfield Zoo. That would depend however, on whether they could find work for someone with back trouble and were not afraid of the liability.

I waited until I had recovered enough to not look like Quasimoto and then took a trip over to the zoo. Once I got there I decided to walk around the park like confines. I had been here many times before, even more than the Shedd Aquarium. I watched the polar bears diving in their rock enclosed pools, the elephants shuffling on silent feet around their large sandy yard, and the dolphins, seals, and walrus swimming in the Seven Seas exhibit. This was the former home of the late Olga the walrus, a crowd favorite, now memorialized with a bronze statue nearby. I gradually worked my way over to the administration building, went inside and asked for an employment application. I took it home and a few days later I mailed it in.

Several weeks went by and there was no response. I knew this was not a good sign, so I continued to amuse myself by working around the house, doing my back exercises, and maintaining my water lily garden, home to my collection of oriental goldfish. After all these years I still liked my fish.

This was how the days passed. The flowers grew and bloomed through the summer, the lawn turned green and then browned in the August sun, then turned green again as the daylight driven heat ebbed and the first hint of color started to edge the leaves. I began to get restless and a little concerned. I started to think I should look for some sales job in the fishing industry, but sales just was not anything I had ever excelled at.

I hadn't had any fish tanks for over fifteen years while I had been concentrating on my pro fishing career, but now I thought it might be fun to get back into the hobby. It at least would help pass the time. My favorite fish had always been the yellowhead jawfish. These are a species of saltwater fish. They are about four or five inches long as adults and have a narrow elongated body that is a light sky blue in color. Their head is either yellow or pearl hued. The reason they appealed to me was that these fish possessed real personality and they had a most unusual choice of housing. The yellowhead jawfish digs vertical burrows in the sand, excavating them like determined little miners, and once done poke their tiny heads in and out of the entrances, resembling a colony of underwater prairie dogs. They always reminded me of Oscar the Grouch from Sesame Street as he glowers out of his garbage can home.

I began to warm up more and more to the thought of setting up an aquarium filled with jawfish, and so for further inspiration I felt a trip to the Shedd Aquarium might be in order. I headed to Chicago.

I drove down the Stevenson Expressway and veered onto Lake Shore Drive. After a few miles I turned onto Solidarity Drive, found a spot not far from the Adler Planetarium and parked. I put enough quarters in the meter to last about three hours and began my walk toward the big rotunda. Lake Michigan lay to my right blowing a cool breeze that swept over the pavement, a messenger from the season to come, reminding one that Fall was close at hand.

Time had really slipped by. I hadn't visited here in many years, perhaps a decade or more, but there was still a familiarity about it. The imposing building looking out over the city and the lake, the thirty seven steps leading to the entranceway, the architecture frozen in time, and the rows of aquariums inside whose glow illuminated the halls and galleries. There was Granddad, the venerable old lungfish, and of course the Caribbean Reef with its resident performer Hawkeye.

There was also a new addition to the building I had not yet seen, the Oceanarium, home to pacific dolphins, sea otters, penguins, seals, beluga whales, and a tide pool. A show was performed several times daily so I put aside some time to sit in the Pacific Northwest theme amphitheatre and catch it.

I sat there by myself waiting for the performance to start and began to thumb through the nicely colored brochure about the aquarium that I had been given when I entered. As I was reading through it, some very small print at the bottom of the page caught my eye. It told of the aquarium's volunteer program. Back when I had been in college I remembered one of my fellow students mentioning that the inside track to a job at the Shedd was to take a volunteer position.

Maybe I though, this is something I could do while waiting to hear from the zoo. Who knows where it might lead. After I returned home I made supper for Salty and myself. Later that night I phoned the volunteer department and left my name and number. I never did hear from the zoo. A week later the Shedd Aquarium called. The year was 1992.

20

ENCOUNTERS

That fall morning as I drove down the highway heading to the Shedd Aquarium for my interview, I was experiencing a bittersweet feeling. While I was excited about the possibility of working at a place I had known all my life and the new experiences that would come along with it, the elation was tempered with sadness. A few weeks earlier my best friend and fishing buddy, Tom Rogalinski, had passed away suddenly of a heart attack at the age of 48.

Tom was a joy to be with while fishing or otherwise. He was always happy for anything good that happened in my life, never jealous or critical, just very easy going and supportive. He and his wife Sandy always made sure I was not alone on any given holiday or birthday. Tom was a heavy smoker and I continually feared something like this would happen. One September morning it did. I knew he would have been anxious to hear about my new career, waiting for my phone call telling him what the place was like, the animals, the fish, especially the fish! He would have lived vicariously through me, but he was gone and I missed him.

I have often heard it said that as one door closes, another will open. One of the first people I met during my interview was someone named Bryan. At that time he was employed in the volunteer department of the aquarium, later in guest services, and ultimately in the Shedd's Amazon Rising Exhibit. Bryan was a fellow fisherman like myself but to describe him as such would be like portraying a heroin addict as someone who likes a good strong cup of coffee every now and then. He fished more days a year than I did and I was making money from the sport! He has had business cards printed up that have the following words on them, "Born to Fish, Forced to Work". He is however a hardworking fastidious individual who would be a prized employee just about anywhere. We became friends as we were certain too and then started fishing together.

During the interview with the aquarium I selected three areas to work in; the lab, where I would be carrying out water quality tests for the animals in the Oceanarium and the Marine Jewels exhibit, which housed clownfish, anemones, and oh yes, yellowhead jawfish. Lastly I was also going to be working in the Tributaries section, a now sadly extinct gallery that was made up of a large number of small home sized aquariums filled with tiny tropical fish from around the world. This exhibit was later converted into a gift store.

I quickly discovered that my back would not hold up under the strain of reaching over so many small fish tanks and after only a few weeks I left Tributaries, which surprisingly enough considering the size of the aquariums was probably the most labor intensive of any other exhibit. I did continue to visit with Bill, the chief aquarist of that gallery who had an interest in WWII aircraft as I did, this was often the topic of our conversations.

The laboratory was the most rewarding job of the three and carried with it the greatest marketability of skills learned for future employment elsewhere. It was quite the rush to go and collect water samples from the beluga whale and Pacific dolphin pools, where it was just myself and the animals in a one on one encounter. The belugas would follow me around the waters edge like friendly dogs watching my every move as I filled the water sample bottles. These bottles were attached to a long stick and then dipped into the water, rinsed three times and then filled. The whales would always swim under the bottles when I was rinsing them enjoying the sensation of water being poured on their heads as they smiled up at me with their built in grins.

If the belugas reminded me of dogs, the Pacific dolphins were reminiscent of cats. They slowly and cautiously swam over to see who was standing over their pool, then having seen me scooted off, not returning. The belugas clearly wanted personal contact, the dolphins passed in the night.

When making the rounds to get water samples I would walk counter clockwise along the back of the large Oceanarium, with the exhibit to my left and a giant picture window overlooking Lake Michigan which was up close and personal to my right. At those times I often couldn't believe where I was, actually working at the Shedd Aquarium and making contact with all kinds of exotic animals and fish. If you would have told me just a few months earlier that I would find myself in this situation, I would have thought you were out of your mind.

Returning to the lab with my samples I would set up a battery of test tubes and begin the procedures necessary to monitor the water quality of each assigned exhibit, then enter the results into a ring binder, all the while improving my rusty laboratory skills. During the hours I was there I would often engage one of the veterinarians, Marty Greenwall in conversation. Marty had a passion for the keeping and breeding of pet killifish and poison dart frogs. He would frequently show me the featured fish parasite of the day under the microscope. Occasionally someone named George Parsons would come into the lab. He was a tall quiet man in his thirties who somewhat resembled George Washington. He was a keeper who I had seen pictured in the Chicago Tribune newspaper, posing with a large octopus that was living in his gallery.

One of the perks of volunteering at the aquarium was that you were allowed to take educational classes offered there free of charge. I took one course taught by George on keeping saltwater aquariums and another on water gardening, where I met a friend of Bryan's named Jim Torelli, who later would often join us on our fishing excursions. Another occasional visitor to the lab was Keith Pamper. I had seen him on television during several Shedd segments on the news. Keith was a skilled scuba diver overseeing the Caribbean Reef exhibit and of course Hawkeye.

On the days I worked in the Marine Jewels exhibit I always arrived early. This gave me some extra time to sit in front of the quarantine tanks and take a look at the various fish waiting to go out on exhibit, usually focusing on the jawfish and their intricate shell and rubble lined burrows. If time allowed I would go and visit Granddad the lungfish laying in his tank, looking like a large brown fire hose, or walk by the Caribbean Reef where Hawkeye would swim up to the glass, watching for any sign of impending food delivery.

Once I started my workday, the first job was to cut and chop food for the various animals and fish in the Marine Jewels exhibit. Brine shrimp, clams, and squid all were diced up and readied for feeding. One day due to heavy traffic on the highway, I had gotten a later start at this task than usual so I had to share space at the food preparation table with two women. One was standing next to me and the other at the far end of the table about six feet away. She somewhat resembled Sarah Jessica Parker. She seemed to be looking at me intently, as if wondering who I was or where I had come from. It was a look that hovered somewhere between friendly curiosity and subtle hostility. She made me slightly uncomfortable although I felt no malice coming from her. Feeling somewhat intimidated, I broke eye contact with her and continued my food preparation, and she resumed her conversation with the other girl. For whatever reason I remembered her face even though I rarely saw her again. When the two women left the room I thought I heard her mention something about a dog she owned. It was named Nickel.

21

ENDS AND BEGINNINGS

While I was enjoying my time at the aquarium, I was continually aware of my current state of employment. It had now been nearly six months since my application was submitted at the zoo and there had been no response. By necessity, I was forced to weigh other alternatives. My collection of home aquariums had continued to grow, now rising to three, all of which housed saltwater fish from the Florida Keys, including my favorite, yellow head jawfish.

As a result of this, a vocation I was starting to consider with increased interest was that of starting an aquarium maintenance service. I had been setting up and maintaining tanks for an assortment of friends and acquaintances for years, why not make a business out of it?

With more time on my hands, I had recently subscribed to a local newspaper, and as part of the deal I was given a free classified ad I could run at any time of my choosing. I decided to place one touting myself as a fisheries biologist-aquarium maintenance service. I called the paper and set it up. The ad would run three days.

On the first day, I received a call from a private party to come over to the house and repair an air pump. It was a small job; I charged nineteen dollars, parts and labor. Not a lot of money, but I had gotten my feet wet, and it paid for a small bag of groceries. The second call came as quite a surprise. It was from the newspaper itself. They had a fish tank in their office, a 55-gallon freshwater aquarium that was home to their pet, a fish called Goldie. They wanted to know if I would be willing to maintain the aquarium in exchange for advertising. Without any hesitation, I said yes. More calls started to come in. I received an added boost when the same newspaper ran a feature article on my business that sported a front-page picture of Goldie and myself. This again resulted in still more calls. One in particular was from a man in Oak Park, Illinois, a theatre director named Nikolai. He had a large apartment building located in the town's historic district not far from Ernest Hemingway's birthplace, and also the studio of the world famous architect, Frank Lloyd Wright. In the courtyard was a fountain pond that Nikolai wanted stocked with goldfish and koi. That job led to still another feature article in Oak Park's hometown paper, The Oak Leaves.

So it went, my business grew and grew, as did my personal collection of fish tanks, now numbering sixteen, sprouting from my bedroom, dining room, and basement. During this time, I had become more and more reacquainted with an interest in Caribbean saltwater fish, which had been kindled in the early nineteen sixties. I had read an article in National Geographic titled, Little Horses of the Sea, by Paul A. Zahl. It was all about seahorses and it described the author's search for these fish. It told of the sea horse pushers of Tampa Bay, Sanibel Island, Tarpon Springs, and the Florida Keys. There, one could snorkel in the grassy shallow waters and observe pygmy seahorses by the tens of thousands. I instantly decided I wanted a saltwater tank with dwarf seahorses and soon started converting my original tank, the pink one my Mom had given me, to a saltwater aquarium. It also created an interest in traveling to the Keys to dive a real coral reef! Now, thirty years after reading the article, I was beginning to consider making my first trip down to that destination.

As my business continued to grow, it was becoming more and more apparent that my stay at the Shedd Aquarium was coming to an end. I just couldn't justify the time spent there as more demands grew on my schedule, so a few weeks before my now confirmed trip to the Keys I ended my time there. It had been a great experience, a life changing one, and as I walked to my truck on that final day, I looked back at the big rotunda with a feeling of sadness. The place had seemingly come in and out of my life as though it was some mysterious focal point. I did not know if I would ever return.

As preparation for my trip, I felt it would be a good idea to go to the local Y.M.C.A. and take a refresher scuba dive before traveling to Florida. My back was still not that limber and in fact never would be, so I was unsure how my diving skills would hold up out in an ocean I had never swam in. The pool dive went off without a hitch, in fact, the instructor encouraged me to take some advanced courses, but I also realized that the pool was not the open ocean. I had felt somewhat stiff in my swimming movement and decided once I got to the Keys to restrict myself mostly to snorkel diving, and when I was comfortable move on to scuba.

In June of 1993, I first set foot in the Florida Keys. Just as with Canada seventeen years earlier, I loved the place right away, although it wasn't at all what I had expected. The string of tiny islands and connected sand spits were much smaller than I had envisioned, with many points where ocean and gulf were only separated by a few tenuous feet. They seemed fragile and delicate, appearing to exist on the edge of ecological disaster and had a feeling of being in a third world Caribbean country rather than being part of Florida. It was a land unto itself, truly the "Conch Republic". I wondered who was the first brave soul to decide to live in this place.

I had driven down the narrow highway, from Homestead, recently devastated by Hurricane Andrew, to Key Largo, Tavernier and soon Islamorada. I thought to myself "Well it took me twenty years but I finally got here!"

I had decided to stay at a place called the Islander Motel. It had been recommended to me by a former Shedd employee who said I would find some good snorkeling around the dock and extensive natural beach that fronted on some good hard bottom community. As soon as I arrived, I unpacked my suitcase and laid my snorkel gear out on the humid, damp, tile covered motel room floor. I clicked on the air conditioner to cool down the room and then took a walk down to the dock to reconnoiter, leaving my dive gear behind.

Walking out onto the old concrete dock, the first thing I was struck by was the clarity of the water. I paused for a minute held onto the railing, and looked below me into the transparent sea. There were small piles of rock everywhere, the "live rock" of which home reef aquariums get their base. Each stone aggregation was punctuated with little stands of marine plants, merman's shaving brush, halimeda, caulerpa, and mermaid's cup sprouted from the granular white sand bottom at every unshaded spot. Blood red Bahama Sea Star glided in open sand paths, their tube feet looking like hundreds of tiny toilet plungers pulling the star along with a suction cup cadence. Horseshoe crabs scuttled mechanically through rubble, plants, and rock obstacles. Needlefish patrolled the surface over the heads of yellow fin mojarra, holding over the bottom, sitting motionless their position revealed only by the shadows their bodies cast on the sand.

Moving further out on the dock I saw a small brown nurse shark sinuously weaving in and out from under the pier followed by an assortment of cowfish, trunkfish, sergeant majors, damselfish, and finally the side to side undulating butterfly dance of a black and yellow striped juvenile gray angelfish. This was all too much for me and I made a quick retreat, scampering back to the room to get my dive gear.

Equipment in hand I returned to the beach at the base of the dock, sat down in the warm ocean washed sand, slid the ankle strap of my fins over my neoprene boots, pulled on my mask, and placed the mouthpiece of the snorkel between my lips. I tilted forward in the shallow bathwater warm sea and pushed off. The temperature gauge on my dive watch read 88 degrees. I began to carefully examine every rock pile and was instantly rewarded with the sight of armies of tiny blue legged hermit crabs, some no bigger than a grain of rice, marching over their surface. Crabs, fish, anemones, vertebrates and invertebrates of every description looked out from each nook and cranny as I one by one discovered their hideouts. Even a pancake shaped walking batfish with its feet like fins revealed itself in the shadow of the dock. At the deeper end of the pier, bonnethead sharks and small barracuda patrolled the pilings.

I was now hooked forever, hopelessly caught in the siren song of this fragile strand of disjuncted islands. I continued to paddle around the ocean for about an hour before exiting the water into the warm body drying heat of the sun. I began to anticipate my first ocean dive two days from now with even more excitement. I was going to be diving on a reef called Looe Key, offshore from Little Torch Key and Big Pine Key. I had made the decision to snorkel dive on the first day to get the feel of the ocean and on the second day switch over to scuba. But first I had elected to take a glass bottom boat trip aboard a boat called the Discovery, currently moored in Key Largo.

The next morning I rose early and walked down to the dock to see what might be working along it. I was rather surprised to sight a six-foot lemon shark and then a bull shark of equal length, followed by an automobile hood sized southern stingray. I was shocked to see sharks of that size so close to shore and walking the dock was rapidly becoming a habit because of the changing ocean theatre that always surprised with a variety of sea going entertainment.

After tearing myself away from fish watching, I jumped into the car and started the twenty or so mile drive up to Key Largo, stopping first for breakfast at the quaint Whale Harbor Dockside restaurant overlooking the charter boat fleet poised to ply the waters for dolphin, shark, grouper, or maybe even marlin.

Finishing my bacon, egg, and fresh squeezed orange juice breakfast, I resumed my trek up to Key Largo arriving soon enough and parking not far from where the Discovery was moored. I bought my ticket and boarded the boat being careful to get a seat nearest the access to the underwater viewing glass.

Dosed up with anti seasick medication, just in case, I sat enjoying the ride as the Discovery made the trip out to Molasses Reef. As we approached that objective the underwater viewing window changed colors from royal blue to a duller more opaque blue possibly with yellow overtones and then to liquid transparency as we began to hover over the white sand bottom adjacent to the reef. The motor was thrown into neutral and we started our drift over the reef proper, which slowly began to reveal its beauty through the viewing glass with the revelation of gardens of purple sea fans and soft corals pulsing in the current. Fish darting here and there stopped and held position indifferent to the audience a few inches away, who were marveling at the colored quilt that is the coral reef. A large barracuda centered himself in the viewing glass apparently as interested in us as we were in him.

I had seen these sights many times on television but this was my first view of a coral reef in person, and it again fueled my excitement about the next days dive on Looe Key, where the only glass separating me from the reef would be that of my dive mask. During the trip back, I replayed visions of what I had just witnessed and mentally began to plan my snorkel dive the following day. I wondered if I would be all right, would my back hold up? Would I be diving alone or with someone? All these questions would be answered in less than a day.

The next morning dawned sunny, clear, and warm. The alarm rang calling me to start my adventure, but I was already awake staring at the clock, waiting for the beep. I washed and dressed quickly, loaded my gear into the rental car, and headed this time down the Keys, toward my destination about fifty five miles away. Anticipation began to build during the more than hour long trip as I passed Indian Key, Robbie's, Hawks Cay, Marathon, The Turtle Hospital, Seven Mile Bridge, Bahia Honda and finally Big Pine Key.

The dive boat was waiting behind the store and I saw about a dozen scuba divers unloading and checking their gear. My eyes scanned the group for other snorkelers like myself, but I found none. It looked like I would be flying solo although I really didn't mind because I wanted to check my skill level without being encumbered by someone else.

The dive boat pulled away from the dock right on schedule and we began the trip out to Looe Key threading through the assortment of cuts, bridges and channels that led toward it, also passing the ultra exclusive Little Palm Island and its tiki hut accommodations that looked like a scene from the movie South Pacific. We continued heading out to sea following in the wash and wake of another dive boat wallowing in the ocean dead ahead of us. Periodically the bow would cut a wave sending up spray that would catch your eyes and lips with a salty string that reminded you indeed this was the ocean we were on. Sometimes flying fish zipped over the water's surface, their giant wing like pectoral fins rigidly held out probing the air currents for any upward lift to prolong their flight. A shy group of dolphin cut across the bow, teasing the passengers by allowing only a fleeting glimpse of themselves. Looking up and out to the horizon I began to make out the distant reef marker that resembled an exclamation point at the limits of my visibility. Closer and closer, we drew until finally we arrived and were floating over the reef resplendent in all its mystery. In minutes I would be jumping into the open sea for the first time since I had seen Lloyd Bridges on Sea Hunt and had crawled under the dining room table with my shoebox scuba tank. Now over three decades later, I would finally get my chance.

Assembling my gear, I shuffled to the stern, sat down at the edge of the ladder deck and put on my fins, my mask and snorkel already being in place. I lowered my legs into the ocean as I sat on the platform and kicked my fins to get the feel of the thrust they would provide, enjoying the sight of them undulating in the water. Pulling my mask down, I did a quick pivot, and descended through the wave-creased surface for a few feet, tucked forward and started swimming. The first clear vision was worth the years I had waited. The profusion of life featuring schools of fish looked like a small metropolis of coral with its reef dwelling citizens busy at work, swimming in large formations, small aggregations, or individuals, all with a purpose of mind, oblivious to one another unless an invisible territorial line was crossed. I could float and hover over choice spots and observe the feeding habits of pairs of French angelfish, rock beauties, or tribes of rainbow parrotfish. Tiny neon gobies cleaned parasites from the gaping mouths and flared gills of black grouper or barracuda many times their size. There was one old grizzled veteran "cuda" easily five feet long, with a hook and fragment of fishing line hanging from his mouth waiting for his turn at the cleaning station. Scanning to my right I saw a trumpet fish and scrawled filefish attempt to unsuccessfully hide from me amongst sea fans and gorgonians, while fingernail sized thimble jellies floated past my glass-covered eyes.

The feel of the ocean itself was also a new experience. The rise and fall of the waves as I floated on the surface created somewhat of an elevator effect when I stared at objects on the sea floor. The water temperature seemed neither cold nor hot, holding between the two nicely, but the current, this was something I had not expected or could have prepared for. It varied from gentle to stiff depending on your position in the water. At some points I had difficulty making headway, while at others I could ride the flow not kicking at all. I began to realize that my dive kick was not what it had been prior to the surgery and I wondered how I would do the following day with the added drag from scuba gear. I would find out in less then twenty-four hours!

The Last Dive

The second day was much like the first; the weather was similar with a slightly stronger wind and heavier chop. The boat left with the same number of scuba divers as the day before accept on this trip I had joined their ranks. As we headed out to Looe Key for the second time, there was not the thrill or anticipation of the initial journey but instead a feeling of apprehension and nervousness. I was second guessing my skills and having doubts about whether or not I could pull this off. The current yesterday had revealed a severe weakness in my ability to move through the water and as I put on my dive gear I felt seriously weighted down and stiff. At that point I knew how David must have felt after King Saul gave him his armor to try on before going out to face Goliath. "I cannot go in these," he said to Saul, "because I am not used to them." So he took them off (1.Samuel, 17:39 N.I.V.). Perhaps the snorkel was intended to be my sling. I was also buddied-up with a man in his sixties and although I didn't doubt his ability, it made me even more uneasy.

Unlike the previous day, the boat anchored right near the reef marker that bordered on a drop off, so I would be looking at some new underwater terrain. Normally I would have viewed this as a good thing but on this day I would have preferred swimming in familiar surroundings. Plodding back to the ladder deck waited down with a tank, regulator, B.C. vest, and movement restricting wetsuit, I felt even less mobile than usual. Entering the water, I was in trouble almost at once. Letting the air out of my vest, I started a slow descent. At about ten feet, after I had reached neutral buoyancy, I attempted to move myself forward from the upright position I was in, to a horizontal swimming attitude, but much to my frustration, I just couldn't get level. I tried with the current, against the current, inflated my vest, deflated my vest. All I could do was go up and down like a yoyo. My final effort resulted in an out of control swimming position, in which my weak rear flipper kick was insufficient to drive myself forward, leaving me like a semi buoyant cork. Feet up, head down, similar to a submerged wheelbarrow moving through the water in a controlled tumble.

I didn't want to torture my elderly dive buddy any longer. The experiment was over, and so were my days of scuba diving. I swam along the ocean's surface and back to the boat. Jettisoning the scuba gear, I returned immediately to the water, now a free moving happy snorkeler, accepting my limitation and grateful for what I was still able to do.

I was not discouraged. I had found my spot. I had a job I loved and was diving in the tropical waters over a coral reef of such beauty it staggered the mind. I was happy with my life, God just didn't intend for it to include scuba diving, and my new love affair with the Florida Keys would only grow over the next ten years.

22

FOLLOWING MALACHI

Since scuba diving was no longer on my radar screen, I began to embrace snorkeling in its place. I started to explore different sites on the shallow side of Looe Key reef and other spots up and down the Keys, like Sombrero Light off Marathon, Alligator reef, whose light I could see from the dock at the Islander at night, as its rhythmic rays pierced the dark, and Molasses Reef, out of Key Largo, whose waters I had first visited aboard the Discovery.

For me the stand out spot among them was once again Looe Key, followed by a close second the Sombrero Light. The problem was, particularly on Looe, that boats carrying only snorkel divers never stayed very long on the water, due to the overall novice level of the dive clientele, some of whom had never even used a snorkel before, tired quickly and or were not that interested in diving. During one particularly infamous trip, the boat I was aboard during a four-hour excursion spent fifteen minutes on the dive site. This just wasn't going to cut it especially now that I had acquired a taste for underwater still and video photography. I had two cameras, a couple of snorkels, vests, a heavy wet suit and a light one, two sets of fins and masks, and my own inflatable dive flag for those frequent beach dives I liked to try. In short, I became probably the best-equipped snorkel diver in the Keys, even if not the most maneuverable. I decided I had to find a better way to go.

I began to laboriously check through an assortment of Keys travel literature looking for boats that could be custom chartered for snorkel diving on Looe Kay. I narrowed it down to two. I called them both, talked things over with each one, and then asked them to send me a brochure. Only one did. His name was Captain John Sahagian of Fun Yet Charters, as in "Are We Having Fun Yet?"

Captain John turned out to be a real find. He would take me not only to the best spots on Looe Key, but to many other unmarked patch reefs that each held a unique variety of fish. I would dive into forests of gorgonians patrolled by plate sized yellow stingrays or over green sea grass beds where I could photograph brilliant red Bahama Stars highlighted by their emerald background. Sometimes he would take me to remote mangrove forests where I could swim between their submerged roots.

And there were times when I wouldn't dive at all, but take up a trade from the past and go fish the flats near the Content Keys for permit or bonefish. Captain John would steadily pole the flats boat in front of and through cormorant and anhinga infested islands, where the birds would make deep guttural calls and the guano smell and heat would blend to create a tropical miasma like that of some exotic African river, where you fully expected to see large crocs slither into the water at the next bend.

John would always help me get my fins on, help me out of the water, or hand my various cameras over the side as I happily snapped away at elusive wet subjects. He always kept an eye on me, probably entertained by my own amusement with tiny things that must have seemed to him rather mundane or common.

Bryan, from the Shedd Aquarium often joined me on my trips, and the three of us would head out to the reef for adventure. Once we hit the water Bryan would go one way and I the other. I to my photography and he to explore every spur, groove, and patch reef possible in the two hours we stayed. I was continually amazed by his free diving skills, while I was always tethered to the surface, never able to dive down very far, he was seemingly everywhere. On one occasion, I was floating over a grotto looking down at some fish about 35 feet below holding over the white sand. I was trying to identify the species when I saw Bryan, on snorkel gear only, swimming below the fish. I must have looked like a rubber raft to him from his vantage point. He surfaced next to me and said the fish I had been looking at were two of the largest permit he had ever seen.

The trips would always be over too soon and I would return home to Salty the Newfoundland and his companion my new dog, a pug named Choppie.

Pugs are one hundred eighty degrees from Newfs. Salty weighed 135 pounds and Choppie 28. Salty liked to swim, walk, or watch you work; Choppie to eat, find a soft pillow to lay on, or play. Owning a Newfoundland is like having something regal and beautiful around; a pug is like owning one of Santa's elves. Pugs are always happy, forever on the search for food, and always ready to sleep in your lap, and you come to love them both, each unique.

When I traveled to the Keys by myself the dogs would stay behind with Janet, a dog trainer friend of mine who would house sit, or I would take the two up to Wisconsin, where they would stay with Salty's breeders, Lee and Dorothy.

On solo trips to the islands I would mostly try to stay at smaller motels as a way to keep the cost of the trip down, always looking for someplace interesting or convenient to my favorite dive site, or restaurants. One place I discovered was in Marathon, twenty one miles from Looe Key. It was an older motel, but it was always very clean and neat. It was quiet and quaint and best of all it was something very unusual, a sea turtle hospital.

The place was home to an assortment of injured turtles suffering from boat strikes, shark attack, fishing line entanglement, or a disease called fibropapilloma that produced ugly sponge-like tumors on the animals.

They were all swimming in what looked like a converted motel pool, or floating in various circular tubs surrounding it. Over in one corner were a couple of green iguanas living in a wooden box house with a small pool. I guessed they might be abandoned pets. Over the days that I stayed there, I became friends with one particular turtle named Coasty who seemed to recognize me and follow me around the edge of the pool. Coasty had been struck by a boat and after the accident had swum into a Coast Guard station, which is how he had gotten his name. Coasty was partially paralyzed and no longer able to dive and so he made the pool at Hidden Harbor Motel his permanent home. Coasty would paddle after me with his front flippers flapping and rears dragging behind. Perhaps he was only looking for food from me, or maybe he recognized a fellow handicapped diver, or maybe I just imagined it.

Often I would see an energetic man with a ponytail riding around the property in a golf cart, seeing that these turtles were being cared for according to plan. He had somewhat of a reverse curve posture and always seemed to be in a hurry.

After diving, my daily routine was to return to the motel, take a shower to wash the salt off, and then go eat at about 2 or 3 o'clock to avoid crowds and get back to the motel for the five o'clock turtle feeding program.

I would go to an assortment of eating places, sometimes the same one, other times somewhere different. One day I went to a restaurant called Brian's in Paradise located in the middle of a strip mall parking lot, sitting like an island not attached to any of the stores, seemingly out of place in the mall, not really part of it. I had been there before. I always liked to order a large orange juice that was the size of a malted milk. It would send you to the bathroom for hours after you drank it, flushing the citric acid from your body, unless of course you were dehydrated after diving in saltwater, which I usually was. After I had finished my meal, I went to the counter to pay my bill. While I was waiting for the cashier I noticed some brochures next to the register. I picked one up. On the cover was a drawing of a turtle below the words "Saving the Sea Turtles". It told of an organization that performed beach patrols and assisted with turtle strandings. It sounded interesting and I decided when I got home I would join. The group was called Save-A-Turtle of the Florida Keys.

After I became a member, I got in the habit of sending checks in the small amount of five dollars once or twice a month as a general commitment to charity and figuring it would help the turtles in some small way.

Soon after joining Save-A-Turtle, I began to receive monthly green newsletters from them updating the members on current activities, along with an assortment of turtle related anecdotes. One newsletter contained something that caught my eye. It was dated March of 1999. Near the bottom of the left side of the page, I was surprised to see my name, and Save-A-Turtle thanking me for my frequent donations, which at the time could only had a cumulative total of maybe one hundred dollars at most.

I thought to myself, "Who are these people that are excited over five dollar checks"? I was never someone who had been singled out for attention in his life, and this small act had a deep effect on me. I thought to myself, "Well, if they are happy with that little bit, maybe I can do more."

One of the ways Save-A-Turtle raised money was through turtle adoptions, where baby turtles could be adopted through donations of ten to one hundred dollars. Ten dollars got you one sea turtle; twenty got you two and so on, up to the one hundred dollar amount for a whole nest of baby turtles. I decided I would start adopting nests and so in 1999 I adopted my first one.

By the summer of 2000 I had adopted five nests. In August of that same year, my dog Salty, missed his birthday by only two weeks. He would have been twelve years old.

23

A STRANGER INVITED IN

Over the years Mike Bier's adventures with Save-A-Turtle settled more into the realm of normalcy and now after over a decade of service he had acquired a much less demanding position. He had become a mailman of sorts. His job was now to drive up to the Islamorada post office and check box 361 for any incoming mail addressed to Save-A-Turtle, open it and then redirect it to the proper person involved. These letters usually consisted of requests for T shirts, memberships, or turtle adoptions of various levels. While scanning through this correspondence he had noticed over the last few years a person from Illinois, who had been sending checks in the amount of five dollars with no instructions or designation as to how they were to be used. Even stranger, for no apparent reason, the five dollar checks stopped and had been replaced with others in the amount of one hundred dollars, requesting sea turtle nest adoptions

The number of adoptions continued to mount with an irregular pattern of regularity until in Mike's opinion they had reached a somewhat significant number. The return address stamped on the back of the envelope indicated that the man was a fisheries biologist from Illinois, and well ... Illinois was certainly not anyplace one would associate with sea turtles.

The mystery man's clandestine activities had also caught the attention of fellow S.A.T. member, Margie Jensen. Margie confided in Mike that she was becoming increasingly concerned about this.

"Mike, I'm beginning to get uneasy about cashing these checks. No one has ever heard of this guy or has seen him anywhere down here. He's not a turtle person that we know of. I'm starting to think he's some little dried up old apple in a nursing home who's lost his marbles and is sending us his pension money. Once his family finds out about it they'll have a fit! I think you better call him and find out who he is"!

"I don't want to call him why don't you do it?", Mike answered. Margie responded, "Maybe he'll take it better from a man than a women if you tell him to stop, the guy could be nuts anyway!" "Well all right", Mike said reluctantly. "I'll call him this weekend."

Contact

One Saturday morning in early spring of 2001, I was down in the basement working on my array of aquariums. My dog Choppie the pug was upstairs sleeping on the sofa, perhaps dreaming of his lost friend Salty. He seldom if ever came downstairs, the curved steps were hard for his small body to negotiate and the place lacked good soft sleeping spots. Salty on the other hand had always shadowed my every move and loved the cool floor on this lower level. I had been unable to find a replacement for my Newfoundland companion for seven months now with no glimmer of hope for a puppy on the horizon. At this point I had contacted about three dozen breeders in the U.S. and Canada with no luck, and with few exceptions, a surprising lack of support or interest in my search from most of them. My hopes were starting to ebb and I was beginning to consider getting a second pug, a black one this time.

The pug people were the exact opposite of the Newf breeders, very supportive, feeling for me in my loss, and ready and willing to help me find a pug puppy if I decided to go that way.

I always enjoyed my free time working in my basement "Fish World", looking at my collection of Florida Keys fish. Angelfish, butterfly fish, wrasse, even a small moray eel I had named Eli swam around me in their glass enclosures. I was draining some water out of one of the tanks when the phone rang. I stopped the siphon, put it into a bucket and headed over to the phone across the room. Looking at the caller ID box I could see the distinct 305 area code I knew was coming from the Florida Keys or Miami area. The name of the caller was Mike Bier. It was a name I had seen before and was familiar with since it had appeared with regularity in the Save-A-Turtle newsletter.

"Hello", I said. The caller responded, "Hi, is this Jim?" "Yes it is", I returned. "Jim, my name is Mike Bier. I'm with Save-A-Turtle of the Florida Keys. I'm calling to see that you actually exist! No one knows who you are or has ever met or seen you. You've become kind of a cult figure down here in the Keys! We were wondering how you had such an interest in sea turtles."

I answered that it was just something that happened and had developed out of my love for the Keys. I told him that I was a fisheries biologist and that was where my main interest lay although in the past I had quite a collection of turtles too. My favorite was the Diamondback Terrapin, a turtle that made the Florida Keys part of its home range. We talked for quite some time, hitting it off at once with our similar interests and eccentricities. At the end of the conversation, Mike invited me down to a S.A.T. meeting if I were ever in the area. I told him that I would try to make one, knowing that I probably would not.

After saying goodbye, Mike called Margie Jensen to give her the report. "Did you find out who he is?" she asked. Mike answered, "Yes, we had a long conversation." "What's he like?", she said. "Well he is definitely not some old guy in a nursing home at all, he's about my age, quite interested in fish and turtles. He just seems to want to help out. The guy is pretty normal, at least as much as we are down here in the Keys. I get the feeling he likes to maintain a low profile and fly under the radar." They ended the conversation both satisfied that the stranger from Illinois was most likely not crazy, but they both were left wondering what they might have found or had been brought their way.

My trips to the Keys continued. I made two that spring and summer of 2001, but I avoided any further contact with Save-A-Turtle, uncomfortable with the attention I had received and enjoying my role as an unknown figure. I continued to send in more nest adoptions encouraged by the interest shown by S.A.T. and the nests had now reached eleven. Each time I adopted one, I received a certificate that told where the nest was located along with a small picture of the emerging hatchlings. The nests were in places familiar to me, like Sunshine Key, Sombrero Beach, Bahia Honda, and Sea Oats Beach. Every adoption certificate was signed by the President of Save-A-Turtle. The first few were autographed by someone named Captain Tina Brown, later by Mike Hall, who I new from the S.A.T. newsletter as Tropical Mike.

Early that Fall, sometime after Labor Day, I received a second call from Mike Bier. He asked if I was planning to be in the Keys anytime during the month of November and said the members would like to meet me at the annual banquet. I graciously refused the invitation saying that I came down to the islands only in May, July, and December. Mike said he understood but that if my plans should change, the invitation was open. I thanked him again knowing full well that even if by some chance I was there during that time, there was no way I was going to attend a dinner comprised of total strangers, being uncomfortable in crowds of even a few people who I already knew. When November finally did roll around I discovered why Mike had been so keen to get me to the banquet. Later that month I received the little green S.A.T. newsletter in the mail that gave details on the dinner. It read, "The Quay hosted the event that drew about thirty members, once again the food was excellent and the company quite enjoyable. At this years banquet the agenda was full of special events with a number of awards presented to members that have made an impact on our conservation efforts." As the story continued, it said that turtle plaque awards had been presented to two people. One was to Captain Larry Parks, and the other much to my extreme shock was to me! I was absolutely taken aback, feeling unworthy of such an honor. As I saw it, all I had done was sign checks, while people who had gotten up at some ungodly hour, day after day to patrol beaches were not being singled out for the hard work they had done. Somewhat embarrassed by the situation, I felt compelled to adopt even more turtle nests, and at the same time trying to figure out some way to "actually" earn an award I had already been given.

Later that year, a few weeks before Christmas, my search for a Newfoundland puppy came to an end. I had contacted fifty five breeders over the year and a half since Salty's death with no success. I was down to what I considered my last shot. It was someone who I had known about early on but had somehow overlooked. The couples name was Donna and Ray and they lived in Sault Saint Marie, Ontario. They were friendly and helpful and said they would have a puppy for me in January of 2002. It would be the beginning of a new year, a special year, a year that began with a journey to the frozen north and ended in islands and sand.

24

JANUARY 2002

It was mid January when I packed my truck with a duffle bag of clothes, a small dog crate placed behind the front seat, and a thermos of water. There was also in the back a boater's life vest, left over from some fishing excursion in the warmer days of the past. I was heading north, up to Sault Saint Marie, Ontario, to retrieve my new pup.

I wondered what he would be like. Would he come to me right away, or would he remain aloof, keeping his distance, unsure of this new stranger who had entered his world a foot above the floor. I had given a great deal of thought to what his name should be, and since he was a working breed with a proud tradition of nautical service, I decided just as with his predecessor Salty, that he too would have a title that would honor that heritage, and so the name Moonfleet's Barnacle Bill of the Conch Republic, call name Barney, was waiting to be bestowed.

I left town on a sunny snowless day that was unseasonably warm for January, hovering in the mid forties. Starting my journey, I headed over the Chicago Skyway toll bridge into Indiana, through the steel town of Gary, and continued eastward. The scenery changed from industrial to rural as Michigan City, Indiana was passed next and I progressed until I crossed into southwestern Michigan.

I had fished this area countless times over the past twenty years and the passing terrain seemed very familiar. Michigan had always been one of my favorite destinations. The State is possessed of a beautiful Great Lakes coastline unbroken around the peninsula, fruit orchards, and an assortment of inland lakes that give it an unmatched appeal. It felt odd to be traveling through the area with no intent of fishing and it brought on feelings of time having passed unnoticed that could not be recaptured. I continued up the west coast and then cut eastward toward Grand Rapids. Turning north from there I drove until just after dark, stopping for the night at the town of Grayling, a small burg named after a fish with an oversized sail like dorsal fin. The lure of staying the night in a town named after a fish was just to appealing.

At this point in the road, there had been no new snowfall, but when I pulled up to the motel and saw the two feet of packed snow and rows of parked snowmobiles in front of the white accented evergreen forest, there was no doubt I was in the Northland. After checking into the motel, I went across the road and picked up a sack of burgers, then parked my truck for the night next to a pristine white snowdrift that was a foot taller than the roof. It was a scene of powerful beauty and silence that produced a feeling of warm coziness and comfort like a visit from a good friend on Christmas eve. Back in my room I watched TV for awhile, checking the weather for the next day and then nodded off. I slept well but during the night I got up a few times to look out the window. The scene below was that of a forest clearing illuminated by the moonlight slicing through the clear crisp sky. It was like looking at a living Christmas card and became even more so when two deer cautiously walked out of the pines and approached a feeding station generously provided for them by the motel. I pulled a camera out of the duffle bag and snapped a few pictures attempting to capture this impossible to capture moment, then I went back to bed, sleeping even deeper than before.

The next morning I was back on the trail early, driving initially through sunlight that reflected off the snow with such glare it would have been painful to drive in without sunglasses. This weather would not hold however and before long it was clouding up. As it did, I was drawing nearer and nearer to the formidable Mackinac Bridge, that traversed the Straits of Mackinac connecting Lake Michigan to Lake Huron. The bridge would bring me to Michigan's Upper Peninsula.

As I drew closer to it, I kept seeing signs every few miles telling, or better stated warning drivers how many miles were left to the bridge. This apparently was to provide the driver with ample opportunity to make good on an escape! There was a subtle coerciveness about this that made my hands tighten on the steering wheel and set me thinking that I had let my last chance pass by.

Finally, off on the horizon, I could see the massive structure rising up from a surprising distance away. This was followed by speed limit signs that instructed, CARS 20 MPH, TRUCKS 15 MPH. In a few more minutes my tires crossed onto the bridge and I began to climb. The hood of my truck pointed up and the uncomfortable feeling looking out the windshield into blank space produced a feeling of driving off into an unknown void. I was sure at any moment I would come to some unseen gap in the bridge and plunge to my doom! Just to add some extra spice to the moment, snow started falling and I could see white caps on the water far below contrasting against the steel gray liquid. The radio station I had been listening to thought this was the perfect time to play Gordon Lightfoot's, Wreck of the Edmond Fitzgerald, and I glanced behind the passengers seat at the forgotten life jacket with increased interest.

I finally found some relief when I pulled up behind a trailer truck and was content to let him lead the way at what now seemed the heady speed of 15 MPH. This is where I stayed, nestled comfortably in the big vehicles wake, until I at last felt the nose of my truck angle downward telling me we were now heading toward land. I was never so glad to pay a toll in my life, thinking that tomorrow I was going to have to cross this thing again on my way back.

The bridge disappeared in my rearview mirror and the miles sailed by as I progressed through parts of the Hiawatha National Forest and the rest of the Upper Peninsula until the Canadian border was in reach. I began to feel like I was approaching an old friend's house for a long overdue visit. I hadn't been up here since July of 1998. Prior to that, I had traveled to Canada at least twice annually for an unbroken string of twenty three years. The national flag of this country with the red and white color setting off the center maple leaf, seemed to have been perfectly created just to contrast with the snowbound land I was returning to, and it stood out boldly. I always felt it was one of the most beautiful of the world's flags.

I checked through customs next, a familiar procedure, although this time when asked the purpose of my visit, I did not say fishing. Instead I responded," I'm here to buy a dog." Without batting an eye the customs official answered, "Welcome to Canada, have a good day, enjoy your dog, I bet it's a Newfie." His clue was my NEWF license plates.

Once I crossed the border, I headed straight away to the dog breeders country house on the outskirts of the town, out to the west on something called Baseline Road. Ray and Donna Overman greeted me at the side door. Entering the house, I was swarmed by a small herd of friendly, inquisitive, bear like animals in black, or black and white coats, with saggy faces and the gentle eyes emblematic of the Newfoundland breed. Donna escorted me into another room and introduced me to a toddling mass of puppies that looked like newborn bear cubs. She had already selected one that she thought would be a good one for me and pointed him out. My eyes looked across the room to a table, under which I saw a furry black face looking back at me. Hello, who are you?, he seemed to say as I approached.

I knelt down to scratch his head and neck, and massage his pink soft puppy toes with their tiny nails. He responded to my touch by spreading the toes, reverse arching his back, and letting out a big yawn, followed by tail wagging. "He's the quietest one in the litter", Donna told me, "very mild tempered and amiable, he should be a good match." I agreed and said I would be back in the morning to pick him up.

"We will have him ready. What are you going to name him?" "Barney", I said. "OK, Barney it is."

That night, back in my motel room I slept soundly, surrounded by snow, red and white maple leafed flags, and memories. Memories of a country that in many ways had become a second home. It was in my blood. It was part of who I was. I also knew that when I left the next morning, I most likely would not return anytime soon, my fishing days pounding around the Canadian wilderness ended by back trouble. And, there was something else. A chain of islands far to the south, scattered over a blue tropical ocean, now provided the call that could not be denied.

The year was young. Who knew what things might come my way?

25

JULY 2002

The next morning I returned to the Overman's to pick up Barney, who was busy patrolling around the kitchen like he owned the place, enjoying his new found freedom in this unexplored room that smelled of pancakes and maple syrup.

We talked for awhile, mostly about dogs, and then mindful of the long trip ahead, I said my goodbyes. Ray picked up Barney and carried him out to the truck for me, plodding through the foot deep snow. I always wondered how hard it was for the breeders to part with their pups. I wondered if it tugged at their hearts, if they were sad to see them go, or if it was just something they had gotten used to over the years. I pushed the passenger seat all the way forward and tilted its back forward also so that I would be able to watch my pup in his crate or reach down to comfort and pet him while I was driving. Barney was lowered into his cage, he looked up at me through its open top and wagged his tail. It was time to leave. Then we were off, starting our new life together. I drove through the frozen quiet town that was still mostly asleep on this Sunday morning, and arrived at the border crossing. The customs agent admired my new pet, checked his vet papers, and then sent us on our way. The Upper Peninsula provided energizing scenery as the distance from Canada gradually increased, the proximity of that nation only hinted at by the French speaking voice I occasionally picked up on the radio. Soon the big bridge lay ahead of us, but it now seemed much less intimidating, illuminated with bright sunlight and surrounded by clear winter air that revealed every detail of its long span. My happy companion sat next to me, and each time I looked down at him, I found he was already looking back at me in a flattering admiring manner, the tail always in perpetual wag mode. We listened to music together. He appeared to approve of my taste, and before long the Mackinac Bridge was fading into memory, dissolving behind us.

I thought it was a good time to stop now so I pulled into a scenic snow covered rest area and liberated Barney from his crate. I wondered how he would react to the leash when I placed it on him for the first time, but he never balked, instead following along happily wherever I led him, taking everything in stride, calm natured, forever looking up with approval.

This is the pattern that continued for the duration of our journey until we at last were home. When I opened up the front door, Choppie was there to greet us. He seemed to approve by in turn wagging his curly fry tail and attempting to play, not sure of what to make of this miniature version of Salty.

The months went by and Barney grew fast, reaching sixty or seventy pounds by the time my summer trip to the Florida Keys rolled around. This excursion was going to be somewhat different however, since I would be traveling solo for the first time in several years, Bryan not being able to get away due to a new addition to his family, a daughter, appropriately named, Coral.

Diving on Looe Key in the summer is usually a real treat. The water temperature hovers in the mid eighties and fish life is at a peak. Schools of them patrol almost nonstop the various coral formations and sea grass beds. Unfortunately for me, thunderstorms which are a near daily occurrence or threat, took hold early in the week washing out any chance for diving. On the bright side, since I was staying at Hidden Harbor Motel with its adjoining Turtle Hospital, I could occupy myself by visiting the various sea turtle residents, like Rebel, Bubblebutt, and of course Coasty. I could fish shop at Dynasty Marine, a tropical fish dealer I used in my aquarium business that also supplied fish to the Shedd, or dine at my favorite Keys haunts. One afternoon while walking around the turtle pool and trying to get a decent picture of "The Big Guy", Tina Brown's pet tarpon, I ran into Sue Schaf who was working in the area. I started a casual conversation with her concerning the problem of sea turtles swallowing fish hooks. I wondered if something couldn't be done about getting the manufacturers to eliminate the plating process on their heavier models. This would in theory allow for quicker corrosion and eventual destruction of the hook, which should lessen the threat to sea turtles and other animals. It was an idea I had thought of and just floated to see what might be the response.

During the conversation, Sue also told me something that surprised me. She said that The Turtle Hospital received many calls from zoos and aquariums looking for sea turtles to add to their collections, but when they were told the only ones available were handicapped unreleasable amputees or boat strike victims who were unable to submerge, they were not interested. I was absolutely shocked when I heard this. I had thought zoos and the like were supposed to be conservation advocates, and in many cases actually touted themselves as such. I did not understand why these institutions would not be interested in turtles like these that had so much potential as ambassadors for educating the public. In addition most of the boat strike turtles in particular looked nearly normal, except for a few scars here and there and of course being semi buoyant. Nearly all could swim, dive, eat, and function like other sea turtles, their disability was only revealed when they rested and floated up to the surface of the water.

I thought this was a rather sad commentary on the mindset of the world's zoos and aquariums. In fact I was quite disgusted to hear such a depressing story.

I put these thoughts temporarily out of my mind when I looked up to the sky and saw the sun. The weather had cracked, at least to some degree and like a curtain lifting on a stage to reveal a new scene, would provide a window of diving opportunity for the next two days. I resolved to make the most of it!

When I loaded my gear and cameras aboard Capt. John's boat on Thursday, July 11, 2002, the weather at nine o'clock that morning was still stirring and unsettled, but it looked like it might clear enough to get in a few hours diving. I wasn't crazy about all the weather fronts blowing through, they tended to stir up the water, lowering underwater visibility. I was also aware as a fisherman that this situation was ideal for bringing big predators up on the reef to hunt, and since I dived alone, this was not a comforting thought.

During our trip out to the reef, our route would take us within a couple hundred yards of a very exclusive resort island populated by tiki hut accommodations and gourmet chefs. Not long after passing that point, some distance off the port side, Capt. John and I simultaneously noticed a commotion on the ocean's surface. The water was roiling and splashing so we decided to investigate the cause, which we suspected was a school of jacks that had herded a swarm of baitfish up to the shallows and were driving them mercilessly. We soon found out how wrong we were when the unmistakable scimitar shaped dorsal fin of a hammerhead shark jutted out of the ocean.

The big fin was a motley ragged thing that was a dirty brown gray color, and it rose from this fish like a Jolly Roger on a mast indicating the owner was a veteran sailor. As the shark pursued its prey, the dorsal cut through the water at such speed that it threw off spray not unlike the bow of a ship, and made a snakelike hiss as it cut frictionless through the sea. The animal exuded bold audacity that evoked fear, but one had to marvel at its power and I held it no malice for being what it was.

There was no more than three or four feet of water below us now and through its transparency I could see fields of twig like red and yellow gorgonians along with the scattered sponges typical of the bottom in this area. I kept scanning the oceans surface all the time keeping my eye on the sinister fin that was obviously focused on some potential victim, its intent indicated by the abrupt directional changes in its path.

Closer we came, and still closer, undeterred the hammerhead still remained locked on its target until we too caught sight of the pursued object. The dull silver flash of a tarpon nearly six feet long completed the story. This shark was attempting to run down, corner, and eat a fish of a hundred pounds or more!

For whatever reason, the hunt ended suddenly, the hammerhead breaking off the chase. Then perhaps bent on vengeance toward us for having disrupted its hunt, the fin slowly turned and headed directly for us and deep water. If it kept true to its current course, it would pass directly in front of our boat. I yelled back to Capt. John, 'That's a BIG shark!", and ran for my video camera, taking it hurriedly out of its underwater housing, then headed to the bow of the boat. Once there I lay flat on my chest at this vortex and draped my arms and camera overboard as close to the water as possible, trying for the best camera angle, oblivious to the possible danger.

I was rewarded with the sight of a hammerhead shark of about twelve or fourteen feet undulating past me at close range. The fish looked old, like some wind beaten pirate on the way back to his sanctuary, and I could almost swear I saw a patch over one of his protruding eyes. At that moment I felt no fear of this strange creature, only awe at its magnificence as I watched it dissolve into the depths until I could no longer see it. On the other hand, this was just the kind of image I didn't want in my head before I prepared to jump unescorted into the ocean at a reef not yet visible on the horizon.

When we finally did arrive at Looe Key it was apparent that the wind and rain of the past few days had taken their toll, lowering the underwater visibility and dropping the water temperature several degrees.

Things felt eerie as I put on my dive gear and noticed there were only a few boats anchored over the whole span of the reef. I felt totally alone as I plunged over the side, sank through the bubble trail and waited for the foam to clear, getting my underwater bearings in the process. The water felt unusually cold for July, and as expected the visibility was quite poor, only about twenty feet, after that everything was a shadowy murk.

Swimming toward the main reef patch I started to observe something unsettling. There was a distinct lack of small fish working around the coral. They were mostly gone with only a few left holding tight to cover, cowering in cracks and crevices. Angelfish, grunts, and wrasse had been replaced instead with numbers of large black grouper and schools of nurse shark accompanied by patrolling yellow jacks. I saw trophy sized permit working in the sand for crabs, kicking up clouds of debris. And then the yellow jacks started circling around me, something that was not normal behavior. I became anxious about what was laying outside my field of visibility. After about twenty minutes of poor photography opportunities, I ended the dive. I couldn't get it over fast enough!

The next day was even worse. A lightning storm had just past when I arrived at the dock, but this would be followed by another couple hours of clear weather before the next storm moved in, at least according to the forecast. Perfect fishing conditions I thought, a good time to be on the water … not in it!

Today there was only one other boat besides ours on the reef and I felt like the Lone Ranger while I was swimming over the sea grass field that led to the main coral patch in a sand crater just ahead. Suddenly out of the corner of my eye I became aware of a large shape materializing out of the shadows off to my right. I stopped swimming, held position and stared at the ill defined shadow advancing toward me, each second growing closer. My heart rate began to rise while I waited for friend or foe to appear, but to my relief the now distinct form of a graceful spotted eagle ray flapping two white spotted wings came into view. It was followed by an entourage of steel colored permit feeding in the sand cloud the ray had kicked up in his wake.

Concentrating on my photography, I worked from coral formation to coral formation, snapping pictures and taking a census of the fish I encountered. All the while I kept glancing behind myself looking for anything trailing me, the image of the large hammerhead from the previous day still clear in my mind. I only had a few shots left on the camera when a forgotten coral patch isolated from the rest of the reef caught my attention. It presented itself as a poorly defined murky gray mound and I was just barely able to make it out in the distance. I decided to investigate.

A few kicks of my fins later I was orbiting around the little reef patch that consisted of a brain coral, some smaller coral species, and an assortment of purple sea fans. I had been here before and knew that this location often held types of fish not seen on other spots. This would be an ideal area to finish off the roll of film, so I began to concentrate and frame up some picture opportunities.

For whatever reason, I decided at that moment to look over my right shoulder. The vision I saw told me it might be a good time to end my dive. The first thing I caught sight of was the large vertical tailfin slowly fanning back and forth as the twelve foot shark swam away from me. My mind began digesting the information and the first thought that came into my mind was, SHARK!. My eyes strained attempting to see through the underwater fog bank that was swallowing up the slow moving gray missile, my brain gathering as much information as it could, like a witness to a crime. I wondered how close he had been when I hadn't seen him. I tried to ID the tailfin and scrutinize the body looking for the telltale spots and bars of a tiger shark or the clear gray of a Caribbean reef shark. It seemed too big for a black tip and too sleek for a bull shark. It was either a very large reef shark or an average size tiger. Maybe it hadn't been as big as I thought, I just couldn't tell in the low vis. Perhaps it was circling even as I looked out into the void?

I started a slow and cautious swimming journey back to the boat, periodically looking in all directions as I passed over sand, grass beds, and open water, all the while providing a perfect target until I sighted the boats aluminum ladder bobbing up and down in the waves, beckoning me back to the surface. When I got in range I grabbed it, held on with one hand and placed my camera into Capt. John's out reaching grasp. I resubmerged one more time, face under water, clicked open my fin straps, and threw the loosed fins up onto the boat, then calmly climbed the ladder until I had escaped the sea and stood dripping saltwater onto the slick white deck.

John, unaware of my little adventure, asked if I wanted to shoot some underwater video. "No", I said. "There is a rather large shark cruising around somewhere out there and I think I'd better not give him a second shot at me! It's really murky!" My good luck continued as we pulled anchor and got underway just in time to be caught in a tropical downpour of epic proportions, with flashes of lightning hitting the blackened sea all around us. Still another accurate Florida weather forecast! I left all my dive gear on during the run back to shore, just in case! I figured if the boat sunk at least I would be properly attired for the occasion. Twenty minutes later as we tied up to the dock, we were bathed in bright sunshine streaming down from a clear sky. Such is the nature of the tropics.

The next day I returned home. Choppie and Barney greeted me at the door. I was glad to be back.

26

YOU DIDN'T CHOOSE ME, BUT I CHOSE YOU

One of the greatest benefits of vacationing is that the traveler often returns with a refreshed mind and body, a souvenir more valuable than any trinket found along the way. This reboot of the mental and physical faculties unfortunately usually lasts only a few hours, days, maybe at best a week, before we are overtaken once again by the mundane trials of daily existence. That is the state I found myself in after my return from the Florida Keys. Back home in Illinois I sat reflecting on the trip, my thoughts always returning to the broken down sea turtles living at The Turtle Hospital. The ones that could not be returned to the ocean. The ones that the zoos and aquariums were not interested in.

That mental picture was conjured up once again when a week later I came across a story in the Chicago Tribune, above which was a photo of the Shedd Aquarium's most famous resident, Hawkeye, the Hawksbill sea turtle. The news clip said that he was celebrating his twenty-fifth birthday or anniversary at the aquarium, I don't remember exactly which, his actual birthday being unknown, as a result of being discovered in that abandoned suitcase a quarter of a century earlier.

Even though I hadn't climbed the thirty seven steps leading to the Shedd's entrance doors in over nine years, Hawkeye looked just as I remembered him, the mercurial personality still clearly evident, undiluted by time and age. I sat and reminisced, caught in the relaxing fog of old but still valued memories that maybe were starting to fade a little, but still mostly there.

A week later, I was once again sitting down, enjoying some quiet time with the newspaper, my dog Choppie sleeping at my side, laying on his back and snoring like an eighty year old man, Barney at the front door, duplicating Choppie's position, guarding the entrance by functioning as a furry doorstop.

I had just returned from a one day fishing trip, and it hadn't been a good one. We had caught fish, lots of them, but it had been a miserable day. Soaking rain had dogged us the whole time, helping me to the realization that fishing did not hold the attraction for me it once did. The weather was quite warm despite the rain and it turned the boat with its soaked carpeting into a humid furnace, bathing us in a coating of bug repellent, sweat, and moisture. My wool socks were sopping wet and my clothes seemed five pounds heavier. I couldn't wait to get home, take a shower, and wash the outdoor stucco I had been coated in down the drain.

That task done, I once again sat down and thumbed through section after section of the newspaper, too tired to really comprehend what I was reading until one article caught my eye. The words popped out from the page and met my gaze. The Shedd Aquarium it said, is saddened to announce the loss of its most famous resident, Hawkeye the sea turtle.

One week after his twenty-fifth birthday he was gone! He had thrilled his last audience and pestered his last diver. The necropsy results gave no indication as to the cause of death other than the obvious obesity of the subject, but to his friends who new him best, they would have told you that maybe he had really tied one on for his birthday bash and that old body just couldn't take it.

I was saddened by the news. He was someone I had known and interacted with, even if only through a pane of glass. The melancholy feeling was followed by reflection as I remembered that transitional part of my life, but then in just an instance an adrenaline shot of an idea jumped into my head. I wondered, would the Shedd Aquarium possibly be interested in acquiring one of the sea turtles from The Turtle Hospital in the Florida Keys?

I immediately went to the phone, excited by the thoughts and speculations that were starting to race through my mind. I called Bryan at the aquarium, and ran my idea by him asking if he thought the powers that be down there would be interested in one of the boat strike turtles at the hospital in the Keys? I had one particular Green sea turtle in mind.

Bryan said it sounded like a good idea and was worth a shot. I was also aware that since he worked in the Amazon Rising Exhibit, he had no decision making power whatsoever on matters like this, but he could be like a senator proposing a bill and get an audience with the right people. I told him to ask his superiors, one of whom was George Parsons, now curator of collections, Keith Pamper, the aquarist in charge of the now turtle vacant Caribbean Reef, and any and all people necessary. I would in turn contact Mike Bier with Save-A-Turtle, run the idea by him, and have him call Sue Schaf at The Turtle Hospital.

I then left Bryan to do his maneuvering and next called Mike. Telling him about the plan I had concocted, he also agreed that it was a great idea and certainly worth the effort. I also said that I thought Coasty, my turtle friend from the swimming pool at Hidden Harbor Motel seemed like a natural choice, but to check with Sue and see what she thought. At this point I wasn't even sure if the whole thing was legal, sea turtles being covered under the Endangered Species Act. We might not be given permission to move a turtle from one State to another, but the project had now been set in motion so I just stepped back a bit, and let things happen.

In less than forty-eight hours I had answers from both interested parties. Bryan told me that the Shedd Aquarium was agreeable to the idea and had given me the green light to proceed. I asked him if they were sure because I did not want to embark on a wild goose chase, disappointing The Turtle Hospital and Save-A-Turtle in the process if the aquarium was not serious. He reaffirmed that they wanted to go ahead. "OK", I said, "I'll make it happen". At that point I felt empowered, as though I had been entrusted with some sort of sacred cause. It was an odd feeling, but a good one. I knew I held all the high ground. I had been given the privileged task of placing a handicapped sea turtle at one of the most prestigious institutions in the world. This turtle had the potential to become a great ambassador for the plight of sea turtles everywhere, not just in Florida. I would not be deterred. I was on a mission.

A few minutes later Mike called. His news was not quite as good. He said he had talked with Sue and she had been very excited to hear that someone wanted a less than perfect turtle for a permanent exhibit, especially a place like the Shedd Aquarium. The problem was that there was a ban on shipping any sea turtles out of Florida that had not been free of the fibropapilloma disease for at least a year. This precaution was to prevent the possible spread of the disease. The sticking point was that none of the permanent resident turtles at the Keys Turtle Hospital had been pap free for that length of time, and that included Coasty.

I was deeply disappointed but as it turned out, all was not lost. Sue had told Mike that there were other sea turtle rehab facilities around the state, particularly one on the west coast, in the town of Clearwater. She also suggested that Mike contact someone named Megan with the Florida Fish and Wildlife Conservation Commission. Sue thought that maybe she could find us a turtle.

Mike sensed my disappointment. "I know you had your heart set on a Keys turtle, so do you still want to pursue this?" I was momentarily deflated and discouraged that I was not going to be able to place a turtle from my adopted home turf of the Florida Keys and also give up on Coasty. I thought for a moment, and then reenergized I answered. "Mike, let's go ahead, this is too good a cause to pass on. Let's find some lucky turtle a nice home. A 90,000 gallon coral reef isn't a bad one!"

"I'll call Megan", Mike responded.

Then I waited again.

I guess about a week went by, certainly no more. I was becoming excited to find out what Megan would come up with and from where? On August 15th, 2002 at three o'clock in the afternoon I received the call I had been waiting for. Mike greeted me with the following words "We've found one, a Green sea turtle. He's a boat strike. He floats but can still dive down. He's living at the Clearwater Marine Aquarium."

"I think his name is Pete!"

27

INTERLOPER

As soon as I was done talking with Mike, I called Bryan at the aquarium. "We've got a turtle", I told him. "What should I do next?" "You need to call Michelle, she's in charge of the Caribbean Reef now, Keith was promoted to chief diver."

I didn't know who she was, so Bryan gave me her number. I dialed it immediately but only was able to get the answering machine. For some reason her voice sounded vaguely familiar. I left my message telling her who I was and that I had been working on a project with the Shedd to acquire a handicapped turtle as a replacement for the late Hawkeye. I continued to say that we had found a Green sea turtle for them. His name was Pete.

It was surprising to me that things had happened so quickly to this point. It had been only eighteen days since I read of Hawkeye's death. But when I waited a day and a half with no return call from Michelle, I began for the first time to have an uneasy feeling that things possibly were not going to proceed as smoothly as it had first seemed. Maybe my enthusiasm for the project was not shared by everyone? I called her once more. This time I made contact.

"Hello, this is Michelle", she answered. I responded with a hello and then gave her my name. Next, restating my story, I told her I had been working with the Shedd Aquarium, Save-A-Turtle of the Florida Keys, the State of Florida, and The Turtle Hospital, attempting to find a replacement for Hawkeye. I explained that we had found one, a boat strike turtle from the Clearwater Marine Aquarium. His name was Pete. The response was not what I had hoped for.

Michelle said that she had already contacted the Brookfield Zoo, which is located in the Chicago suburb of the same name, and less than ten minutes from my home. The zoo had four healthy Green turtles that were on loan from the State of Hawaii. They were part of a program in which young sea turtles hatched at Sea Life Park in Hawaii, were sent to various zoos and aquariums on the mainland. There they would be captive reared for a year or two, during which time they could work as tiny ambassadors, raising the public's awareness of sea turtles.

Ideally, after that time period, they would be sent back to Hawaii and then released into the wild. That was the program Brookfield Zoo was participating in as explained to me.

I have to say, upon hearing this, as a biologist myself, I thought it a completely crackpot idea. Taking healthy animals out of their home waters, shipping them thousands of miles away to a captive environment, then sending them back years later to be released into the wild seemed ill conceived to say the least. I thought to myself that apparently none of these people had read Joy Adamson's book, *Born Free*, about an orphaned lion cub named Elsa, who was semi captive raised and then reintroduced back to the wilds of Africa. The book told of the great difficulties encountered by Joy and her husband George while trying to accomplish the task. At any rate, I could not understand why Michelle was so bent on pursuing turtles, that by law, would have to be returned sooner or later to Hawaii.

I also let her know that the State of Florida, Save-A-Turtle, and The Turtle Hospital, were very excited about placing our turtle Pete, and how disappointed they would be if the project fell through now after getting the green light from the aquarium. Michelle seemed unswayed by this, although she said she understood. Still, her plan was to try for the Brookfield Zoo turtles from Hawaii. Michelle was now waiting to hear from the zoo, who in turn had contacted Sea Life Park for permission to move the turtles to the Shedd Aquarium. She seemed to me to have her mind made up and I had pushed my case about as far as I could at this point, so I reluctantly said, "Well, OK, keep me posted on what happens."

After the phone conversation, I had the distinct feeling that Michelle hoped I would go away

Mistake! Mistake! Mistake!

> "I wish to have no connection with any ship that does not sail fast; for I intend to go in harm's way"
>
> John Paul Jones
> U.S. Navy, War of Independence

28

END RUN

The Sea Life Park turtles that Michelle was hoping to transfer over to the Shedd Aquarium, were for all purposes, stranded on the mainland at the Brookfield Zoo, as were turtles at any other facilities, zoos, or aquariums around the continental United States participating in the Hawaiian program.

The normal procedure that had been in place was that after the sea turtles were returned to Hawaii, they were all then released into the wild on the Fourth of July, as part of a promotional event called, "Turtle Independence Day". This happy occasion was always covered by the media, and Michelle herself, when working at Sea Life Park, had actually participated in several of them.

All this was the procedure when everything had gone right, and up until this point it had, but for this last group of turtles, things would not go as planned. Something called pharyngeal nodules had been discovered in the throats of a few of the sea turtles. These polyp like growths were a cause for concern because they may have been an early indicator of some new turtle disease. So, the Brookfield Zoo turtles and all other participating animals from other aquariums or zoos, were now in limbo, unable to move back to Hawaii for fear of disease introduction into wild populations around the island. A veterinary analysis would have to take place and an all clear given before any transfer could happen. At the time, none of these facts were known to Michelle or myself. Pete on the other hand was patiently swimming around his pool at the Clearwater Marine Aquarium, ready to go. Then, still another unforeseen obstacle came to light. In a little over six months, the Shedd was scheduled to open its new multimillion dollar exhibit, The Wild Reef. This several hundred thousand gallon attraction featuring a simulated Pacific coral reef, would be housing assorted species of shark, coral fish, and one particularly large grouper, the one hundred fifty pound plus, Bubba, who interestingly enough had just recovered from a bout with cancer. Also of note was the fact that Bubba had almost Hawkeye like beginnings, except in this instance, instead of being discovered in an abandoned airport suitcase, Bubba had been left to fend for himself on the steps of the aquarium, swimming in a bucket of saltwater. That had been eighteen years ago.

The end result of all this was that the Shedd was not particularly focused on sea turtle acquisition at this time, so between that and Michelle's quest, things started to become lethargic, advancing little or not at all. As if this was not discouraging enough, a friend of mine named, John, who had been to both the Florida Keys and Hawaii, told me, "If you think things happen slowly in the Keys, wait until you start dealing with Hawaii!".

Not content to sit around with hands in pockets, I started to consider ways of getting things moving again, at least at some discernable pace. I began to kick about the idea of doing an end run around Michelle and going directly to her supervisor, George Parsons, now the Curator of Collections. I knew this move would not make me popular with her and if our positions had been reversed, I would probably have felt the same way. On the other hand I didn't think she was getting a real feel for what we were trying to do, and once she did, ... if she did, I could win her over, a kind of "Try it, You'll like it!", situation. At any rate, by this time it had become war. It was Pete and myself against the powers that be, and I was prepared to sail into harm's way.

Then, out of the blue I got a break. As it turned out, George Parsons was a tenant in a building owned by none other than my fishing buddy and dive trip friend, Jim Torelli. Jim had fished on several occasions with Bryan and myself and was employed at the Shedd in the engineering department. Even better, another tenant of the same building was Dr. Marty Greenwall, the aquarium's fish vet, who I had worked for in the lab nine years earlier. Fate had given me an inside track to Michelle's boss.

A change in tactics was in order. I wasted no time in calling George. I told him about Pete, who as it turned out, he was already familiar with, thanks to Bryan. I tried to impress on him what a good project this was and how the Shedd would be the first zoo or aquarium to step up to the plate and take on a handicapped turtle as a permanent exhibit. George was very receptive to the idea, but I knew him to be a quiet person and he seemed uncomfortable about pushing the idea to his superiors, or overrule Michelle. I again reiterated that the Hawaiian turtles would eventually have to go home, and the Shedd would be in the same position once again, no turtle, while Pete would be theirs. I followed by saying, "You need to press this program with the board of directors George, we can't allow it to fail, this could open up other homes for more sea turtles." He answered that he would do his best, and also asked if I had any pictures of Pete? I said I would call Clearwater and have them send some. With that the conversation ended. I had a good feeling that I had started to convert George. He seemed to have "gotten it". He was someone I could work with who understood what we were trying to do along with its importance. George would lay all our cards on the table, and we held all the high ones. The following day I called the Clearwater Marine Aquarium and was put in touch with the sea turtle department and a man named Glenn. I brought him up to date on our project and he seemed vaguely aware of it, having been informed by Megan with Florida Fish and Wildlife. I asked him if he could send some pictures of Pete, which he said he would. Then I told him that I felt we were currently running in place, but I was confident we would succeed. I ended by saying, "Don't worry we'll find Pete a home." His answer was, "Well, he's already got one here."

Now, that was a response that I didn't expect, or know how to take. It seemed kind of tepid at best. Was he skeptical we would be able to pull this off? Or, was he just not that enthusiastic about sending one of his turtles up north, even to a home eighty to ninety times larger than Pete's current enclosure?

I knew if I was persistent we would eventually reach our goal, but the lack of enthusiasm was just beginning to wear me down when I got my first bit of good news in three months. It came attached to of all things a fishing trip, to the Saint Joseph River in Michigan. Bryan, Jim Torelli and myself were set to travel up there and I would be driving. We would stay overnight, fish, then return home the same day. The plan was for me to pick up Bryan, and then Jim at his Chicago home, which was of course where George and Marty also lived. Before we left for Jim's place, Bryan tipped me off to some valuable information. "George said he has decided to go with Pete, but told me not to tell you so you won't bug him." "I won't even mention it.", I responded, all the while jumping up and down on the inside. At that point I really didn't care if I caught any fish at all on the trip.

Bryan and I drove over to Jim's house which was not far from U.S.Cellular Field, where the Chicago White Sox play. This was the first time I had seen his home and it was an interesting sight to say the least.

Jim has made a hobby of buying older vintage homes with potential and character, and then rehabbing them. I had witnessed his skill in this line of endeavor first hand at another home in LaGrange, Illinois, and the result was without question first class, but to say his work was cut out for him with this particular house would have been an understatement. The place was well over a century old and had an iron spiked fence surrounding it which gave it somewhat of a medieval appearance. It had an air of lost elegance waiting to be rediscovered that made one wonder who the former occupants had been. On the other hand it looked like the current residence of the Addams Family and when Bryan knocked on the door, I was certain Gomez or Morticia would answer. Instead it was George.

Since Jim was not home yet, George proceeded to take us on a tour of the ancient building, which oddly enough started in the basement. Once we had descended the creaking steps to that level, he opened a thick wood chip padded door that I immediately recognized from my trips to the Canadian outback as being the entrance to a long abandoned ice room, a room that had been out of use since the invention of the refrigerator. Inside this archaic musty enclosure stood various fish tanks containing Marty's collection of poison dart frogs and their tadpole young. As we spoke, one escaped amphibian happily hopped across the floor, oblivious to the three giants that had just entered its world. Sandwiched in between the frog apartments was a collection of odd twisted looking plants that seemed to be searching for a stronger source of light, not unlike a man groping about in a dark room looking for the wall switch.

The next subterranean room we entered housed a large Rubbermaid tub containing what looked like a dozen or more gray lizards busily scurrying around the confines of their plastic bounded world. At that point I said to George, "Do you guys ever bring any women down here? I've got sixteen fish tanks, two dogs, and a half dozen turtles and you're starting to creep ME out with all this weird stuff!"

Jim showed up just as the tour was starting to get interesting, and the walk through the Little Shop of Horrors came to an end. We departed for Michigan with the unstated acceptance for one another that only comes from the shared passion for all things that fly, swim, walk, creep, or crawl. We don't consider ourselves odd, just unique or momentarily out of place.

Our fishing destination was only two hours away. Bryan mentioned somewhere along the way that the only thing holding up Pete now was waiting to hear from Hawaii or Brookfield, and on that front as usual, nothing was happening. A trip to the zoo was in order.

"It seems to be a law of nature, inflexible and inexorable, that those who will not risk cannot win"

John Paul Jones

29

IMPASSE

It was mid November when I received the pictures of Pete from the Clearwater Marine Aquarium that George had requested. There were eight color photographs assembled on a one page document showing our turtle from different angles. From what I could tell, he looked like a perfectly normal specimen. You could see the wicked scar from the boat strike wound he had suffered that was located on the very back edge of his shell at about the 6:30 position. Other than that, he gave every appearance of being a handsome Green sea turtle.

I wanted to learn more about him, so I called Megan at Florida Fish and Wildlife and asked if she could send over the stranding report on Pete. A few minutes later it was clicking through my fax machine. I looked it over carefully and with much interest, like a prospective parent trying to learn as much as they could about an adoptive child, hoping to gain whatever insight I could draw from the page in front of me.

Reading along at each entry slot on the form, I found out more and more with each line as the incident started to take shape. Pete was found on July 1, 1998, at the mouth of Fish Hawk Creek west of a place called Dismal Key, near the town of Goodland, which was located in the heart of the Ten Thousand Island area of Southwest Florida, about ninety to one hundred miles northeast of the Keys. He had been found back in the mangroves by a man named Matt Finn. The turtle was unable to submerge or dive down. Pete had been transferred to a conservation specialist named Maura Kraus, who had in turn transferred him to the Clearwater Marine Aquarium.

I began to sense that this turtle had a story surrounding him, and since Maura's phone number appeared on the report, I decided to give her a call, see what she could tell me, and also if she might get me in touch with Matt Finn. My intention was to work up some kind of biography on Pete so when he came to the Shedd, they would have some background information on him.

When I talked to Maura and told her what we were hoping to do with one of her turtles, she was extremely excited that one of her "babies", was going to such a good home as the Shedd Aquarium. During the conversation I also asked her if there were anymore photos of Pete. Maura said that she was sure Matt had some and then gave me his number. I learned that he was a marine biologist doing fisheries work so I was anxious to talk shop with him, turtles or not.

When Matt Finn answered the phone, I was greeted to the sound of a voice that had somewhat of a southern twang, although the accent was not quite fully embraced. I introduced myself and told him that a certain sea turtle he had found back in 1998 was about to make a big trip up to Chicago. He became intrigued at once, marveling at the events he had set in motion almost five and a half years earlier on that hot July morning. I asked if he had any pictures of Pete and he said that he did. He told me more about himself and I became interested in the news that he was doing research on jewfish, A.K.A., Goliath grouper. We talked about the animals we had come to know and our various pets. Our collections of dogs, fish, and turtles were discussed. I learned his wife was from Tomahawk, Wisconsin, a place I had fished many years before. She even knew the name of the family that had owned the resort where I had often stayed. Before the chat ended he invited me down to his area if I was ever in the neighborhood. I told him I just might take him up on that offer.

A few days later, a new set of pictures arrived. Looking them over, I saw a man that looked somewhat like Jimmy Buffet holding up a turtle, which of course was Pete. Matt was wearing a Real Tree camouflage baseball cap and a blue tee shirt that set off the colors of the freshly rescued sea turtle. With each photo, I found myself becoming more and more emotionally invested in the project. Pete was transformed from a name on a piece of paper to a living breathing creature, a creature who I was determined to find a new home for. Accordingly I felt the time had come to try and build a fire under the Brookfield Zoo since they had been silent for the last three months as to the disposition of their Green turtles. I took the ten minute drive over to the park.

I knew the sea turtles were part of an exhibit called the "Living Coast", so I made the long trek over to that area. Walking had become an enjoyable pastime for me and the Zoo provided a lot of scenic panoramas as I made my way over to the target and this also allowed me time to mentally define my strategy along the way.

Arriving at the exhibit, I entered the building and started walking through it, passing tanks of jellyfish, penguins, and fish, before spotting the competition paddling up and down in their aquarium. I sized the turtles up and felt no particular malice toward them knowing that they already had homes far away in the Pacific Ocean. Continuing to wander around, it wasn't long before I found what I was looking for, an unsuspecting tour guide or docent as they are called at the zoo. I struck up a conversation with her and commenced to tell her about our sea turtle project. Then I asked her if she could get one of the keepers for me so I could inquire about what was happening with their turtles. The trusting guide was very helpful and before long was back accompanied by a friendly looking person who introduced herself as Patty.

Next, I once again told my story about what we were attempting to do, transfer a turtle from Florida, a handicapped one, over to the Shedd Aquarium. She looked at me, shook her head, and responded, "Never going to happen!", dismissing me somewhat. At that point, the negativity surrounding the project for the last four months was starting to take a toll on me, so I shot back quickly with some amount of sternness, "Oh no, no, no. We already have a turtle set to go approved by the State of Florida. We're being held up because we are waiting to hear from YOU and Hawaii!"

She seemed surprised that I had all the information I did and responded rather meekly that they had contacted Hawaii several times and gotten no response. "Well, give me the number. I'll call them right now!", I said. Her answer was that she did not have the number or know what it was.

With that I gave her a Save-A-Turtle brochure and told her when the zoo's turtles returned to Hawaii to contact us and we would get them some new ones! I left the zoo now more determined than ever. Pete would be going to the Shedd Aquarium! If I had to go down with the ship, so be it!!

30

UPS AND DOWNS

Several years prior to Project Pete as we were now calling it, I had discovered the therapeutic value of recreational walking. This exercise helped lower cholesterol and blood pressure, keep weight down, and most important of all in this instance, provided an escape from the continuing frustration of the turtle project. I would select various places and venues for the walks which I liked to extend for about a mile or two. Sometimes the stroll might even include the Shedd Aquarium area if I could find a parking meter nearby, but that wasn't very often. My favorite place however has always been Oak Park, Illinois, a suburb west of Chicago.

The foremost reason for this is the place reminds me on many levels of Key West. There are no surrounding ocean waters, sand beaches, or palm trees, but there are quite a few subtle similarities. The town is very liberal and quirky and in the summer hosts an array of outdoor restaurants, where one might see someone dining with their dog, or sitting with a parrot on his or her shoulder as they sip coffee, or read a paper. I can gain anonymity and blend in to the crowd of people who are doing the same thing I am, walking just for the fun of it, just as in Key West.

Oak Park is the birthplace of Ernest Hemingway. The vintage home is located appropriately enough on Oak Park Avenue, and just down the street there is a Hemingway museum, both quite the tourist attractions, just as his home on Whitehead Street in Old Town Key West also is. A few blocks from Papa's Florida residence, bounded by a black iron fence, we have the Truman Annex, where President Harry Truman spent many months, during the span of his term in office.

Oak Park's Pleasant Home Historic Sight, has a similar looking black iron fence surrounding it, and walking along its stretch brings to mind a hot summer stroll next to the Key West Truman counterpart where you might be traveling between Mel Fisher's Treasure Museum and back to the Hemingway home. Perhaps finally there is the turn of the century architecture in and around the Oak

Park Historic District, more widely spaced than in Key West's Old Town but in both cities the stately elegance is well preserved.

In Oak Park, I always walk alone, usually through the business district and its peripheries, over a route I have laid out and modified over time. It takes me past an assortment of shops, bookstores, and restaurants. Sometimes I run into people I know or even the occasional celebrity disguised in caps and sunglasses.

I said I walk alone. That's not entirely true. Barney sometimes accompanies me when the weather permits and that would be a cool or cold day. On those occasions, we take a more secluded route through the more affluent adjoining town of River Forest, usually passing by a koi pond,(had to get those fish in there), then to the post office, mailing a letter or two in the process.

Barney does not really see the point in all this walking. I know he only does it to be with me, tolerating it if he must, unlike his predecessor Salty who couldn't wait for the opportunity, but Barney humors me anyway.

In this way I passed many evenings while I was waiting for things to develop on the sea turtle front. I would walk, think about Pete down in Clearwater, then walk some more, perhaps momentarily distracted by someone passing on the other side of the street but then refocusing quickly, always trying to think of some new angle to move things along.

The days were growing shorter now, early darkness and the occasional snowflake were often my companions during the Oak Park journeys where white strings of Christmas lights started to make their annual appearance along Lake Street. Fall was in full swing and Thanksgiving was coming along with Barney's first birthday. After that I would again be heading down to Florida for my yearly dive with the manatees of Crystal River, a quaint town located about an hours drive north of the Tarpon Springs Sponge Docks.

I had discovered the joy of swimming with these walrus like creatures several years earlier and rapidly became addicted to it. How could one not be? It was like taking a swim with a friendly dog or group of them. There are all kinds of rules involved with manatee snorkeling which will be recited to you by your guide. The main one being that you cannot touch a manatee or dive down on one. No harassment of any kind is allowed. But, and here's the thing, if the manatee approaches you and initiates contact, the human is then allowed to touch it with one hand. To the snorkeler, there will be no doubt when this fortuitous event occurs. A gray friendly looking bewhiskered face will appear out of the freshwater murk and tentatively scan you the alien form in front of it. The manatee's face radiates a trustful gentleness that freezes you in place as you float at the waters surface gently sucking air through your snorkel, contemplating what sort of being this flippered dirigible is.

The gray round face with the tiny searching eyes approaches closer, then closer still, until the whiskers brush your dive mask and your own eyes make contact with those of this wild animal that is like no other.

You are now allowed to touch the manatee, or better still from the animal's point of view, scratch it! Your hand begins to run across the rubbery skin, stroking and scratching, feeling the patches of dead barnacles or the tiny solitary hairs protruding here and there, telling you that yes, this is a mammal. There are remarkably elephant like toenails on the ends of each flipper and as your scratching effort reaches a good location, the manatee will guide your hand with one of these appendages to a particularly "itchy spot".

Each manatee has a distinctive personality. Some come for a quick visit and scratch, then leave. The big males often will only acknowledge you in passing as they head to the daytime feeding areas, but then there are those, the special ones, that follow you around like affectionate dogs, looking for just one more good scratch, begging for attention, accompanying you throughout the duration of your dive, faithfully swimming at your side.

But, all is not bliss. There is one disturbing aspect to the experience. In your interaction with the manatees you soon discover that virtually every one of them, with the exception of most babies, is marked to some extent by an assortment of scars, deep gouges or cuts. These are motorboat propeller wounds in various states of healing, caused by collisions with fast moving watercraft. Sometimes the animal is nicked, sometimes hurt, and sometimes killed.

As I examined the variety of man inflicted scars and lacerations on these gentle, slow moving animals early one morning in December of 2002, I couldn't help but think of Pete, who had met a similar fate. I wondered if he had suffered much pain and how long he had floated on the ocean's surface, helplessly pushed along by the wind and waves. I wondered if the sun burned his skin or hunger tortured him as he dissolved in and out of consciousness. I wondered if he had ever been able to grasp what had happened as he drifted, his days of diving ended forever.

I had never met Pete, but that was about to change, because you see, after I was done with my manatee experience, I would be driving the hour and a half route down highway 19, to the Clearwater Marine Aquarium, where he had perhaps, been all along patiently waiting for me.

I recognized him right away when I saw him in his concrete tank. He looked just like his pictures, and there was his unmistakable Loggerhead companion

Pinky. The aquarium itself was a peaceful place. It was small and unassuming. It had a feeling of serenity about it, possibly due to its off the beaten path location.

Pete was swimming around in his blue colored pool unaware of me looking downward, being lifted up. His enclosure was divided by a bridge or walkway at the center. I had called ahead and told the man named Glen I was coming to see Pete, but he said he wasn't sure he would be there. Instead an enthusiastic young woman named Tammy Langer came out to greet me.

She introduced herself and then asked me if I would like to meet Pete? I said I would and we then walked down to the access gate leading to the dividing walkway. "Do you want to pet him? It's OK, you can!",she said.

Tammy swished her hand in the water and over he came, swimming in his signature tail up, head down attitude. I placed my hand on him and ran it over the weathered shell, feeling its contours and the prop wound scar at the very back that ran jaggedly inward. Next I touched his front flipper, the right one, gripping it slightly like a soft handshake, one of the same flippers that had guided him through miles of ocean to places only he knew. Both of us had traveled a long way to intersect at this place in time. Now we had touched. Our stories were now joined together.

"It will be great to see him in his new home where maybe he will be able to dive down!" Tammy said. I just smiled, enjoying the moment, knowing that nothing was certain at this point. I took a few pictures and left my new friend saying, "I'll see you again soon Pete."

Returning to the car, I started the long drive down to the Florida Keys where I would be attending the Sea Turtle Rehab Symposium at the Turtle Hospital in Marathon, hosted by Ritchie Moretti. Turtle experts from all over the country and the world would be congregating at that location but there was one person in particular I was hoping to meet, Megan, Pete's locater from Florida Fish and Wildlife would be attending.

After the symposium, which starts at about 9:00 a.m. and ends around 5:00 p.m., Save A Turtle sponsors a cookout on the grounds of the Turtle Hospital and Hidden Harbor Motel for the attendees and interested S.A.T. members. Picnic benches are placed along the outdoor sea turtle rehab pools and a variety of tasty fare is served up courtesy of head hamburger chef Pat Wells, who is usually assisted by Herb and Yea Bernett, Margie and Don Jensen, Patty Anthony, Tropical Mike Hall, and of course my friend, Mike Bier.

The atmosphere is singularly remarkable as you sit in the semi lit evening, right next to pools and tubs of recovering sea turtles, cooled by tropical breezes eminating from the adjacent ocean, gently fanning the appreciative crowd.

Megan seemed to recognize me right away, perhaps from my voice or maybe the Newfoundland dog tee shirt I was wearing. I asked her how she had liked the symposium and she answered that it had gone well. I learned she was an Illinois native like myself and that she would be coming up to the Chicago area for Christmas. Megan said that if there was any way she could help with the project when she was up North, she would be glad to. I filed this fact in my brain for possible future use. She struck me as a person who could give a good account of herself, which might come in handy somewhere down the line.

The Monday after the Symposium weekend, I was still down in the Keys, in Islamorada, intending to go fishing. Before I left I thought I would call Bryan at the Shedd and give him an update on how things were going turtle wise down in the lower latitudes. I excitedly related all my stories. His response was not in kind. "Bad news", he said. "I came into the office today and saw the pictures of Pete on one of the tables and I said to George, looks like we're going to get Pete?" George answered, "Well, I don't know, Michelle still wants to go for the Hawaiian turtles."

I absolutely hit the roof! "This is just ridiculous, I said. "The people down here in Florida are very excited about this whole thing and we're still playing games with sea turtles that are sooner or later going back to Hawaii! It just doesn't make any sense!" I was learning that few things did in this project. "I can't believe this! Do you think it would help if I got Megan to come down to the aquarium? She's offered to and will be in town for Christmas."

Bryan said to hold on and he would run down to George's office and ask him. He returned quickly and told me that George thought it could possibly help things along. "Good!", I said. I hung up and wasted no time in calling Megan. She agreed to come down to the Shedd Aquarium. The date was set. The meeting would take place December 27, 2002. It would include George, Megan, myself, and Michelle. I would finally get to meet the mystery woman who had been my competition!

31

TO GOOD TO BE TRUE

Megan had given me her home phone number in Illinois, so around suppertime on December 26, I decided to give her a call to make sure everything was still a go. I had just finished grilling some hamburgers outside in the snow for the dogs and myself, a rare treat for that time of year. Choppie and Barney continually ran up and down the back porch stairs, monitoring my cooking progress as they awaited the forthcoming manna that they knew would soon arise from "WEBER", the God of charcoal fire.

When I got hold of Megan at her parents home, she told me she was all set for the visit to the aquarium, although she had not been down there for several years and was not sure of her means of transportation or where to park. I detected what I thought was a slight uncertainness in her voice which made me uneasy, having been disappointed so many times before, I was getting a little gun shy. I guessed that she had most likely flown up from Florida and did not have a car, so the prospect of borrowing one and driving down into the heart of Chicago surrounded by heavy traffic was not a pleasant prospect. This was also a vacation for her, accordingly, I did not feel good about pressing hard to make sure she showed up.

After our call ended, I became more and more worried that the meeting was going to fall through at the last minute, which could easily cause the whole project to collapse. I would have offered to pick her up at her home myself, which was located about forty five minutes to the west, but I really didn't know her that well and didn't think she would accept the offer. I kept stewing over the problem when all of a sudden the potential solution hit me.

One of my aquarium customers, George Jacobs, owned one of the largest limousine services in the Chicago area and for that matter the country. George was an animal lover, so I called him and told him what was up with my sea turtle project of which I had been giving him regular reports on over the past several months. I also brought up Megan's transportation predicament. As I expected,

George came to my aid. A limo would pick her up at her home, bring her to the aquarium, then return her. Megan arriving at the Shedd in a limousine would have the added effect of showing the aquarium that we were serious about this "turtle thing".

On Friday morning I arrived at the Shedd aquarium earlier than the appointed time as is my usual habit, and then sat down on an old table around the corner from the security guards office. I thumbed through Pete's biography and stranding report to refresh my memory, which really didn't need it at that point. Only a short time passed before Megan came walking around the corner.

We greeted each other and I showed her some of the documents I had brought with me while we waited for George Parsons to come over from his office and escort us to the Caribbean Reef exhibit. All the while I was mentally loading up ammunition for the expected confrontation with Michelle, but my initial plan was to unleash Megan on her, then stand back and look for a target of opportunity if one came my way.

We climbed to the top of the Caribbean Reef exhibit and the meeting between George, Megan, and myself proceeded according to plan, George asking various questions concerning the suitability of the exhibit for Pete, with Megan answering. Things could not have been going better. It looked like a done deal, as though there had never been any question that Pete would be coming to the Shedd Aquarium, but then George said the words that snapped me out of my happy trance. "Let's call Michelle up here to see what she thinks." I thought to myself, "I KNEW this was too good to be true!"

The three of us were standing at the top of a set of stairs overlooking the artificial reef. At the base of these same steps was a heavy brass door that served as the entrance to the exhibit. I heard the latch click and saw the knob turn, followed by the door swinging open. I watched with anticipation. In the open doorway entrance a women appeared who looked somewhat like Sarah Jessica Parker.

I knew who she was instantly, even after nine years. It was the same woman I had seen at the food preparation table, the one who had looked at me with such an odd expression, the one with the dog named Nickel! "So this is her!", I thought to myself. Michelle greeted everyone with a smile and joined in the discussion immediately. She was very up beat, going along with everything we had been planning. I thought, could this be the same Michelle I had been dealing with for all these past months? Then she looked at me closely at one point and said, "You look familiar." George quickly stepped in and answered, "You and Jim were volunteers at the same time." "I thought I recognized you.", she responded.

"So how did you get into this line of work?" "It's a long story", I answered. "I'd probably have to write a book to explain."

So it was agreed in principle, Pete would be coming to the Shedd Aquarium. After the meeting had ended, Bryan gathered with Megan and myself out in a secluded stairwell for a covert conference. Bryan asked how things had gone? I answered him that it had been quite productive. Megan reiterated and said she felt it was about seventy percent a done deal. Bryan then asked the big question, "How was Michelle?" "Actually, I was pleasantly surprised," I said. "I was ready for this evil woman to come riding in on her broom and take a couple of spins around us! She turned out to be very nice and helpful."

There was nothing to do now but wait for the final word from the Shedd Aquarium.

32

BARRY

It was January of 2003, a new year had dawned, and along with it came increased hope that Project Pete was now finally going to come to fruition. I had been at this job for six months, doggedly maneuvering, dodging, and weaving, attempting to keep the house of cards from collapsing. The little plan we had conceived that should have been completed in two weeks had stretched from one year into the next, and despite the positive response at the December meeting, we still had not heard a peep from the Shedd Aquarium. It was like the drip, drip, drip, of Chinese water torture, and we could do nothing but wait.

The reason for the delay was most likely I told myself, that the aquarium would be opening in April its highly touted new exhibit, The Wild Reef, and concentrating all efforts on that. Actually, the fact of the matter was that it would be better if Pete arrived after all of the hullabaloo of the Wild Reef opening had subsided somewhat. That way we would more likely get maximum exposure for our turtle.

There was also something about the Wild Reef that I was taking personal pride in. I would have a friend swimming around in it on a daily basis, but this was not a human being in dive gear, he was a fish, and I had named him Barry.

In 2001, the last time Bryan and I had been to the Keys together, we had stayed at a motel in Islamorada. The place had a long dock that jutted a good distance out from the shore into the tropical ocean. Along its underwater structure one could find almost every variety of fish living in these islands. Even some of the rarest and oddest species could be counted on to show up sooner or later. One fish that was always present was the barracuda.

The motel dock was certainly not home to the "big boys" typical of the offshore reefs, at least not to our knowledge, but as you glided over the sunlit white sand bottom adjacent to the pilings, one would often spot tiny, one inch long, missile shaped fry of some sort. A closer examination revealed that the little fish were actually minuscule barracuda.

Since one of Bryan's passions when diving was collecting marine life for his fish tanks, I asked him if he would catch one of these guppy sized critters for my home aquarium. A few hours later, swimming in a bucket, was the miniature predator, presented to me by Bryan. I don't generally name my fish, but this guy just called out for it. I decided to call him Barry, the "Cuda".

Much like our turtle Pete, a barracuda fry's chances of surviving to adulthood are very slim, much worse in fact than those of a sea turtle. Everything works against them, even the elongated missile shape that serves the adult fish so well as a means of streamlined, explosive, flesh severing attack, conversely in the hatchling barracuda, facilitates ease of being swallowed.

When first encountering a barracuda fry holding over the sea floor, it will freeze in position hoping to avoid detection. Then at the slightest movement, it will dart off in the blink of an eye, apparently scared out of its wits, a far cry from the brash, toothy grin of the adults who hold their ground, daring you to approach before giving way ... maybe! Barry behaved in a manner befitting his youth, cowering in the bucket and later the plastic bag that carried him on the plane.

After arriving home I placed him in his very own 38 gallon tank where he took up residence in some plastic plants vacated by the previous occupants, a herd of seahorses.

It was entertaining to watch his brain work as he ventured farther out from his sulking position in his secret lair and got the lay of the land, swimming around his new habitat, checking at each turn for any predators that might take his life ... but, there were none. His confidence rose as he grew larger, dining several times a day on the live brine shrimp I brought him.

Even at his current tiny size, I could see the miniature needles sticking out of his jaw that would become the fearsome dentition of an adult barracuda. As his size increased, Barry's diet progressed from the shrimp to baby guppies. He would craftily stalk the quarter inch long fish approaching closer and closer, from plant stem to plant leaf, seeking just the right opportunity. Then exploding forward like an uncoiling spring, he would seize the unlucky guppy crosswise in his jaws turn it and swallow. This action was invariably followed shortly after by the expulsion of a miniature cloud of pinhead sized scales.

At first, Barry would only eat one or two guppies at a time, soon it became a dozen or more until his menu was changed over to frozen silversides minnows danced in front of him on a clear plastic feeding stick. These he wolfed down with apparent relish. Barry kept on growing until after a year in captivity he had reached about six or seven inches and had the beginnings of the signature barracuda toothy smile. It was time for him to move on to a new home.

After returning from Florida in the summer of 2002 and only a few days after Hawkeye's death, I called Bryan up and told him Barry was ready to move over to the Shedd, where he would eventually, the plan was, be housed in the new Wild Reef exhibit. I netted my friend out of his home and placed him into a five gallon bucket. Later Bryan picked him up and transferred him to the aquarium's quarantine department, where he continued to grow, reaching I was told, around eighteen inches.

I restocked his now empty tank with some more sea horses, but it was just not the same. I missed the little "Sea Wolf" that had lived in the aquarium just off the foot of my bed for the past year. I eventually took the tank down altogether, replacing it with a habitat for a small tortoise. It always amazes me how we get attached to our pets, even a sneaky looking little fish, or perhaps some beat up sea turtle.

The first month of 2003 was almost over now. It was Friday, the 31st of January. I returned home from work, said hello to Choppie and Barney, and swept some light snow off the front steps before checking my phone messages. There was only one. It was from Megan. The Shedd Aquarium had called. They had told her to send Pete!

33

WORTH THE WAIT!

Back at the aquarium in Clearwater, Pete continued adapting to life outside the wild. It had now been nearly five years since he had miraculously survived the boat collision and the memories of his past life in the free ocean had certainly faded. His daily routine of swimming with his friend Pinky, eating, sleeping, and looking up at the visitors was the accepted pattern for each day. Lately however, Pete had noticed increased attention from the aquarium staff in one form or another. He had been removed from the water a few days ago, measured front to back and then side to side. Later he had detected what was the faint sound of wood being sawed and cut. It was a sound that he himself did not recognize. It was the sound of Pete's shipping crate being assembled.

Up north in Illinois, the days dragged by like thick molasses in cold weather as I waited for the turtle's shipping date to be finalized. I constantly expected the floor to cave in on the project at any minute or on any day. The first glitch came when Pete's medical records were not received according to schedule and I had to put out a fire with an irate pencil pusher who threatened to scuttle the whole project even though he had no authority to do so whatsoever. I gave him a stern lecture on Pete's unfortunate history, having little tolerance for his manner, then immediately called Florida. The medical records arrived a few days later. This illustrated what a precarious path we were on and getting Pete up to Chicago was becoming more and more like walking a tightrope. Then on March 29th I received a call from Bryan that nearly gave me heart failure. He said the words I had dreaded, "I've got some bad news." I thought, "Oh no, here it comes, they've changed their minds!" But the bad news came in an unexpected form. "Barry is dead!", I heard him say. "They moved him to the new exhibit and had a malfunction in the filtration system. He didn't make it."

This was definitely one of those good news bad news situations. I was greatly saddened by having lost the little friend I had raised with such care and for so long. On the other hand I was relieved to also hear that everything was proceeding according to plan on the turtle front, although still at a slow pace. I consoled myself with the thought that if Barry had been left in the wild, he would have most likely been eaten by a larger fish long ago, but his loss was still very discouraging. "All right Pete, it's all up to you.", I thought.

Finally on April 17 my luck changed. I received a call from Michelle of all people. She told me that Pete's flight from Florida had been confirmed. He would be arriving in just six days on April 23. She invited me to ride along with her to O'Hare Airport and pick him up. I considered it an honor and gratefully accepted.

In a Little While You Will See Me No More

On the morning of April 23, 2003, Pete the Green sea turtle, who had been through so much adversity and had overcome such overwhelming odds since the day he had first fought his way from the nest to the ocean, who had survived a near fatal boat collision and had doggedly clung to life baked by the summer sun, who had the good fortune to be found and nursed back to health and had adapted to a life far away from his natural home, was about to make his final journey.

Early that morning he was lifted out of the pool that he had shared as home with his Loggerhead companion Pinky for the last time, lovingly petted by his old friends at the Clearwater Marine Aquarium, and laid in his padded shipping crate. A damp, sea foam green, bath towel was placed over him to keep our turtle cool and moist during the flight. It was not unlike the towel that had been placed on him by Matt Finn so many years ago, before his trip from the Ten Thousand Islands to Clearwater. Finally the wooden lid was placed on his crate and fastened down with several Phillips head screws. Now, covered in darkness, Pete made a few attempts to move around a little, but shortly found this to be an unsuccessful venture. He settled down. Five years in captivity had taught him that to struggle was fruitless. Patience and persistence, the survival ethic that had served him so well before, would now hopefully pull him through again. The sensation of movement began to transmit itself through the crate walls, as cracks of light illuminated his bed here and there as if they were beams from some distant lighthouse guiding him homeward. Eventually, Pete relaxed, and fell into a deep sleep, exhausted but at peace, perhaps dreaming of the past, both the near and far distant.

Me and My Swiss Army Knife

That April morning in Chicago I awoke to a beautiful, cool, spring day. The sun's beams shone through unencumbered by clouds or humidity and helped increase the sense of excitement. I decided to call Sue Schaf at The Turtle Hospital in the Keys to see if she had any tips for me that might be helpful to know. She was reassuring, and her always calm, upbeat, encouraging demeanor was just the security blanket I needed. Sue always came through.

She assured me that everything would go smoothly, but just to be aware that the turtle would probably be especially buoyant after an airplane flight and to give her a call if we needed any help.

Pete's flight was scheduled to arrive at 5pm, so I got down to the aquarium at about 3 o'clock. I wasn't taking any chances. The usual situation is that I am early for everything. If I am not on time, I am most likely sick,.... possibly dead!

Just as I was entering the aquarium's back door, who was coming out but none other than Michelle. With over three hundred employees on staff, I thought, "What are the chances of this?" She told me she would be gone a couple of hours and to meet her in the aquarist's office then. She was on her way to the veterinarian to pick up her cat Minnow, who had undergone some sort of procedure to remove a foreign object from her throat. Michelle showed it to me and I recognized it as a chewed up ballpoint pen cap, a work of art duplicated by Salty, Choppie, and Barney, on several occasions. I told Michelle what I thought it was, but she seemed skeptical that I was correct. I had the distinct feeling at that point that God Himself would have to descend from Heaven and back me up for her to take seriously any observations I might have on anything in particular right then. Hmmm, I observed, "Do we have a refreezing of the glacier that was the Michelle of old?" I hoped not.

While I waited for her return, I passed the time sitting with Bryan at his desk, talking about fish, fishing, or fish related subjects, before the conversation turned to Michelle and her cat. He said, "Do you know what the vet bill for the cat is? A thousand dollars! For a cat she found on the loading dock!"

I took this bit of news with a great deal of interest. What kind of person could this be I thought, who would spend that kind of money on what had previously been a feral cat? I knew she wasn't wealthy. Michelle obviously had a great deal of compassion for animals and a strong nurturing instinct, but still, she was not connecting with Pete. Why? Could I be the obstacle? I filed all this information in my brain hoping that maybe I could use it at some point to my advantage. For the first time I was beginning to wonder what we may have found here.

A few hours later, Michelle returned along with her one year old son Kobe, and two women volunteers from the Shedd. We all jumped into the van, everyone sitting in the seats up front, except me. I was on the floor in the rear. We headed off to the airport immediately, but first stopped for fuel at a downtown Chicago gas station. The two volunteers went inside, leaving just Michelle, her son and myself in the vehicle. Apparently, this was just the opportunity she had been waiting for. She turned around and looked at me with an icy stare and said, "You know I didn't want this turtle!" At that point I felt like a poker player who knows he is holding a royal flush! "Yeah, why was that? The Brookfield Zoo turtles have to go back to Hawaii. Pete is yours!" She turned around and never said another word.

Once we got on the road the traffic was of course heavy, it being rush hour. Nothing about this project was going to come easy! To kill some time, I asked my captive audience if they would like to hear the first few chapters of a book that I had decided to write about Pete and the story of how he came to the Shedd Aquarium. They all said they would with a somewhat surprised look on their faces, so, I started reading to the other four as we drove along. I began with the words, "The sun rose early this time of year, having nearly reached its summer solstice....

I continued the narrative. Everyone was silent as we went along and I couldn't tell if they were listening, or just looking out the window as the "crackpot" in the back rambled on. When I finished the first chapter, I asked if I should continue or wait for the ride home. I calculated that this way if I was boring them, it would provide an easy way out, and I just would not resume on the return trip, exiting gracefully. Much to my grateful surprise, they all asked me to keep reading.

The time past quickly despite the turtle slow traffic that Michelle had to navigate the tugboat like van through and before long we were rolling into the cargo pick up area at O'Hare Airport. We backed up to the loading dock, Michelle went inside, and in short order the overhead door began to lift like a curtain on a stage.

The scene revealed inside was that of a man driving a forklift that held a large wooden crate nestled in its prongs. He pulled up to the back of our vehicle and commenced to lower our parcel down to the level of the van.

It became evident that this method of loading was not going to work since the floor of the vehicle was a good foot or two lower than the edge of the loading dock. The forklift driver and I apparently came to the same conclusion simultaneously as the two of us grabbed for the rope hand holds on either side of the crate and began to manually load the parcel into the van. My foot slipped briefly just as I got to the edge of the dock but I thankfully caught my balance and we slid Pete's container inward until it came to rest on the van's bed. I jumped back into the rear of our vehicle and sat on the floor in a semi prone position laying next to the wooden box that was now ours. I noticed it had several shipping labels on it, one of them with the turtle's name, PETE, in bold letters. We got underway quickly, heading back to Chicago, Michelle, her son, and the two volunteers up front, as for me, I was laying on the floor next to Pete's crate in the back. I wouldn't have wanted it any other way!

Upon arrival at our destination, the crate was once more unloaded and then placed on a wheeled freight cart, after which it was rolled down around and through the tangle of hallways that make up the interior of the Shedd Aquarium. After traversing the Pentagon like maze, we boarded a freight elevator.

A few floors up we exited into still another series of halls, passing by some of my old work areas that I hadn't seen in a decade. I could never have imagined back in 1993 that the next time I set foot in the place it would be as a valet for a handicapped sea turtle. Incredible!

Pulling up to what Michelle said would be Pete's quarantine tank, we slid the box onto the floor. The lid was held down with Phillip's head screws, so consequently, we found ourselves in need of a matching screwdriver. Since of course none was available in the immediate area, Michelle went off on a hunt around the aquarium to find one. While she was away, I reached into my pocket and took out my favorite Swiss Army knife which I always carry for just such emergencies. The trusted red jackknife had accompanied me for over a decade on countless fishing trips to Canada and other northern locales. I examined its familiar worn features, then unleashed the Phillips screwdriver nestled between the various other blades and gadgets that are the trademark of these versatile tools. Slowly I began to undo each screw, raising one after another upward an inch or so, sufficiently high for one of the volunteers who had found some pliers to finish off the job. Like an assembly line we proceeded around the edge of the crate until all of the screws were removed and placed on a nearby table.

One of the volunteers then asked if we should take the lid off? To which I replied, "No, let Michelle do the honors, she is Pete's mom now!" That is a move I will never regret.

Not long after, Michelle arrived and gave the OK for the unveiling. With great anticipation, the lid was lifted off. As the interior of the crate was illuminated, the sight we were presented with was that of a Green sea turtle laying motionless in his foam padded crate, covered with a sea foam green bath towel.

"Is he alive?", one of the volunteers asked. "Yes he issss …!", said Michelle. Bathed in light for the first time in many hours and like someone wakening from a long nap, Pete slowly raised his head and looked directly at me as I filmed this special event.

From that moment, frozen in time, there are two things that I know I will remember and carry with me for the rest of my life. One is the absolute thrill of knowing that the very first thing Pete saw when he arrived from his long journey, was me standing over him. The second is the sound of Michelle's voice as she oohed and awwed over her new "Baby", as she called him. She looked at the green bath towel and said, "Oh look, He's got a "Blankey." I knew from that point on that I could trust Michelle to take care of Pete, and that he had melted the soft heart that I had known all along must surely be there. He was in good hands. There was only one more thing for me to do.

We now had to figure out how to get the one hundred twenty five pound turtle off the floor, up in the air several feet, then over the edge of the quarantine tank and into the water. The four of us speculated on several methods, including sliding him onto a board, lifting that up, and then sliding him burial at sea style into the tank.

Finally, I decided to take matters into my own hands. I told Michelle to let me step into the crate, straddle the turtle, get a grip on him and feel for the weight, then lift him up myself.

She agreed, so I stepped into the padded box placing my feet on either side of Pete, who seemed to be taking this all in with amusement. I grabbed his shell at the three o'clock and nine o'clock position, tightened my grip, and started. The feel was not unlike lifting an air conditioner with flippers, but despite my bad back I felt strengthened, and the turtle rose easily from my feet to knees, to belt, then chest, at which point the other three jumped in and we all pushed our turtle over the top of the tank and into the water. Pete sank like a stone, but to everyone's relief, surfaced quickly and took his first gasping breath of air while he reacquainted himself with his swimming skills. For about a half an hour we all watched, the others amused by Pete's tail up swimming posture which just as Sue suggested, had been made even more buoyant by the airplane flight. Questions, answers, and speculations were the topic as we watched until it was at last time to leave. Michelle turned to me and said, "I'll keep you posted and check back with you when we plan to do any medical exams before he's released." I responded, "Thanks, I appreciate it, but that's not necessary, he's yours now. You're his mom. I know you'll do a good job." As we left, she turned and said to her turtle, "Don't worry Pete, this isn't your final home, your new one will be a lot bigger."

I couldn't help but think that the quarantine tank he was in was just as large as the exhibit he had been living in for the past five years in Florida and that Michelle had taken to mothering our turtle like a duck takes to water. She had unexpectedly become a pleasant surprise. It was the end of a magical day. I returned to my truck, exiting through the back door of the now vacant Shedd Aquarium and into the clear night. The Chicago skyline illuminated the horizon like some exotic jewelry glowing from every direction as I drove home that night. At my door I was greeted as always by Choppie and Barney. We all went to bed and I slept well for the first time in months.

I hoped Pete did too!

34

REVELATION

The next morning, still filled with excitement from the previous day, I called Bryan at the aquarium to learn how Pete had made it through the night. He told me that as soon as he had arrived at work, he had gone over to see the new turtle and how it was doing. Pete was swimming around in the quarantine tank and calmly taking everything in stride. This shouldn't have been a surprise considering all the other hurdles he had overcome in the past. The guy's a trooper, I thought. He's settling in.

After a few weeks had passed it was decided the time had come for Pete to undergo a more extensive medical examination. Accordingly, he was scheduled to have an MRI screening at Saint Mary of Nazareth Hospital. The designated day arrived and our turtle was loaded one more time into the van, this time by a crew of people that included Bryan among others. Pete was laid on his back with his head placed on a foam pillow support to keep him calm and immobile during the ride over to the hospital. Once there he was transferred to a gurney and rolled over to the MRI machine.

A hitch in the plan was evident soon enough when an attempt was made to slide the turtle into the MRI and it became apparent that he was not going to fit. Now what? A quick call was made to another local hospital and Pete was loaded up once again and whisked over to medical facility number two, where this time an attempt would be made with a larger CAT scan machine instead of the MRI. The fit was perfect and the exam was successfully carried out. Pete was reloaded and made the seventh and final van ride of his career back to the aquarium, where he was returned to his tank, probably wondering what to make of all this!

A few weeks later in May, I was once more down in the Florida Keys, diving, fishing for tarpon, and also I would take the opportunity to attend my first Save-A-Turtle meeting.

The featured presentation was given by Tony Redlow from the Florida Fish and Wildlife Conservation Commission. The topic was artificial beach lighting and how it can disorient sea turtle hatchlings. One interesting anecdote he related concerned just such a group of baby turtles, who hatched out and then proceeded to head straight for a Coke machine, gathering around its base attracted by its electric powered moonlight glow. They were later rescued as were another troop of turtles that entered a very surprised elderly man's back door and congregated around the soft glow of his TV set. There were no Coke adds on so it was definitely the light that attracted them and not the soda. Sorry Madison Avenue!

After the lecture, Mike Bier took time to introduce me to fellow Save-A-Turtle members, Margie and Don Jensen, Herb and Yea Bernett, Patty Anthony, Jeanette Hobbs, Jeri Sears, Pat Wells, outgoing President Tropical Mike Hall, and of course Sue Schaf.

The next day, after a stop over at Pigeon Key, I returned to my room at the Hidden Harbor Motel. I had brought my Mom along this time, and before we went to dinner I decided to call home and check my phone messages. One of them was of extreme interest. It was once again from Michelle. She relayed to me what the results of the CAT scan had shown.

Natalie Mylniczenko, one of the veterinarians at the Shedd, had examined the CAT scans for any apparent cause for Pete's buoyancy disorder, but like so many before her, she could find nothing to pin it down. An old healed fracture had also been discovered, and interestingly enough, there seemed to be what looked like a coin lodged in the turtle's esophagus. Finally, there was still one more message from Michelle, and it was a stunner! The CAT scan had revealed that Pete was a female!

Return

A week or two later I was back home, still digesting all the new information concerning our turtle. I was working on one of my fish tanks, home to a rather large French angelfish that I had grown from a half dollar sized, yellow striped juvenile, to a regal dinner plate sized adult. I was cleaning a filter when the phone rang. I went over to it and saw that the call was coming from the Shedd Aquarium. It was Michelle, giving me the latest update. I had to give the woman credit. She had been true to her word about keeping me up to speed on any developments.

Michele told me that a procedure was going to be performed to remove the coin from Pete's esophagus. It would be a fairly simple task that should be routine. Oh, and one more thing! It had been decided that the turtle would be renamed according to whatever the denomination the coin turned out to be, the odds on favorite being, Penny. It came as no surprise to me that Michelle was rooting for a nickel. She felt that it would be as if her departed dog Nickel had in some way returned to her.

I couldn't help but think that with all the turtle had been through, and all the serendipitous events and occurrences that needed to fall in place for Pete to be where she was now, what would be a more appropriate ending. I was certain what the outcome would be. I answered Michelle, "You KNOW it's going to be a nickel!"

As it turned out, the coin's identity started to generate quite a bit of interest around the aquarium, so a betting pool was generated. Guess the denomination and the date, win the money.

The operation was performed. Interestingly enough, Natalie the veterinarian was the winner. The coin was a 1975 nickel. The Shedd Aquarium had a new star to follow in the footsteps of Hawkeye. Nickel the sea turtle was born. How could it have been anything else?

35

HOME

I was told by Michelle to be down at the aquarium at 7:00am. The date was July 22, 2003. Nickel's coming out party. Today she would finally be released into the 90,000 gallon Caribbean Reef exhibit with all its schools of fish and rows and grottos of coral. For the first time in over five years, Nickel would possibly be able to find something that had been lost, her life in the ocean. How would she take to this new artificial sea? Would she possibly be able to recapture what life in the wild had been like? Or was that memory too distant, too faded, only a smoky wisp, something not to be regained. All these questions would be answered in a little over an hour. Michelle showed up right on time and found me sitting near the same old table I had been at seven months earlier, where I had waited for George Parsons and prepared to do battle with her. She wore a teal blue polo shirt with the Shedd Aquarium logo embroidered on it, and khaki cargo shorts, the typical uniform of an aquarist at this institution. My own outfit consisted of cargo pants, also khaki, and a yellow Outer Banks polo shirt with the Save-A-Turtle of the Florida Keys emblem on the pocket. The latter was a gift from Mike Bier. Something to suit the occasion and represent the home team. After a little while of killing time in the cafeteria, I was led up to Nickel's quarantine tank. I carried my video camera with me, hoping to document the event just as I had the arrival. This was the first time I had seen the turtle who we now know as Nickel since I had lifted her from the shipping crate. It seemed like a long time had passed since that special April night.

    Nickel's transfer crew had gathered and it included Bryan, and Keith Pamper among others. I began filming as the group led by Keith started to commiserate on the best way to catch the 125 pound turtle and remove her from the water.

    Michelle next climbed up on the catwalk that bordered the tank, crouched down and with a landing net, attempted to shepherd the unsuspecting Nickel, over to the waiting arms of Bryan and Keith. This did not go well at first. Our turtle obviously sensing that something was up, steadfastly refused to play along.

At one point, Bryan got what he thought was a good grip on her only to have the turtle break away and in the process thoroughly drench him with rather cold saltwater, soaking him to the skin along with the dark navy blue Shedd polo shirt he was wearing.

Michelle kept working the water with the net, like someone stirring a large pot of soup with a ladle. A few months earlier I would have likened her to a witch stirring her cauldron waiting for the rest of her coven to arrive! I didn't think of her that way anymore.

Finally the moment of opportunity presented itself. Keith and Bryan were finally able to gain a hold on her shell and flippers and in a quick but labored move, whisked Nickel out of the tank, flipped her on her back, and laid her on a waiting cart. Michelle hopped off the catwalk and watched the proceedings, nervously wiping her hands on her cargo shorts, using an almost childlike back and forth paddling motion, swinging her arms in the air.

The caravan of people then made its way through the labyrinth of halls that led to the Caribbean Reef tank, exiting through a set of doors into the semi lit rotunda interior where the miniature ocean that is the exhibit glowed like an unobtainable icon that now was at last in reach. A crowd of Shedd employees had gathered around and ringed the exterior of the tank in order to witness the event.

As Nickel and her entourage approached the entrance, the familiar brass door was opened and she disappeared from my sight while she was carried up the steps to the top of her new home. At that point, the crowd was too large for me to get more than a few feet up the steps, leaving me in a very poor position to view the big event, so my ears strained for clues as to what was now happening. In just a few seconds I could tell by the spontaneous cheer from the surrounding crowd that Nickel had just made her entry into the water. The Caribbean Reef was without a turtle no longer!

Quickly I descended the few steps and ran to the front of the exhibit. I am sure that some jaded biologists or scientists would say that animals do not experience emotion, that they can't experience feelings. Well, they are most assuredly wrong! What my eyes were treated to can best be described as nothing other than a living creature experiencing pure unadulterated joy!

There was Nickel, swimming excitedly through schools of silver lookdown fish, she chased the cow nose rays, explored the coral, descended to the bottom and dug in the sand! She didn't know which way to turn first. The turtle who had been written off was doing just fine, convinced she had miraculously some how returned home. If a sea turtle could hyperventilate, Nickel seemed to be doing just that!

Bryan showed up having disappeared for awhile, now wearing a teal colored shirt like Michelle, his water soaked one having been replaced. Michelle called over to him, "That color looks good on you." in a mocking but good natured tone.

"How cool is this!", he said to me, and I had to agree. I asked him if he had a mint of some kind? "My mouth feels like the desert!" He found a peppermint candy somewhere that filled the bill.

The next point of excitement came when the news media began to arrive. Probably the first on the scene was FOX TV, followed by NBC, CBS, ABC, WGN, and CNN, along with photographers and reporters from the print media, the Chicago Tribune, and Chicago Sun Times newspapers.

NBC did the most extensive story. I first recognized Kim Vatis, a reporter and sometimes co-anchor for that station. She was wearing a red outfit and looking at our turtle with a great deal of interest, and then the camera lights clicked on and she began to tell the Chicago television audience the story of Nickel, our star turtle. Michelle was also bathed in those same lights, detailing what Nickel's life would be like at the aquarium, describing the turtles survival as a miracle to millions of viewers. Meanwhile all the other cameras, a whole row of them, were pressed up against the glass all focused on one thing, Nickel. It looked like Mayor Daley was holding a press conference!

I stayed in the background. Nickel and Michelle were the stars now. It was their time to shine. But hidden in the shadows, I enjoyed and lived in that moment. Taking it all in. Well paid! I watched the children and their parents as they pressed up against the glass to get a better view, pushing through the enthralled crowd, there small hands pointing at our turtle. The scene was surreal.

I guess it was about an hour before the crowd started to thin out a little. Michelle had left. I hadn't seen her go. Bryan was also no where to be found. I took the opportunity to slip out the back door, the same one I had escorted Pete through back on that clear spring evening. It was now mid summer. Stepping outside, I was at once warmed by the late morning sunshine. It felt good. It felt like I was in the Keys! I hoped that was how it felt for Nickel.

She in turn had changed my life also. Nothing would ever be the same again. Standing there I reached into my pocket, my fingers first encountering the familiar weathered old Swiss Army knife, soon to be retired to a place of honor in my bookcase. My hand continued on, grabbing a handkerchief. Withdrawing it, I unfolded the cloth and wiped the Lake Michigan humidity from my glasses. Then I looked up and my eyes fixed on the stately rotunda that my old friend

"Pete" was now living under. What a privilege it had been to be part of this! An unforgettable adventure!

I couldn't help but think that even as I stood there, somewhere out on the far away ocean, alone, silhouetted along the blue horizon by the tropical sun, washed by the effervescent mist that sprays from the breaking waves, another Nickel, another Pete, persists against any number of life extracting forces. It to refuses to give in, inhaling the good air scented of the ocean, fighting defeat, hoping for salvation. There would always be more injured turtles. That is the way things are, but we do what we can. We do what we must. I took the handkerchief and wiped my glasses once again, and this time also my eyes. Nickel was home at last!

EPILOGUE

◆

August 2007

There is only one thing constant in life, and that is that things constantly change. In the five years that have passed since I came to know Nickel the sea turtle, much has. As a result of the Shedd Aquarium's commitment to the placement of a handicapped turtle in a featured exhibit, other facilities became interested. This" Nickel Effect", as I like to call it has caused an increased awareness of other non releasable turtles, and now several more have found homes in zoos and aquariums around the United States. Hopefully, the thinking is starting to change on what kind of animals, be it sea turtles or other creatures of the land, sea, or air, can and should be placed on public display. Much work remains to be done.

Nickel herself, the sea turtle that nobody wanted, has now gone on to become the most recognized animal celebrity at the Shedd Aquarium. Her image is often seen on refrigerator magnets, key chains, tee shirts, and mugs and tumblers of various designs. She is often seen during TV segments swimming in the background or right up front on center screen, maybe taking a cue from her predecessor Hawkeye. The argument can be made that Nickel is possibly the most famous sea turtle in the country. Certainly a long way from the near lifeless creature found floating under the mangroves back on that July day.

Perhaps the greatest change has come to the Florida Keys. An always precarious place to live, it became even more so in the fall of 2005 when the islands were relentlessly pelted with hurricanes, the worst of them being Wilma in the month of October. The storm did great damage to The Turtle Hospital and Hidden Harbor Motel. Loss of important equipment and the demoralizing effect of extreme flooding was eventually overcome, and no turtle patients were lost. The Motel however, was never reopened. The Turtle Hospital itself, is now open to the general public and depends on tourism, government funding, and of course the support of Ritchie Moretti for its continued existence.

Save A Turtle's work still goes on, although its colorful members are aging and new blood is desperately needed. Becoming involved with them continues to be one of the best things that ever happened in my life. It was an unforgettable ride!

Sadly, Barney, my Newfoundland dog, has a life that may be way too short. He developed health problems and has difficulty walking. I help him up the stairs with a sling each time we go out, his tail still perpetually wagging even through the pain. He is the most devoted and loving of my three wonderful dogs. When the time comes, he will lay at Salty's feet in a quiet pet cemetery, where I visit often.

Choppie, the pug, is now a gray faced senior citizen. His hobbies remain as always, sleeping and eating He warms my own feet every night from his favorite spot on the foot of my bed.

And Nickel? Well, thinking of her, warms my heart everyday. She will always be the first and most special of my turtle friends. There are others like her now. Living in their own new homes. But those perhaps, are stories for another day.

Jim Gamlin, Used Turtle Salesman

978-0-595-44650-6
0-595-44650-7

Printed in the United States
129721LV00003B/106-216/A